# THE MYT?

## ALSO AVAILABLE FROM BLOOMSBURY

*Epistemology: The Key Thinkers*, edited by Stephen Hetherington
*Free Will and Epistemology*, by Robert Lockie
*Problems in Epistemology and Metaphysics*, edited by Steven B. Cowan
*Radical Skepticism and the Shadow of Doubt*, by Eli Hirsch
*Technic and Magic*, by Federico Campagna

# THE MYTH OF LUCK

Philosophy, Fate, and Fortune

## Steven D. Hales

BLOOMSBURY ACADEMIC
LONDON • NEW YORK • OXFORD • NEW DELHI • SYDNEY

BLOOMSBURY ACADEMIC
Bloomsbury Publishing Plc
50 Bedford Square, London, WC1B 3DP, UK
1385 Broadway, New York, NY 10018, USA

BLOOMSBURY, BLOOMSBURY ACADEMIC and the Diana logo are
trademarks of Bloomsbury Publishing Plc

First published in Great Britain 2020

Cover design by Louise Dugdale

A catalogue record for this book is available from the British Library.

A catalog record for this book is available from the Library of Congress.

ISBN:   HB:     978-1-3501-4928-1
        PB:     978-1-3501-4929-8
        ePDF:   978-1-3501-4930-4
        eBook:  978-1-3501-4931-1

Typeset by Integra Software Services Pvt. Ltd.
Printed and bound in Great Britain

To find out more about our authors and books visit www.bloomsbury.com
and sign up for our newsletters.

To my family: Vanessa, Holly, and Everett,
whom I am lucky to have.

# CONTENTS

# LIST OF FIGURES

# LIST OF TABLES

# ACKNOWLEDGMENTS

I have talked about luck with a lot of people, including Nathan Ballantyne, Kevin Ferland, Scott Lowe, Christy Mag Uihdir, Duncan Pritchard, and Lee Whittington. Audiences at Bucknell University, University of Edinburgh, Universidad de La Laguna, Universidade do Porto, Stevens Institute of Technology, Università degli Studi di Torino, and William Paterson University helped me polish pieces of the material herein.

I worked out more technical versions of a few of these ideas in "Luck Attributions and Cognitive Bias," *Metaphilosophy* (45, 2014), "A Problem for Moral Luck," *Philosophical Studies* (172:9, 2015), "Why Every Theory of Luck Is Wrong," *Noûs* (50:3, 2016), "Dispositional Optimism and Luck Attributions: Implications for Philosophical Theories of Luck," *Philosophical Psychology* (31:7, 2018), and "Moral Luck and Control," *Midwest Studies in Philosophy* (43, 2019).

Several generous souls read some or all of the chapters in draft, and I appreciate their comments and observations. Thank you Olivia Best, Richard Brook, Drue Coles, Jeff Dean, Tobey Scharding, Eric Stouffer, and Jessa Wood. Many of the ideas in Chapter 6 are the result of collaborative work I have done with my friend and psychologist colleague Jennifer Johnson. I'm glad she was willing to help out a philosopher. My long-time friend Tim Johnson is always my most diligent critic, for which I am ~~always~~ usually grateful. My wife Vanessa not only read and commented on the entire manuscript, but she very patiently listened to me talk about my hopes and fears about it. Finally, I am thankful to Colleen Coalter, my editor at Bloomsbury, for believing in this project.

# 1 LACHESIS'S LOTTERY AND THE HISTORY OF LUCK

*"How complex and misleading a thing is luck!"*
**—MENANDER, UNIDENTIFIED FRAGMENT, C. 300 BCE**

Luck is a golden thread woven through the tapestry of the history of ideas, uniting gods and gamblers, philosophers and theologians, logicians, astrologers, emperors, scientists, and slaves. All have feared ill fortune and hoped for good luck, all have wondered what the fates have written in the book of their lives. Much of who we become is due to chance and yet we tell ourselves that we are self-made and our lives are wholly due to our own choices. Or when we have hard times we write it off to bad luck instead of our own mistakes. Even what we know and understand about the world around us is often just good fortune, not due to our own praiseworthy effort. We struggle to predict and control the events around us, and try to foresee what the future will bring. Most of all we attempt to explain our own lives to ourselves, and sort out what was chance and what was our own doing. Humanity has thrown everything we have at implacable luck—novel theologies, entire philosophical movements, fresh branches of mathematics—and yet we seem to have gained only the smallest edge on the power of fortune.

The present book will argue that we have been fighting an unconquerable foe. It's not that as soon as we solve one problem with luck that two more appear, like new heads from a decapitated hydra, but rather that the monster is altogether mythological. We cannot master luck because there is literally nothing to defeat: we will see that luck is no more than a persistent and troubling illusion. There is no such thing as luck. Recognizing that fact will help us focus our energies on related phenomena that *are* real, like fortune and chance. What's more, we'll see that in a very real sense that we make our own luck, that luck is our *own* doing, our *own* perspective on how things turn out. Cleaning our mental house of dusty old concepts that we're hanging onto because we keep hoping that they will one day be useful—that is liberating. To give up luck is to regain our own agency in the world.

# The Myth of Er

Why did we ever think that luck was a vital notion? Let's trace out the history of luck, and start with Plato. "Plato" was a nickname meaning "broad," a reference to his beefy wrestler's build, and he stands in antiquity shouldering the entirety of the Western philosophical tradition upon his mighty frame. One of the many pleasures of reading Plato is that you get this sense of nascent rationality emerging out of an older mystical tradition. The golden age of Greek philosophy (fifth to fourth centuries BCE) arrives a mere 300 years after Hesiod's origin stories of the gods in his *Theogony* and Homer's tales of heroes, demigods, and monsters in the *Iliad* and *Odyssey*. Plato's dialogues are at once filled with subtle and ingenious logic—indeed, they are the very invention of the Socratic Method—but then in the next passage one makes a left turn into the arcane. The end of the *Phaedo* reads like a Lonely Planet travel guide to Hades ("A good walk starts at the River Acheron and will take you past the new souls at the Acherusian Lake and down to the pit of Tartarus. Be sure to try the ouzo at a nearby taverna."). We owe the legend of Atlantis to Plato: he is our oldest, original source on Atlantis and presents it seriously in *Timaeus* and *Critias*. In *Phaedrus* Plato even depicts the Egyptian gods Thoth and Amon as just as legitimate and credible as the speaking oaks at the sanctuary of Zeus.

Plato's most famous dialogue, the *Republic*, is an extended discussion about the nature of justice, how to live a harmonious life, and the ideal political state. Yet the *Republic* wraps up with a curious folk tale of the afterlife that has come to be known as the Myth of Er. Not everyone appreciates Plato's juxtaposition of reasoned debate and credulous recitation of the supernatural. The classicist Julia Annas characterizes the Myth of Er as a "vulgar, painful shock" and "a lame and messy ending" to Plato's masterpiece.[1] But Er's tale embodies the complex weaving of luck, fate, fortune, chance, choice, and destiny that we see in our own lives and in how we understand gambling, free will, moral responsibility, scientific discovery, social egalitarianism, and the nature of knowledge in the modern day.

Er was a Pamphylian warrior killed in battle. He was piled up with the other corpses for nearly two weeks until finally brought home and laid upon a funeral pyre. As the mourners came with the torches, Er sprang to life, as good as new, to relate what he had seen in the afterlife. (Plato does not comment on whether the attendees were at all surprised by this turn of events.) Er reported that after his death he journeyed with a large company of other souls to a "mysterious region." In this place was a one-way tunnel leading into the Earth and another coming out of it, and there were two similar passageways leading up into and down from the sky. Judges sat before the entrances, deciding which souls were allowed to take the heavenly skyway and which were sent down the chthonic subway, and they affixed tokens of passage to each of the souls. Coming out of the road from the heavens was a procession of clean and cheerful travelers, whereas those exiting the underworld tunnel looked squalid and dusty. The judges did not allow Er to move on, but singled him out as an observer to recount what he had seen. All the souls newly delivered from Tartarus (the deep abyss of suffering) or the Elysian Fields (the halcyon isles of the blessed) mingled with the freshly deceased as in a festival meadow, swapping stories and striking up acquaintances. The mingling souls spent a week there before being allowed to move on. The whole affair is reminiscent of an international airport, with passport control officers who decide which stamps and visas to issue and where you are allowed to travel, the first-class passengers who arrive at the gates fresh and jaunty, and the rest who are haggard and weary. But everyone is trapped in the concourse for a week.

On the eighth day, Er and the others were sent on a five-day journey to a great pillar of rainbow light which fastened the heavens and the Earth. Plato's description of the cosmos here is complicated, with nested colored whorls spinning in the vault of the sky, but the key element is that this is the Spindle of Necessity, turning on the knees of the goddess Ananke (Lady Necessity). She is attended by her daughters, the three Fates: Lachesis, who sings of the past, Clotho, who sings of the present, and Atropos, who sings of the future (it is hard not to see the Fates presaging Dickens's Ghosts of Christmas Past, Present, and Future). The travelers were directed to Lachesis, who held a box full of lots, like tickets to a raffle. Also in the box were patterns of different kinds of lives—short lives, long ones, tyrannies, lives of physical beauty or bodily strength, lives of low birth or high, exiles, beggars, even lives of animals. The prophet of Lachesis threw out the numbered tickets, and everyone (except Er, who was just watching) picked up the one that landed at their feet. Then the prophet tossed out the patterns of lives. Based on the number you drew, you got to choose the kind of life you would have when returned to Earth and reborn.

Certainly Er's tale has much in common with other, later, accounts of the afterlife: that there is an afterlife, that you will be judged on the basis of your virtues and vices, and that you will be rewarded or punished. One part that did not catch on widely in the West was the idea of reincarnation. Early Christianity, for example, toyed with the idea of reincarnation for a few hundred years—the sixth-century theologian Origen of Alexandria was its most prominent defender—but ultimately rejected the doctrine as heretical. According to Er one spent 1,000 years in either Elysium or Tartarus before rejoining the migration of souls back into bodily forms. That too Christianity rejected to make rewards and punishments eternal instead. Classical Buddhism took these ideas in a somewhat different direction: deeds while living determined your *karma*, like bookkeeping entries in the ledger book of your life, and *karma* determined your life upon rebirth. There was no punishment or reward in an afterlife, but an automatic recycling back into the world.

Plato advises us to choose wisely in picking the kind of life we want to have upon rebirth. #1 in Lachesis's lottery, freshly arrived from a millennium in heaven, chose to be a great tyrant upon rebirth, apparently failing to read the fine print of the job description, which included eating his own children and other horrors. Others chose to be a swan, a lion, a nightingale, and other animals. A well-known "buffoon" chose to be an ape. Plato emphasizes that we are responsible for our own lives, and that it is up to us to pursue wisdom and live virtuously. The prophet of Lachesis declares that the blame for a poor life rests on the one who chose it, not on the gods, and that even the soul who drew the last number in the lottery still has the opportunity for an acceptable life. According to Er, the final pick in the lottery went to Odysseus, who, after his previous life of stress and responsibilities, poked around the remaining possible lives until in the corner he found one for an ordinary, unambitious citizen. He was reportedly satisfied.

You might well wonder, though, how much of this "every possible life is minimally decent" is just divine propaganda. Despite the assurance of the gods, our lives seem very much out of our control, even whether we are able to adequately aim for a just life. Lachesis's lottery itself is random; what number you draw helps determine which of the patterns of life remain for you to choose from. And not every life is as good as every other. Some are manifestly worse, and if you have the final number in the drawing, the options remaining to you may be unappealing—like being the last person at a box of donuts and nothing tasty remains. So what life you get to have is chance as much as choice. Even what you can make of that life is partly due to luck. Plato seems to recognize this when he says of the various possible lives that "the choice of a different life inevitably determined a different character." The kind of person you are able to become may largely be fixed by the kind of life you have and the circumstances you are in.

Suppose that you get your numbered ticket in the afterlife, and these lives are available to you. Which do you choose?

1  You are a rich business despot. You will be divorced several times, your employees all hate you, and your children will fight over your estate.

2  You work in a factory, making parts for the robots that will eventually take over your job. Your back hurts.

3  You are a suburban parent, with a decent ranch-style house, three kids, and a spouse you usually get along with. You pay your bills and your job is OK. You could lose a few pounds.

4  You are a hippie who thinks organic gardening and yoga will undermine global capitalism.

5  You are a philosopher who insulted most of the prominent citizens in your town. You never got along with your spouse, never published, live in poverty, and will be executed by the state.

All of these lives have their pros and cons, but it would be foolish to suppose that the kind of person you become—the development of your character—is just the same whether you are a hippie, factory worker, autocrat, suburban parent, or Socrates. As University of Oklahoma football coach Barry Switzer famously said, "Some people are born on third base and go through life thinking they hit a triple." Other factors that affect the goodness and value of your life also seem like a matter of luck: whether you are born with a heart condition or not, if you are shot in a firefight or just missed, whether you invested in Microsoft at the right time or the wrong one. Moreover, these vagaries of fortune are not evenly distributed. It may be that upon us all a little rain must fall, but some people are hit with Hurricane Katrina. Even the degree to which we can be credited for our knowledge may be the result of fortune. Er was no one special—just a random fallen soldier from an out-of-the-way spot—but he was picked to witness the design of the afterworld and return to tell about it. Er's understanding is not really attributable to a virtuous intellectual character, his assiduous reasoning, or his relentless inquiry. He was merely lucky to be favored by the gods.

When the reincarnating souls had chosen a new form of life, they paraded before the Fates and Ananke herself, so that the goddesses could ratify the destiny of their lots and choices and make the web of their destinies irreversible. Only then could they drink of the River Lethe, forgetting their travels in the afterlife, and return to the world of flesh and blood. The idea that the patterns and ends of our lives should be locked in by fate and necessity is at odds with the conception of our lives as either subject to chancy luck or under our volitional control. How can we be responsible for who we are and how things turn out for us when on the one hand we have an inescapable destiny foreordained by the gods and on the other it is just good luck or bad?

While the Myth of Er nicely raises some of the core questions of the present book, we needn't accept Plato's theories of an afterlife, or really any theories of an afterlife at all, for these questions to be pressing in our own lives. To what extent is your life the result of your choices, the exercise of your skills, and the implementation of your will? How much of what happens to you—your successes and failures, where you live, what you do, whom you love—is simply luck? Can you count on your beliefs as trustworthy knowledge, or are you merely lucky if they are true? Some find it comforting to suppose that our lives are planned in advance, that they are essential components of a cosmic order. Perhaps even then it is luck whether the Fates have ordained that you are a big cog or a little one.

## Tuche and Fortuna

For the Greeks, luck was personified as Tuche (or Tyche), the goddess of luck. In *Olympian Ode 12*, the great Greek poet Pindar wrote:

> Savior Tuche, daughter of Zeus the Deliverer, I pray to you ... But men's hopes are tossed up and down as they voyage through waves of empty lies. No man on earth has yet found out from the gods a sure

token of things to come; man's perception is blinded as to the future. Many things fall out for men in ways they do not expect: sometimes their hoped-for pleasure is thwarted, sometimes, when they have encountered storms of pain, their grief changes in a moment to profound joy.[2]

Depictions of Tuche sometimes showed her with a ship's rudder, indicating that it was she who steered our lives. However, as the playwright Menander of Athens noted, "Tuche's current is swift to change its course."

While Tuche was portrayed as unpredictable and changing, she was an agent of cosmic balance too: bad luck brings down the haughty and good luck raises the downtrodden. There was a fatalism in the worship of Tuche, though. You can trust in your luck or you can employ your skills and foresight to plan for the future, but either way Tuche is mercurial, undependable, and has the final say. Polybius, the Greek chronicler of the Roman Republic, confirmed, "for it is quite the way of Tuche to confound human calculations by surprises; and when she has helped a man for a time, and caused her balance to incline in his favor, to turn round upon him as though she repented, throw her weight into the opposite scale, and mar all his successes."[3] In *Girl Pipers*, Menander is even more direct: "Tuche ... destroys all logic and runs counter to our expectations, planning other outcomes. Tuche makes all efforts futile." In *The Changeling* he lectured:

> Stop reasoning; for human reason adds nothing to Tuche, whether Tuche is divine spirit or not. It's this that steers all things and turns them upside down and puts them right, while mortal thought is just smoke and crap. Believe me; don't criticize my words. All that we think or say or do is Tuche; we only write our signatures below.[4]

In the face of Tuche's overarching power, all we can do is admit our mortal helplessness and hope for our own good fortune. As Theophrastus, Aristotle's successor at the Lyceum, wrote in *Callisthenes*: "Life is ruled by Tuche, not wisdom."

Greek Tuche morphed into Roman Fortuna, and was the subject of widespread public worship in the empire, with many temples erected in her honor. During the time of the transition to the Imperium under Augustus, Quintus Horatius Flaccus—better known as Horace—was Rome's leading lyric poet. In *Ode 29 "To Maecenas"* he wrote:

Fortune, happy in the execution of her cruel office, and persisting to play her insolent game, changes uncertain honors, indulgent now to me, by and by to another. I praise her, while she abides by me. If she moves her fleet wings, I resign what she has bestowed, and wrap myself up in my virtue, and court honest poverty without a portion.

Fortuna is nothing if not unpredictable, and all we can do is show gratitude when she favors us and stoicism when she does not.

Plutarch, a Greek historian and citizen of Rome in the first century CE, acknowledged the power and influence of luck in success of Rome itself. In "The Fortune of the Romans," he illustrated that luck was present at Rome's very beginning—it was good luck that the twins Romulus and Remus were fathered by the god Mars, that when the king ordered the twins killed a kindly man instead deposited them safely on the shaded banks of the Tiber, that they were suckled by a she-wolf, that they were fed by a woodpecker, and that they were not discovered by the malicious king as they were reared and educated. Plutarch suggested these machinations were all a "furtive and shrewd device of fortune."[5] Plutarch is less enthusiastic than some other writers about ascribing all successes and failures to luck, and tried to argue in his short essay "On Tuche" that it's best to not give up entirely in the face of chance, but to use our intellect and talents to our advantage. Yet it's clear that Plutarch was pushing back against a well-established passive defeatism about the power of luck.

Fortuna was praised in good times and cursed in bad. From the Middle Ages comes an anonymous collection of poems known as the *Carmina Burana*, which includes the famous "O Fortuna." These were the years of the Black Death, when close to half of Europe's population perished from an inexplicable and swiftly lethal disease, and the remainder eked out a hardscrabble existence.

> O Fortuna,
> like the moon
> you are changeable,
> ever waxing
> and waning;
> hateful life
> first oppresses

and then soothes
as fancy takes it;
poverty
and power
it melts them like ice.
Fate—monstrous
and empty,
you whirling wheel,
you are malevolent,
well-being is vain
and always fades to nothing,
shadowed
and veiled
you plague me too;
now through the game
I bring my bare back
to your villainy.
Fate is against me
in health
and virtue,
driven on
and weighted down,
always enslaved.
So at this hour
without delay
pluck the vibrating strings;
since Fate
strikes down the strong man,
everyone weep with me!

It's best to cover your bases when it comes to luck. When the first Christian emperor, Constantine the Great, built "New Rome" (Constantinople), he made sure that it included a temple to Fortuna.[6] You can't be too careful. Fortuna was depicted astride a great wheel, which as it turns lifts men from the bottom of society to the very top and then round again, dropping them from the pinnacle of success back down to penury. We are strapped to the wheel of fortune, the "whirling wheel," and our fate is firmly in her indifferent hands.

# Submission to Luck: Lucky Charms

So what can we do? Traditionally there were three main responses to the role of luck in our lives: submission, rebellion, and denial. The first option attempted to propitiate Fortuna or redirect her ill luck to others and capture her good fortune for ourselves. Luck was commonly regarded as a fungible quality, a mysterious natural force in the world that might be used or replenished. Many natural forces oscillate between depletion and renewal: physical strength, willpower, powers of concentration, sexual desire. If your luck is like these other qualities, then it should be conserved and used sparingly. Gamblers at the end of a winning streak are said to have used up their luck, but one on a losing streak is due for a win because her luck has built back up and she is due for a success. Athletes don't want to waste their luck on a spectacularly fortuitous play during practice but instead save it for the game.

The ancients knew that some natural forces can be stored or bound in objects—the power of magnetism could be carried about in a lodestone, the salvific potency of *aqua vitae* could be had by distilling wine into a concentrated tonic. So too it became a widespread and long-standing belief that luck can be protected or augmented with talismans, amulets, and potions. Birthstones, for example, have been part of Greek history and culture for more than 4,000 years and are viewed as good-luck charms. There are lucky birthstones for each month as well as for each of the signs of the Zodiac.[7] Horseshoes, forged out of the strongest known metal by elemental fire and with a shape like the fertile crescent moon, are also widely considered to be talismans of luck, and have been since the pre-Christian era.[8] In Druidic Ireland, the shamrock, the rare one clover in 10,000 with four leaves instead of three, was regarded as a good luck charm that would provide health and yield spiritual insight.[9] Petronius, a Roman courtier during the reign of Nero, describes a dinner party at which a small statue with an amulet around its neck was placed on the table to bring the diners good luck.[10] Sigmund Freud, as one might expect, claims that all the lucky charms of his day are all easily recognized as genital or sexual symbols.[11]

The idea that luck can be harbored in a physical object has persisted in popular culture. In J. K. Rowling's best selling *Harry Potter and the Half-Blood Prince*, Horace Slughorn, potions master of the wizarding school Hogwarts, brewed Felix Felicis, or liquid luck (the Latin translation of the name is more like "the luck of luck" or "lucky luck").[12] Liquid luck is a magical potion that makes the drinker lucky for a period of time, during which all of their endeavors are successful. Felix Felicis doesn't endow the imbiber with any special talents or powers or allow the impossible, but instead guides the drinker through the pathway of possibilities so that he always chooses the optimal action. When Harry drinks the brew, he is filled with confidence and able to invariably make the correct decisions and perform just the right actions in an increasingly implausible (but not impossible) set of circumstances.

Specific days of the week were supposed to contain luck as well. In *Works and Days*, Hesiod gave extensive advice about which days are the luckiest for a male to be born, which are luckiest for a female to be born, or for castrating a bull, threshing grain, yoking oxen, shearing sheep, and other activities. He wrote that lucky "days are a great boon for those on earth. But the others are random, doomless, they bring nothing. One man praises one kind of day, another another; but few are the ones who know."[13] In his *Natural History* (book 7, chapter 40), the first-century Roman scholar Pliny the Elder relates that the Thracians were in the habit of putting either a white pebble or a black one into an urn depending on whether it was a lucky or an unlucky day. By 2000 BCE the Egyptians had worked out entire Calendars of Lucky and Unlucky Days, with every day of the year associated with various relationships and interactions among the Egyptian gods and goddesses. These calendars, which were in use for nearly 3,000 years, provide very specific guidance for good fortune: do not eat or drink this food on this day of the month; do not kill this animal; do not travel on the river on this day; do not allow a bull to pass you; do not work at this occupation on this day; no construction of houses or boats on this day, etc.[14]

Not only was good luck to be acquired and protected, but bad luck could be repelled. For example, a belief in the evil eye continues to be widespread across the Mediterranean. The evil eye is not necessarily a malevolent glare; it could be someone who involuntarily brings bad luck, like an accidental and dangerous superpower.[15] It could be warded off with a variety of totems, mostly ones with some kind of fertility significance. Examples include the Fig Hand, an amulet dating to the Etruscan period, which was a closed fist with the thumb inserted between the middle and index fingers and symbolized heterosexual intercourse. Another, the Horned Hand, is now popular as a vaguely Satanic emblem of rock and roll rebellion, but formerly was symbolic of the horned head of a bull, which in turn was seen as magically potent due to its resemblance to a woman's reproductive organs.[16] Amulets representing the divine phallus, or *fascinum*, also served to ward off the evil eye. One Roman mosaic makes the point explicitly, depicting a phallus ejaculating into a disembodied eye.[17] Even today you can find the *nazar boncuğu*, a blue glass bead with a black dot in the middle of a white center, for sale in the bazaars of Turkey. It too is believed to be proof against the evil eye.

Another means of deflecting bad luck was by publicly courting contempt as a protection against hubris. The reasoning went that if misfortune is attracted by self-praise, then it must be repelled by self-mockery.[18] Royal households would retain a fool or jester to humorously mock and disillusion the king, thus warding off bad luck. Societies could rid themselves of misfortune by designating a scapegoat who would shoulder the whole burden of whatever bad luck had befallen them—plague, invasion, famine—and punish the scapegoat with beatings or exile. In this way the bad luck was also driven out of the community. James Fraser provides an extensive discussion of scapegoating and the transference of bad luck in his magisterial anthropology of religion, *The Golden Bough*.[19] *The Golden Bough* was published in Victorian England, and caused quite a controversy by pointing out that Christianity followed many commonplace religious archetypes, including the fact that the death of Christ is also the familiar tale of a scapegoat: the sacrifice of one individual to remove the ill fortunes of others.

# Rebellion against Luck: Stoicism

The second approach to manipulating Fortuna was rebellion, the strategy of the Stoics. Fortuna's wheel turns for us all, and so people from every stratum of Hellenistic society embraced the philosophy of Stoicism— from Epictetus, a deformed Greek slave in the first century CE to the Roman Emperor Marcus Aurelius. The Stoics attempted to defy the power of Fortuna by refusing to recognize things in the outside world as having any hold over us. A Stoic sage is insulated from misfortune because he does not value the objects of the external world, and believes it is virtue alone that ensures the good life. For the Stoics, emotions are to be distinguished from actions; you *undergo* emotions—they are things that happen to you—but you *perform* actions. The proper attitude toward the emotions is to not be buffeted and controlled by them, but to be self-sufficient and even-keeled. The Stoics tried to live apathetically, meaning in its original sense unmoved by the *pathê*, or passions.

Epictetus argues that human misfortune is the result of frustrated desires, and that the key to serenity (*ataraxia*) is to stop desiring what is not within our control. Our bodies, our possessions, our reputations, and social status are all subject to ill luck, but we are harmed when we lose our assets or our status only when we misjudge the value of those things. We must come to see such items as merely on loan from the gods and not our permanent property.[20] Stoic philosophy is a medicine for the soul, one that aims to cure the contingencies of fortune through, as the scholar Martha Nussbaum argues, the therapy of desire.[21] It is when we limit our expectations for the future and recognize that the self-sufficiency of virtue alone is needed for the good life that we can appreciate Marcus Aurelius's "rule to remember in the future, when anything tempts you to feel bitter: not 'This is misfortune,' but 'To bear this worthily is good fortune.'"[22]

As an advisor to the tyrannical Emperor Nero, the Stoic philosopher Seneca had a lot to be stoic about. When Nero, in a fit of pique, ordered Seneca to commit suicide in 65 CE, he made vivid Seneca's repeated counsels against trusting one's luck. In his *Moral Epistles* Seneca warns that the so-called gifts of Fortuna are really snares, and advises that "the wise man is sufficient unto himself for a happy existence, but not for mere existence. For he needs many helps towards mere existence; but for a happy existence he needs only a sound and upright soul, one that despises Fortuna."[23]

To the extent that Stoic tactics won the battle against Fortuna, it was a pyrrhic victory. Stoics thought the only way to inoculate oneself against the vicissitudes of chance was by eradicating the passions altogether—not just fear, distress, jealousy, and anger, but hope, love, and joy as well. It is one thing to abjure wealth or fame, but even having children, having friends, and having political rights and privileges were declared worthless because they could be cut off by accidents beyond our control.[24] The doctrine of radical self-sufficiency and inner virtue precluded seeing ordinary human bonds as legitimate components of a good life. When even love and family must be sacrificed in the war against Fortuna, the price may be too high. It is no surprise that in their own time Stoics were derided as "men of stone." The question then is whether to capitulate to chance and concede to our own contingency, the fragility of human relationships and our standing in the world, or to embrace the philosophy of stone.

# The Denial of Luck: All Is Fated

The third and final strategy to deal with luck was denial. While the Stoics wanted to beard Fortuna, another long-standing tradition tried to dismiss her altogether. We saw this alternative earlier in the Myth of Er—instead of luck, chance, and caprice governing our lives, perhaps our destinies are foreordained by the Fates, and secured by Necessity. From our own ignorant and shortsighted perspective, the future is an undiscovered country, full of surprises, misfortunes, and good luck, but those future events may all be essential components of our unknown fates. We may not know what is around the corner, but the gods know what is around every corner. What we see as luck, the gods see as the inexorable unfolding of the world. Put another way: you may not know what will happen later in the book and be surprised by twists and turns of the plot, but the author knows, and is not surprised.

Recall that in Sophocles's *Oedipus Rex* (429 BCE), Oedipus is born to King Laius and Queen Jocasta of Thebes. Laius is told by an oracle that he is doomed to die by the hand of his own son, so to escape his fate he binds the infant and orders him killed. Oedipus is left to die from exposure on a mountainside, but instead is found by a shepherd who takes the infant to Corinth, where he is adopted by the childless King Polybus and Queen Merope. Later Oedipus is told by the oracle at Delphi that he is fated to kill his father and mate with his mother. Believing that Polybus and Merope are his biological parents, Oedipus flees Corinth to escape the prophecy. On the road to Thebes, he meets Laius and several other men, and they quarrel about whose chariot has the right of way. A fight breaks out, and Oedipus kills Laius in the street, thus unwittingly fulfilling half of his foretold destiny. Further down the road Oedipus meets the Sphinx, a monster that has been terrorizing Thebes by refusing passage and killing all travelers who are unable to answer her famous riddle. When Oedipus solves the riddle and defeats the Sphinx, he is rewarded with the kingship of Thebes and the hand of the widowed Queen Jocasta. Thus Oedipus satisfies the prophecy completely; despite the efforts of both Laius and himself, all attempts to run from his destiny only led directly to its fulfillment. In the tale of Oedipus, nothing is a matter of luck, not meeting Laius on the road, not besting the Sphinx. Everything that happens is foreordained.

The idea that we are powerless to avoid our ineluctable fate is a common theme. According to *Mark* 14:17-30, Jesus prophesied that Judas Iscariot would betray him to the Sanhedrin and that Peter would deny him three times before morning. In both cases, there seems to be nothing Judas or Peter can do to avoid their destiny. Similarly, in Fudail ibn Ayad's *Hikayat-I-Naqshia*, a ninth-century Arabian Sufi tale, a man sees Death in the morning marketplace in Baghdad. Terrified, the man leaps on a horse and gallops to Samarra, only to find that he does indeed have an appointment with Death, but it was in the afternoon, in Samarra. Sisyphus, the legendary first king of Corinth, cheated death by binding Thanatos (death) and refusing to return to the underworld. Duly angered, Zeus decreed that Sisyphus be eternally doomed to push a great boulder to the top of a mountain in Hades, only to have it roll back down again. Albert Camus famously imagines Sisyphus embracing his fate, scornful of the gods, the absurd hero happy in a perpetual struggle that he cannot escape.[25]

If fatalism is right—used here in the metaphysical sense that the future is fixed and unchangeable, not the psychological sense of fatalism as resignation in the face of some expected event—then it does seem that luck has no role in our lives. There are two strands to this line of thinking. One is that the gods have planned the future and that our actions are predetermined for us. Thus if God picked Judas to betray Jesus from the get-go, then Judas could not have done anything differently. Judas didn't choose freely, nor was he the victim of bad luck, any more than Oedipus or Sisyphus. The other strand of fatalist thinking does not depend on predetermination at all or on a sense of the gods leading us by the hand from one action to the next. All we need is a little logic.

The Greek logician Diodorus Cronus (fourth to third centuries BCE) provided an early fatalist argument, the so-called Master Argument. The Master Argument was sufficiently famous even in Diodorus's time that it was hotly debated at dinner parties. Indeed, Diodorus himself was so well known for his work in logic that, according to the Alexandrian poet Callimachus, even the ravens on the rooftops recognized his dominance, cawing out his criterion for conditional propositions.[26] No clear statement of the Master Argument survives, but it seems to have gone something like this.[27] Every true past tensed statement is necessarily true. For example, "Socrates was snub-nosed" is true and unalterable; there is nothing we can do to change the past, or make true sentences about the past into false ones. Time-traveling rhinoplasties are out of the question. It is true now, true then, and true at every point in time that

"Socrates was snub-nosed." From the fact that "it was true that Socrates was snub-nosed" we can prove that it is necessarily true that Socrates was snub-nosed.

You might be inclined to suppose that statements about the future are different; they are not necessary, and the future is still contingent in a way the past is not and remains open to other possibilities. So "the final American president will be snub-nosed" may or may not be true; there just isn't a fact of the matter yet. What are we going do with a past tensed statement that refers to some future fact? Consider this pair of sentences:

- It was true in 1776 that the final American president will be snub-nosed.

- It was true in 1776 that the final American president will not be snub-nosed.

If every statement of the form "It was true that X" expresses a necessity (as in the Socrates example), then one of those two sentences must be necessarily true. Either it is a true and unalterable fact of the past that the final American president will be snub-nosed, or a true and unalterable fact of the past that the final president is not snub-nosed. Either way the snub-nosedness of the final American president turns out to be a necessary truth after all. Thus, if "the final American president will be snub-nosed" is true, then it is necessarily true. Likewise, if "the final American president will *not* be snub-nosed" is true, then it is necessarily true. We may not know what the future holds—whether the final president's nose is snub, button, aquiline, or even Michael Jacksonish is currently a mystery to us—yet nevertheless there is right now a set and fixed future which awaits us. At least if Diodorus is right.

Early Christian theologians reached a similar conclusion by reflecting on God's omniscience and what that implies about his knowledge of the future. Boethius, a Roman philosopher of the early sixth century CE, discussed this issue in the fifth book of his *The Consolation of Philosophy*. Boethius lived at the very end of the Roman Empire, as it collapsed under barbarian invasions, and perhaps his philosophy of divine foreknowledge did bring some consolation. In his succinct formulation:

If God sees everything that will happen, and if he cannot be mistaken, then what he foresees must necessarily happen. And if he knows from the very beginning what all eternity will bring, not only men's actions but their thoughts and desires will be known to him, and that means that there cannot be any free will. There couldn't be any thought or action that divine providence, which is never mistaken, did not know about in advance.[28]

Since God is omniscient, he infallibly knows every fact about the past, present, and future. Therefore, God infallibly knows everything that you will do, every action you will perform, and everything that will happen to you.

What we perceive as the future is every bit as rigid and necessary as Diodorus Cronus thought it was; Boethius only reasons his way to the same conclusion from a different starting point. Note that unlike some earlier discussions of fate, Boethius does not assume that there is any kind of divine plan or design. God is not compelling any actions at all; he simply *knows* precisely what you will do and that alone proves the necessity of the future. Where does this leave luck? Boethius, following Aristotle, argues that nothing is truly a matter of chance; nothing is random or uncaused. Luck is merely "the unexpected result of causes that come together of things that were done for some other purpose." When Terry Herbert, an English metal detector enthusiast, went poking around a farmer's field in Staffordshire in 2009 and found an Anglo-Saxon hoard of nearly 4,000 golden objects that were twelve centuries old, it was only good luck because he did not expect it. Antiquities specialists think that the hoard was buried to hide the artifacts during a time of danger. Likewise, Herbert's presence in that field was not chance—he intentionally went there with his metal detector, hoping to find something of interest. Their mutual presence in that field was the result of causes that come together of things that were done for some other purpose; it wasn't caprice or causeless chance. While from Herbert's point of view finding the Staffordshire Hoard was a matter of luck, it was not some whim of Fortuna's. After all, God knew all along that Herbert would strike it rich.

Boethius was troubled by the implications that divine omniscience poses for free will. If God infallibly knows everything that you will do, then it is impossible for you to do anything other than what God knows you will do; you have no choice. Your doing anything other than what God knows you will do would undermine his infallible knowledge, which of course is impossible. Therefore, you have no choice in what you will do. Yet if you have no choice in what you will do, then you are not free. For many Christian theologians this was a serious problem, since they thought that God could not properly judge us after death if our choices in this life were not made freely.

Not everyone was bothered by this issue, though. In the sixteenth century, the French Protestant reformer John Calvin embraced Boethius's conclusions, writing, "the Providence of God, as taught in Scripture, is opposed to fortune."[29] Calvin acknowledges that it is "an erroneous opinion prevailing in all ages, an opinion almost universally prevailing in our own day—viz. that all things happen fortuitously." He lists several cases that people would ordinarily describe as good or bad luck, like a wondrous hair's-breadth escape from death or falling in among robbers, and declares that they are all governed by the secret counsel of God. The true doctrine of Providence, he claims, has not only been obscured, but almost buried by the worship of Fortuna. "There is no place left in human affairs for fortune and chance," he declares, "that which is vulgarly called Fortune, is also regulated by a hidden order, and what we call Chance is nothing else than that the reason and cause of which is secret."[30] There is no luck and there is no fortune, because God leaves nothing to chance.

The doctrine of divine foreknowledge has led to some absolutely terrifying theologies. The American colonial divine Jonathan Edwards, for example, argued at length that all truths are necessary ones, and that God knows them all, including every future act you might desire, will, or perform.[31] Apparently this knowledge has left God quite angry at us. Here's a sample from Edwards's delightful sermon "Sinners in the Hands of an Angry God":

> Natural Men are held in the Hand of God over the Pit of Hell; they have deserved the fiery Pit, and are already sentenced to it; and God is dreadfully provoked, his Anger is as great towards them as to those that are actually suffering the Executions of the fierceness of his Wrath in Hell … the Devil is waiting for them, Hell is gaping for them, the Flames gather and flash about them, and would fain lay hold on them … [and] there are no Means within Reach that can be any Security to them … all that preserves them every Moment is the mere arbitrary Will, and uncovenanted unobliged Forbearance of an incensed God.[32]

Ironically, with Calvin and Edwards we have come full circle. Fatalism was supposed to strip Fortuna of her powers by showing that everything happens by necessity and so there is no room for luck. Now it looks like she has the upper hand once again. Some of Calvin's later followers were satirized as the "frozen chosen": from time immemorial God selected them for a heavenly afterlife, but since their selection happened long before they had performed any deeds or even existed, it had nothing to do with merit or desert. Likewise, Edwards did not think that we all go to Hell, despite how much we deserve it. In another sermon he writes:

> When the saints in glory … shall see the doleful state of the damned, how this will heighten their sense of the blessedness of their own state … When they shall see how miserable others of their fellow creatures are … when they shall see the smoke of their torment, and the raging of the flames of their burning, and hear their dolorous shrieks and cries, and consider that they in the mean time are in the most blissful state, and shall surely be in it to all eternity; how they will rejoice![33]

What, then, is the difference between the saints and the sinners? For Edwards, the saved deserve the same misery as the damned, and it was nothing but sovereign grace that elevated them to bliss. God arbitrarily, capriciously selects some for his heavenly banquet (served with a side of schadenfreude), and drops the rest into the pit. A few are lucky that God favored them and the rest are unlucky, but either way Divine Providence turns out to be no more than Fortuna under a new guise.

# Luck and Gambling

Luck and fate are surprisingly intertwined, not just in the matter of fatalism and divine foreknowledge, but in the case of gambling, where there is a long tradition of using chance to discover what is non-chancy, already determined, or fated. This peculiar collusion between Tuche and the Fates is seen throughout the history of gambling. Filed and sanded *astragali* (the ankle bones of sheep, antelopes, deer, or similar animals) are the precursors to modern dice, and have been found in abundance at archaeological sites from France to India. They are thought to have been used by shamans to divine the future. Modern-style dice, numbered as ours with opposite sides summing to seven, have been discovered in ancient sites in Egypt. Dice games like backgammon and the Royal Game of Ur date back at least 5,000 years.[34] Even the gods gamble, only for greater stakes. Zeus, Poseidon, and Hades drew lots for shares in the universe, with Zeus drawing the sky, Poseidon the seas, and Hades the underworld.

The divinatory use of proto-dice, like *astragali*, seems to have preceded dice-based games used for entertainment. With Tarot cards, though, the reverse is true. Painted or block-printed playing cards were originally invented in China in the early medieval period. From there they spread by trade on the Silk Road or by Mongol conquerors to Persia, Egypt, and finally Europe. There was little or no standardization, and many different types of card packs were put to use. The Tarot dates to the early fifteenth century, and was originally just another type of deck of cards used for gaming. By the eighteenth century it had acquired its mystical associations with the occult, through imaginary links to ancient Egyptian or Hermetic symbolism.[35] Giacomo Casanova, one of the world's most famous lovers, noted in his diary that his Russian mistress was obsessed with using cards to predict the future, and remarks that it was one of the reasons he left her (well, that and her "extreme jealousy" regarding his other amorous liaisons).[36]

Thomas Aquinas, the greatest theologian of the Middle Ages, bent his considerable intellect to examining the role of gambling and its place in the Christian life. In his book *On Lots*, he recognized that gambling is not merely a recreational pastime, but that people use the casting of lots to find out information that they are unable to discover by their own intellect. Aquinas makes a distinction among the use of lots as divisory, consultory, and divinatory.[37] The divisory use was to settle disputes, or to make communal decisions in matters of controversy. In *Numbers* 26:52–56, Yahweh orders the use of lots to divide the land of Israel. The open land must be divvied up somehow, and given equal claims of merit, random selection is a reasonable way to go. Similarly, all four canonical gospels report that the Roman soldiers used lots to divide up Jesus's garments. Thus a lottery ensured that they all received their fair allotment. More recently we toss a coin to see who receives the kickoff at the start of a football game, or draw cards to see who starts as dealer in a poker game. There is no particular benefit to receiving the kickoff or dealing first, but some impartial method of starting the game is needed.

The consultory use of lots was to distribute honors and benefits or assign punishments and risk. Aquinas reminds us that in the *First Book of Kings* Saul was elected king by lot. In the *Book of Jonah*, when Jonah's ship is nearly capsized by a violent storm, the sailors drew lots to determine who was to blame, and Jonah was selected. Here we see the use of luck to pick a scapegoat: Jonah's number comes up and he is tossed into the raging sea, taking away the danger from the community of sailors back on board the ship. A more modern example might be a platoon leader who has his troops draw straws to see who must clear a dangerous tunnel. Not everyone can go into the tunnel; the task cannot be evenly divided. Yet someone must go, and random selection seems fairest. Luck is thereby consulted to determine the course of action.

Most controversial is sortilege—the divinatory use of lots to ascertain the future or determine the will of the gods. Attempts to discover our destined ends through the use of auguries, portents, and omens no doubt predate history itself. One famous example is when Julius Caesar drove south to the Rubicon River leading the *Legio tertia decima Gemina* (the 13th Twin Legion). At the time, Caesar was governor of a northern province. Past the river was Roman territory proper. Roman law stated that it was forbidden to enter Rome as a military commander at the head of troops, instead of disbanding and entering as peaceful citizens. Caesar, indecisive as to whether to lay down his command or cross the Rubicon with the legion and spark civil war, threw dice to reveal his fate. When he crossed the Rubicon, Caesar was widely reported as declaring "Alea iacta est!" (the die has been cast). His subsequent victory in war saw him anointed Dictator for Life and marked the turning point from the Republic to the Empire.

Even in Caesar's time sortilege was subject to sharp criticism. His contemporary, the Roman statesman and orator Marcus Tullius Cicero, wrote in *On Divination*, "the casting of lots? It is much like playing at morra, dice, or knuckle-bones, in which recklessness and luck prevail rather than reflection and judgment. The whole scheme of divination by lots was fraudulently contrived from mercenary motives, or as a means of encouraging superstition and error."[38] Cicero's critique made little headway against the appeal of using luck to apprehend the divine plan. When John Wesley, the founder of the Methodist Church, tried to decide in 1737 whether he should marry, he turned to the casting of lots. When he found out that marriage was not in the cards, Wesley did not agonize over it, but instead was able to cheerfully say "thy will be done."[39] His continued bachelorhood was not bad luck, but fate.

Little advance was made in the mastery and understanding of luck until the Renaissance and the development of probability theory. Gambling was directly responsible for the development of probability theory—if there is anyone who wants to subjugate luck, it is gamblers. In the early sixteenth century, Gerolamo Cardano traveled to Pavia, Italy, to enroll in medical school. Like most students, he was not flush with funds; but he did discover that he had an exceptional head for gambling, and before long he had won enough to put himself through school.[40] Cardano decided to write down his gambling insights, and produced the first treatise on probability, *Liber de Ludo Aleae* (*Book on Games of Chance*) in which he discusses cards, dice, backgammon, and other games. The mathematics of his day was primitive: the = sign had not yet been invented, and + and — were brand new. Cardano still gave it a go. In line with the adage that "in the land of the blind the one-eyed is king," *Liber de Ludo Aleae* was not published until long after his death. Cardano didn't want his gambling opponents knowing his secrets.

Even the greatest scientist of his age, Galileo Galilei, worked on problems of gambling. His arm was twisted a bit by his patron, the Grand Duke of Tuscany, who was apparently devoted to the gaming tables. Games played with three dice were popular in Galileo's day, and the Grand Duke had played so much dice that he had noticed a slight discrepancy in the frequencies of certain numbers. In particular, he noticed that the dice summed up to ten more often than they summed to nine. This was puzzling to the Duke. The chance that any particular face of a die turn up is the same as any other face, furthermore there are six possible ways for the three dice to sum to nine:

(621), (531), (522), (441), (432), (333)

And there are six ways for the dice to sum to 10:

(631), (622), (541), (532), (422), (433)

So why should ten come up more often? Galileo was busy sorting out the mysteries of the universe and wasn't pleased to take time away to address someone's petty gambling problem. Nonetheless, he dutifully solved it, writing, "Now I, in order to oblige him who has ordered me to produce whatever occurs to me about the problem, will expound my ideas."[41] Galileo's answer was that not all combinations are equiprobable. (631), for example, is six times likelier than (333). There is only one way to throw (333): first die is a three, the second die is a three, and so is the third. But with (631) you could throw (136), (163), (316), (361), (613), or (631). There are twenty-seven ways of rolling a ten with three dice, but only twenty-five ways of rolling a nine. Galileo concluded that with three dice rolling a ten was 27/25, or about 1.08, times more likely than a nine.[42] Ten didn't turn up more often than nine because of some inexplicable preference of Fortuna's; it was just straight mathematics.

In 1654, Antoine Gombaud, a French raconteur and inveterate gambler better known as the Chevalier de Méré, was bothered by a long-standing and more difficult puzzle known as the Problem of Points. The problem is this. Suppose two players of equal skill and opportunity play a fair game for fixed stakes, but are forced to break off play before the game's conclusion. What is the fairest way of dividing the stakes? For example, suppose two equally skilled tennis players bet $100 on the outcome of a best of three sets match. One player is up 7–5, 1–2 when they are rained out. How should they split the $100? Or suppose two players place equal bets on who will win the best of five coin tosses and one player has won two tosses and the other one toss when the game is suspended. How should the pot be divided? It looks like any adequate solution requires peering into the future to see how the players will fare. In addition, a fully acceptable answer must be wholly generalizable to any kind of game—dice, cards, whatever—and to any length of play.

The Chevalier had an inflated sense of his own analytical ability, to such an extent that true intellects like the polymath Gottfried Leibniz laughed at his airs.[43] Nevertheless, he at least had enough sense to take this conundrum to his smart friends. The Chevalier approached the mathematical virtuosos Pierre de Fermat and Blaise Pascal with the Problem of Points and asked if they could figure out how to solve it. Pascal, who had inherited a bit of money as a young man and enjoyed gambling himself, happily took on the task. In the subsequent exchange of letters between Fermat and Pascal, they not only solved the Problem of Points, but also developed the idea of expected value and laid down the foundations of probability theory. If we cannot know the future for certain, we at least have the tools to determine what is likely.

Mathematicians thought they had pulled back the curtain, as in *The Wizard of Oz*, to reveal the great and terrible power of Fortuna as nothing more than a little man pushing levers and pulling knobs. Pierre Rémond de Montmort, a French nobleman who contributed to probability theory during the reign of the Sun King Louis XIV, wrote in his *Analytical Essay on Games of Chance* (1708),

> [Most men] believe that it is necessary to appease this blind divinity that one calls Fortune, in order to force her to be favorable to them in following the rules which they have imagined. I think therefore it would be useful, not only to gamesters but to all men in general, to know that chance has rules which can be known … [44]

If mathematics is the language of the book of the world, as Galileo famously said, then probability theory is the language of Fortuna's journal.

By the eighteenth century, mathematicians felt entitled to proclaim themselves the conquerors of luck. In 1718 the French mathematician Abraham de Moivre published one of the first textbooks on probability theory, *The Doctrine of Chances: or, a Method for Calculating the Probabilities of Events in Play*. In it he declares:

> If by saying that a man has had good Luck, nothing more was meant than that he has been generally a Gainer at play, the Expression might be allowed as very proper in a short way of speaking: But if the Word good Luck be understood to signify a certain predominant quality, so inherent in a Man, that he must win whenever he Plays, or at least win oftener than lose, it may be denied that there is any such thing in nature.[45]

In the Myth of Er we saw a tangled nest of ideas regarding luck, fate, and choice. In the two and a half millennia since then, thinkers have used every tool in the shop to try to tease those ideas apart and find some way of understanding their role in our lives. We appealed to the gods, used charms and talismans, and declared our stoic self-sufficiency. Now it is fair to say that contemporary mathematicians and scientists regard the matter of luck to have been completely settled by probability theory. To be sure, it has been a hard-won and magnificent achievement, and in narrow spheres like gambling it is the key in the lock of chance.

Still, many puzzles remain, and much of the rest of this book will examine them in detail. Here is a preview of some coming attractions. If the fatalists like Diodorus Cronus and Boethius are right, then everything that happens is probability 1. How then could anything be a matter of luck when all is certain? Or consider a wealthy miser who against all odds leaves his fortune to charity. You might say that the charity was lucky to have received such a bequest, but from the miser's perspective it wasn't luck—he knew all along the terms of his will. Was it luck or not? Or if probability is supposed to measure human expectations and not the objective chance of events in a fated or determined world, then what shall we make of the optimist who always expects to win the lottery? If she is destined to do so and expected it all along, there does not seem to be much room to say that her win was improbable.

Some things that are quite probable seem lucky, and other things that are improbable do not. For example, it is very probable that you win at Russian Roulette, if you are nervy enough to play: you have an 80 percent chance of winning. Nevertheless, if you pull the trigger on an empty chamber when the bullet is in an adjacent one, it still feels awfully lucky to have come away unscathed. Or imagine a rock shattered by a bolt of lightning. It is very unlikely that that particular rock should be hit by lightning, but it does not seem like bad luck. Bad luck for whom? The rock?

Even more, the mathematics of probability seems ill equipped to explain the varieties of fortune we saw in the Lachesis's Lottery, where the kinds of lives we have, or the sorts of people we become, seems largely a matter of luck. The circumstances of our births, the travails of our fortunes in the world—how can we fix the prior probabilities and make the calculations? There may also be a worthwhile distinction between how fortunate or unfortunate we are and how lucky or unlucky we are. Augustus was fortunate to be the nephew of Julius Caesar and his adopted heir, but it wasn't a matter of luck, and it certainly wasn't improbable.

The interplay between luck and skill also remains a mystery. Playing sports, getting a job, finding love—how much of our success or failure at these things should be assigned to luck and how much to talent, effort, and skill? The probability calculus does not offer an obvious solution, despite what has been promised on its behalf. Even gambling with dice or cards—the very thing that probability theory was designed to solve—is in part the luck of the draw and partly the talent of the players. How can we parse the contribution that each makes to the outcome? All these pieces of luck, chance, fortune, fate, and skill coalesce into the intricate mosaic of our lives, and despite the tremendous and venerable effort that has been made to square our accounts with Fortuna, there is still much to do in reckoning the character of luck.

# 2 LUCK AND SKILL

*"No victor believes in chance."*
—FRIEDRICH NIETZSCHE, *THE GAY SCIENCE* §258 (1882)

The eighteenth-century Croatian polymath Roger Boscovich (Ruđer Bošković in his mother tongue) thought it was a serious mistake to suppose that "there is anything that is in itself truly fortuitous; for, all things have definite causes in Nature, from which they arise, & therefore some things are called by us fortuitous, simply because we are ignorant of the causes by which their existence is determined."[1] Like Montmort and de Moivre before him, Boscovich was sure that "Lucky Events" was just the signpost at the swamp of our ignorance, which modern science was in the process of draining.

Boscovich was influenced by Newton's great development of mechanical laws that allowed people to explain and predict a whole range of phenomena. Why do cars move forward on dry pavement but spin out on icy roads? Newton's third law gives us the answer. It states that when one body exerts a force on a second body, the second body simultaneously exerts a force equal in magnitude and opposite in direction on the first body. This is what allows cars to drive: the road pushes back on the car just as much as the car pushes the road. In a sense, the road propels the car forward as the tires push backwards on the road. On an icy road, there isn't enough friction for the car to produce the action force needed to cause a reaction, so the tires spin and the car goes nowhere.

Not only could Newton address such homely examples, but his mechanics reached out to the heavens. The motion of the planets around the sun is a stable, predictable pattern, but why? Planetary orbits are an example of a two-body problem: determining the repeating path of two objects that only interact with each other. Classical mechanics could solve this problem too. Newton's first law tells us that a body remains at rest, or moves in a straight line at a constant velocity, unless acted upon by a net outside force. So imagine spinning in a circle while holding a string with a golf ball attached at the end. When you let go of the string, the weight flies off in a straight line instead of continuing to spin in a circle. When you are holding the string, it constrains the motion of the golf ball—which, basically, is going as straight as it can. The Sun's gravitational attraction constrains the motion of the Earth in the same way (ignoring Earth's gravity and that of other local bodies, which are negligible by comparison). Instead of the Earth flying through space in a straight line, the Sun's gravity grabbed it like a string on a golf ball, and around we go. Before Newton you might have thought that it is just bad luck to slip on ice, or good luck that the Earth is in a nice stable orbit, but that would be because, in Boscovich's words, "we are ignorant of the causes by which their existence is determined." But as soon as we know about those mechanical causes and laws, our belief in luck fades away.[2]

One problem with this optimism concerns nonlinear systems. For example, Newtonian mechanics could deal nicely with two-body problems like planetary orbits, but are completely stymied with three-body problems. Suppose there are three interacting bodies, like a trinary star system, or an iron pendulum suspended over three magnets arranged in a triangle. You might expect that the patterns and regularities of their revolutions around each other can be worked out with some effort. In fact, in certain special cases, they can be worked out. But there is no general formula for predicting the future locations of bodies in a three-body problem. If you set the pendulum in motion it will not settle into any predictable configuration; it will swing back and forth between magnets A and B for a while, then switch to B and C, only to jump back to A.[3] A three-body problem isn't like a two-body problem, only a bit more complicated; it is so much more complex that no general solution has been found, and the prospects for one are dim. Needless to say, things get even worse for n-body problems when n>3.

The quagmire is chaos. Stand at the top of the 2425' Yosemite Falls and toss a ping pong ball over the edge. In fact, toss ten different colored ping pong balls in, as close to the same spot as you possibly can. Even though they went in at the same place, the balls do not wind up at the same place. In fact their final destinations will be wonderfully far from each other, and it will be impossible in advance to foresee their exact final locations. Each jet of water over the top is like another ping pong ball—interacting with each other, merging, colliding, slowed by rocks or sped by gravity, aerated, windblown, a billion nodes intersecting every moment with those colored balls tumbling to their ultimate end. Likewise, extraordinarily fine differences in the initial parameters of two weather models will swiftly lead to radically divergent weather predictions. And much the same is true with forecasting the stock market, fish populations, and many other dynamic systems. The constant interaction of the securities traders or the ever-changing conditions of aquatic environment amounts to an incessant resetting of the initial state of the system; the true initial conditions cannot be recovered, like finding the prime factors of very large numbers. Even something as humble as the swirling patterns of cream in one's coffee are nonrepeating and more or less unmodelable beyond fairly general parameters.

## Slaying Laplace's Demon

Still, one might think that no matter how chaotically unpredictable things may be, they are still deterministic, and thus neither a matter of chance nor luck. In 1814, the French scientist Pierre-Simon Laplace famously wrote:

> We ought to regard the present state of the universe as the effect of its anterior state and as the cause of the one which is to follow. Given for one instant an intelligence which could comprehend all the forces by which nature is animated and the respective situation of the beings who compose it an intelligence sufficiently vast to submit these data to analysis it would embrace in the same formula the movements of the greatest bodies of the universe and those of the lightest atom; for it, nothing would be uncertain and the future, as the past, would be present to its eyes.[4]

All we need is a snapshot of the universe, one so finely detailed that we could tell the position and momentum of every particle and we could in principle figure out the entire future history of the universe and everything in it. Well, maybe we couldn't figure it out (the fine details of chaotic interactions being beyond our small simian brains), but a vast intelligence could—perhaps a future supercomputer with full knowledge of all the forces and laws of nature. At least, that's the Laplacean dream.

However, Laplace's Demon (as the hypothetical superintelligence is often called) is not physically possible. That is, the existence of such a being is inconsistent with the laws of nature. A proper demonstration requires that we consider the practical limits of computability. Before we try to tackle the greatest bodies in the universe and the lightest atom, let's look first at something humble, like board games. Could a computer perfectly predict the outcome of games like chess, or the ancient Chinese board game of Go? That is, are those games solvable? Some games are. Tic-tac-toe is solvable: there are only 26,830 possible games and it can be proven that every real game can be driven to a tie. Chess is stupendously more complicated; the total number of possible games of chess that can be played (its game-tree complexity) is on the order of $10^{123}$. By comparison, there are around $10^{80}$ atoms in the observable universe. Go makes chess look simple. If we assume a standard 19x19 Go board and that the average number of moves in a game is 200, there are $10^{768}$ possible games of Go. The longest possible game—presumably between two boneheads making relentlessly dumb choices—takes $10^{48}$ moves, which gives a staggering $10^{10^{171}}$ possible games. The ratio of possible Go games to possible chess games is many orders of magnitude larger than the ratio of the size of the entire universe to the size of a single atom.[5]

Could any physical being solve Go? Another way to ask the question is to ask for the specs of the most powerful imaginable computer. Computers can be built out of pretty much anything, including Tinkertoys[6]—the key feature is the use of energy to flip something from a 0 to a 1, the most basic logical operation. In our everyday computers, this takes the form of switching on a transistor, but it could be changing the state of a subatomic particle, like inverting a nuclear spin. It turns out that the number of elementary logical operations per second that a physical system can perform is limited by the system's energy, and the amount of information that the system can register is limited by its maximum entropy.[7] Well, the universe as a whole is a physical system. Surely the most powerful computer has everything the universe has to give; indeed, it is the universe itself. So what can it do? Assuming that nothing can compute faster than the Planck time (the incredibly short time scale at which gravitational effects are of the same order as quantum effects), MIT physicist Seth Lloyd has estimated that at most the universe could have performed $10^{120}$ basic operations on all its informational bits since the Big Bang. Given some further calculations about entropy, there are between $10^{90}$ and $10^{120}$ (assuming gravitational fields can contribute entropy) bits of information in the universe.[8] The greatest physically possible computer has at best performed $10^{120}$ operations over $10^{120}$ bits since the beginning of time.

Presumably the ultimate computer could solve Go with fancy algorithms that can prune away certain game branches that are obvious losers or isomorphic with other branches. In fact, Google DeepMind's computer AlphaGo does something like this and is now superior to all human players. Can the ultimate computer solve Go by brute force? Well, to do so it would have to consider every possible game and then develop an optimal move response map, a bit like planning a trip to Houston by first looking at all the roads in North America. That's not efficient, but it is effective. Assume that looking at each game counts as one basic operation. That means $10^{10^{171}}$ operations, which is way, way more than the universe has ever done. How long the universe will last is an open question in cosmology, and is dependent on settling several things, including the expansion acceleration due to dark energy. At present, however, it looks like the universe doesn't have enough time to perform $10^{10^{171}}$ operations before Armageddon.

The usual way that people dismiss Laplace is to cite the intrinsic stochastity of the quantum world. Determinism is false because atomic-scale events, like radioactive decay, are essentially probabilistic—there's a 50 percent chance that an atom of Krypton-85 will decay to Rubidium in the next 10.73 years, and that's the end of it. Yet that swift dismissal misses the larger picture. Even if we ignore quantum indeterminacy and suppose we live in a wholly deterministic world, even if we forget about complicated things like the three-body problem, waterfalls, or the swirls of cream in a cup of coffee, the Laplacean dream is dead. The whole universe can't even solve a rule-governed board game like Go by brute force. Unless we are ready to posit supernatural agents, there are vast realms of future events that cannot be predicted in principle. Those events may not be truly random, in the sense of uncaused, but they are fundamentally unpredictable, unknowable, and in that sense deeply chancy.

The developers of probability theory and Enlightenment science cheerfully declared that Fortuna was dead, although (to borrow from Nietzsche), given the way of men, Fortuna's shadow lives on in the way that we casually interpret our experiences as lucky or unlucky, and so we must vanquish her shadow too. Contemporary mathematicians and probabilists think that they have eliminated luck, and the better we internalize regression to the mean, grasp the law of large numbers, or skirt the gambler's fallacy, the more we shrink the domain of luck.[9] "Luck" becomes a mere placeholder for our ignorance and just as Ben

Franklin's humble kite brought low the mighty thunderbolts of Zeus, so too with probability and Fortuna.

However, an analysis of luck in terms of probability does not thereby eliminate it; that sort of attitude now seems like hubristic overreaching. Boscovich may be right that we call some things luck because we don't understand how they come about, but his stance does little to eliminate the reality of luck in a chaotic world where the details of the future are beyond all possible determining. Instead of concluding that probability theory has eradicated luck, it is more reasonable to see it as a *theory* of luck. That is, luck is a perfectly real phenomenon, but it is to be understood in terms of what is improbable, the calculation of which is the very point of the axioms and theorems of probability. While this book will be arguing that luck is not real, it is not so easily dismissed as the mathematicians think. It is a much longer road to get safely to that skeptical conclusion.

# A Probability Theory of Luck

Most of what happens to us is improbable, but much less is a matter of luck. You get up in the morning and put on a pink dress shirt—an uncommon choice since you tend to prefer blues and blacks. You make a cup of a tea, which you rarely have, but you are out of coffee. Then you stick a couple pieces of pumpernickel in the toaster, and reflect that of all the breakfast options in the world, from Asian congee to Scottish haggis, pumpernickel toast is an unlikely selection. Even restricted to your own kitchen, there was yogurt, granola, eggs, or even waffles, which you might easily have eaten instead. The likelihood of pumpernickel toast was not high. After breakfast you step outside to a cool and drizzly day. The forecast had been for partly sunny and warmer weather, and only a low chance of cool rain. You get into your car and take the freeway to work, noting a blue 2007 Subaru Legacy in front of you as you look for your exit. Not very likely for *that* particular car to be in front of you. Yet out of the millions of combinations of car colors, makes, models, and years, a 2007 blue Subaru Legacy wound up in front of you. Driving past the Dunkin Donuts drive-thru, you see that it is sparsely attended—a surprise since it is a popular location and cars are typically backed up to the road. You don't stop, though, and continue to work. As you pull into your parking lot, you notice an empty spot near your building, which seldom happens. You make sure to take it.

This little vignette is shot through with the improbable—your shirt color, breakfast selection, the weather, other cars in traffic, the customers at Dunkin Donuts, even the parking at work. At least, it is presented that way. However, what is the assumed background comparison to establish what is probable or not? For example, is it really improbable that you have pumpernickel toast for breakfast? If the comparison reference class is "all the possible breakfast foods in the world," then, yes, it is unlikely that pumpernickel toast would emerge out of that vast sea of possibilities. If the reference class is "all possible breakfasts in your kitchen," a much more modest selection that doesn't include haggis or congee, then pumpernickel toast is more probable. Maybe that's still the wrong way to think about it. Perhaps we should just consider how likely it is that you have pumpernickel toast given the fact that's what you really wanted for breakfast this morning. In other words, the proper frame of reference is "the breakfast food in your kitchen that you want most," in which case it is quite probable that pumpernickel toast is your selection.

So which is the right way to think about it? Is there a right way? In the study of probability, this is known as the reference class problem, and will be revisited in a bit. Yet even setting the reference class issue aside, there must be more to luck than mere (im)probability alone. It might be unlikely that you put on a pink dress shirt this morning, but it's not a matter of luck. For one thing, you decided to put it on. Or the paucity of customers at Dunkin Donuts—again, maybe it was probabilistically surprising at a popular location, but you weren't planning to stop there, so what makes it either lucky or unlucky for you? It certainly seems less a matter of luck than finding a convenient parking spot close to work. The difference is that the parking spot *matters to you*, and the line at the donut shop does not. Taken on its own, probability can't be the whole story about luck. Most things, probable or improbable, as in the vignette above, just aren't a matter of luck. If you flip a penny and get five heads in a row, that's certainly unlikely (there's about a 3/100 chance of getting five heads in a row), but you're not lucky for having done so. Not unless it matters to you in some way. If you have a bet riding on the coin tosses, that's different; then the five heads will be lucky (if you wagered on heads) or unlucky (if you wagered on tails), but otherwise it is really a matter of non-luck. Adding a significance requirement allows us to attach luck to an agent. Without it, who exactly is lucky or unlucky? An even easier way to see this is to consider an improbable event without agency: suppose a lightning bolt turns some atmospheric oxygen ($O_2$) into ozone ($O_3$).

That doesn't seem to be an issue of luck at all; the air certainly didn't care one way or another. The lightning may have been improbable, but it was not luck. So in addition to an event's being improbable, another necessary condition for luck (good or bad) is that the event *matter* in some way.

An additional motivation for a significance condition on luck is that it allows us to figure out whether someone has been subject to good luck or bad luck. It is not enough to know that an event is chancy, or that a chancy event affects someone, we need to know whether it affects them in a good or bad way. If Heloise and Abelard are playing blackjack against each other, and Heloise is dealt Jack-Ace, that's very improbable (about .5 percent) and certainly matters for Heloise. Obviously it matters just as much for Abelard too, just inversely. Without establishing that not only is the low chance of Jack-Ace significant for both Heloise and Abelard, but that it affects her in a good way and him in a bad way, it can't be sorted out who is lucky and who is unlucky.

A third reason that we need a significance condition for luck is that without it, we cannot adequately explain degrees of luckiness. For example, suppose that both Jean-Paul and Simone play the lottery. Jean-Paul plays a lottery with a 1/10,000,000 chance of winning, and so does Simone. The only difference between the two lotteries is that Jean-Paul's lottery has a top prize of only $10, whereas Simone's lottery has a top prize of $1 million. If Jean-Paul wins he is lucky, but if Simone wins, she is much, much luckier. That fact can't be explained by probability alone: the chance of winning was the same in both lotteries. The difference is that a $1 million prize is of much greater significance than a paltry $10 payout.

Is this significance condition one that comes in degrees or is it more of a threshold concept? If it is a threshold concept, then equally improbable events that are sufficiently important or significant to someone above a boundary degree are equally lucky. Below the boundary, they are more a matter of non-luck. For example, suppose that both Jean-Paul and Simone are dirt-poor and can barely afford their next pack of Galoises. Winning any amount of money over $5 would be significant to either one of them. So when Jean-Paul wins his $10 in a 1/10,000,000 lottery and Simone wins her $1 million in a different 1/10,000,000 lottery, they are equally lucky: they both beat the same odds, and they both won a sum above the significance threshold. But, of course, that's absurd. They aren't equally lucky, precisely because winning $1 million is so much more significant than winning $10, even if we grant that winning any amount of money is a worthwhile thing. So the significance requirement must be variable, just as probability is.[10]

The University of Pittsburgh philosopher Nicholas Rescher writes, "luck … involves three things: (1) a beneficiary or maleficiary, (2) a development that is benign (positive) or malign (negative) from the standpoint of the interests of the affected individual, and that, moreover, (3) is fortuitous (unexpected, chancy, unforeseeable)."[11] Rescher recognized that the significance of the lucky event and the probability of its occurrence are inversely proportional. A mildly improbable event of real significance (like getting a new job when you are one of four finalists) is lucky, but not as lucky as a greatly improbable event of the same significance (like getting a new job when you were just one of 200 applicants). An unlikely event with little significance has low levels of luck associated with it (like finding decent parking on a spontaneous trip to Manhattan), whereas an unlikely event with high significance is much luckier (like finding decent parking in Manhattan when you are running late for a show).

Rescher offers this formula[12] to measure the amount of luck ($\lambda$) in an event E, given a level of significance for that event ($\Delta(E)$):

$$\lambda(E) = \Delta(E)^{*}pr(not\text{-}E).$$

The occurrence of a mildly improbable event that is very important might be just as lucky as a very improbable event that is only somewhat important. Very important, very unlikely events are the luckiest of all. No luck whatsoever attaches to events that are wholly unimportant or are certain to occur. Rescher's formula assumes a very simple linear relationship between probability and significance, for which he offers little argument. Is something really twice as lucky if it is twice as unlikely? Perhaps luck scales logarithmically, as many perceptual scales do, such as loudness (decibels) and earthquake shaking (Richter scale). In that case the right formula is $\lambda(E) = \Delta(E) * \log(pr(not\text{-}E))$. Or the connection between luck and significance could be a power law dependence. Just as the area of a square is multiplied by a factor of four when its length is doubled, a mildly improbable event that is very important might be an order of magnitude luckier than a very improbable event that is only somewhat important. In short, it is best not to rush into pseudoscientific formulas that offer illegitimate precision.

How well does the basic notion of a probability theory of luck hold up? The first test for it is to examine whether it helps distinguish skill from luck. Are successful people just in the right place at the right time, elevated by caprice, or do they make wise choices and work hard? Are our failures to be chalked up to bad bosses and faithless friends, or to our own defects of character and intellect? If a theory of luck is to do anything, it needs to help us get a handle on these questions, and determine just how much of our lives is due fundamentally to ourselves, and how much to randomness.[13]

# Winners and Losers

In 1892 Baron Manfred von Richthofen was born into a noble Prussian family of diplomats and military men. His uncle Walter was an émigré to the American West who built a sumptuous German-style castle near Denver, and his distant cousin Frieda was the wife of English novelist D. H. Lawrence. Richthofen was an exceptional gymnast as a child, and a devoted hunter of wild game such as elk and boar. He began military training at the age of eleven and by nineteen had joined a Prussian cavalry squadron. The trench warfare of the First World War made traditional mounted cavalry units obsolete, so Richthofen was reallocated to various support positions, winding up in supply. Eager for combat, Richthofen applied for reassignment, writing, "I have not gone to war in order to collect cheese and eggs, but for another purpose" and was subsequently transferred to the Imperial German Army Air Service. Originally a mere observer on reconnaissance missions, after an inspirational meeting with flying ace Oswald Boelcke, Richthofen began pilot training in 1915.

He swiftly started downing enemy planes, diving from above with the sun behind him. A disciplined tactician, Richthofen had strict rules for his squadron, including orders to fire first on the enemy's gunner instead of the pilot and to never run from an attack you have started. Richthofen began painting his planes red, a move which both captured the imagination of the German public and inspired other flying squadrons to paint their aircraft in identifiable unit colors. Probably the best known fighter pilot of all time, the Red Baron is credited with eighty confirmed kills, making him the most successful ace of the First World War. His biography is a résumé of talent and aptitude—the family history, athleticism, hunting skills, early military training, personal courage, and flying success. Yet when he was decorated with the Iron Cross, he wrote a letter to his mother in which he remarked "If I should come out of this war alive, I will have more luck than brains." Four years later the Red Baron died in aerial combat, and was treated by the enemy British to a formal burial with full military honors. Was his death bad luck? On the one hand, it was wartime and he was a high-priority military target, so dying seems like a very likely outcome and not a matter of luck at all. On the other hand, he was the best pilot of the war with an impressive pedigree, and shooting down the Red Baron was like winning Wimbledon against Roger Federer in his prime. So perhaps Richthofen was wrong: if he had come out of the war alive, it would have been attributable to his tremendous skill (his brains), not luck.

It is difficult to parse the relationship between skill and luck. One well-discussed example is Bill Gates. Gates was clearly very smart and driven, but also had the good fortune as an eighth-grader in the 1960s to have unlimited access to an early time-share computer programming terminal. Gates himself doubts that fifty other people in the world at that time had the opportunities he did to program and get instant feedback.[14] Later, after founding Microsoft with Paul Allen, Gates worked with IBM to provide the operating system for their new personal computers. IBM was pessimistic about how well their new PCs would sell, and so they allowed Microsoft to retain the rights to the operating system MS-DOS rather than spending the money to buy them out. Instead IBM provided a royalty to Microsoft for each new IBM PC that used Microsoft's operating system. Ultimately this deal was worth hundreds of billions of dollars, only flowing into the pockets of Microsoft instead of IBM. So was Gates's wealth due to hard work and ambition or good luck?

Or consider Nick Hanauer. Hanauer describes himself as a .01%er, a proud and unapologetic capitalist who owns multiple homes, his own plane, a yacht, and a bank. Hanauer made his money as a venture capitalist and entrepreneur, and has been involved with over thirty companies, including aQuantive, an Internet advertising company which Hanauer founded and sold to Microsoft for $6.4 billion in cash. Hanauer believes that what sets him apart is a tolerance for risk and an intuition about what will happen in the future. When the Internet came along Hanauer saw the handwriting on the wall for big box stores, realizing that once people could easily peruse all the world's goods from the comfort of their living rooms, brick-and-mortar shopping would be an endangered species. So Hanauer jumped at the opportunity to become the first nonfamily investor in Amazon.[15]

In his letter to his mother, the Red Baron showed a humility about his successes and prospects, recognizing a role for luck in his wartime fate. Gates too is circumspect about his life, remarking that "I had a better exposure to software development at a young age than I think anyone did in that period of time, and all because of an incredibly lucky series of events."[16] Hanauer is explicit about his good fortune: Jeff Bezos, founder of Amazon, was his friend and took Hanauer up on his offer to invest in whatever Bezos wanted to do. Hanauer argues that entrepreneurs in Somalia or the Congo aren't less ambitious or smart than he is, but they are *unlucky*. They are born into poor countries and have impoverished customers. So they are selling fruit by the side of the road instead of captaining their own yachts.

The modesty displayed by Richthofen, Gates, and Hanauer is not often shared by successful people, who frequently assign all personal achievements to their own meritorious effort. To intimate that luck was involved is to undermine the legitimacy of their attainments, and thereby undercut the sense of agency, of ownership, of their actions. Unquestionably, it requires both innate talent and massive drive to achieve at the level of Olympic athletes, Nobel laureates, or captains of industry, and highly successful people can be testy when it is suggested that their accomplishments were helped along the way by a big scoop of luck. This point is well illustrated by Cornell economist Robert H. Frank, who has written several items in the popular press defending the role of luck in our life trajectories.[17] Frank recalls this interview with an angry and defensive Stuart Varney, host of the TV program *Fox Business News*.

Professor, wait a minute, do you know how insulting that was when I read that? I came to America with nothing thirty-five years ago. I've made something of myself, I think, with nothing but talent, hard work, and risk-taking. And you're going to write in the *New York Times* that this is luck? … That's outrageous! Do you know what risk is involved in coming to America with absolutely nothing? Do you know what risk is involved trying to work for a major American network with a British accent? A total foreigner? Do you know what risk is implied for this level of success?[18]

It is easy to find other examples. In a more temperate vein, the nineteenth-century American Transcendentalist Ralph Waldo Emerson remarks that "commerce is a game of skill … good luck is another name for tenacity of purpose."[19] Modern business guru Peter Drucker writes, "Luck, chance and catastrophe affect business as they do all human endeavors. But luck never built a business. Prosperity and growth come only to the business that systematically finds and exploits its potential."[20] In Drucker's strangely asymmetric view, a business might suffer from bad luck, or fail due to a calamity, but flourishing, progress, and prosperity are wholly due to laudable effort. The greatest active American athlete, tennis champion Serena Williams, has claimed that "luck has nothing to do with it, because I have spent many, many hours, countless hours, on the court working for my one moment in time, not knowing when it would come."[21] As Tammy Bleck, a columnist at the *Huffington Post* pithily put it, "My success, anyone's success, isn't preordained or acquired by a stroke of luck. Hell no. It isn't who we know, but rather who we are, that makes the difference in our life path … What does luck have to do with success? Not one damn thing."[22]

It is not hard to see why these successful people furiously dismiss any role for luck. To agree that their achievements were even partly due to good fortune is diminishment, a lessening of rugged individualism and a concession of frailty. What's more, it suggests that they might not be wholly entitled to their station and possessions, since the portion that results from capricious chance was not in any sense *earned*. Which means that those undeserved goods could be taken away and redistributed by the fickle winds of fortune. No accomplished person likes *that* idea. The sociologist Max Weber succinctly explains, writing in 1913:

> The fortunate is seldom satisfied with the fact of being fortunate. Beyond this, he needs to know that he has a *right* to his good fortune. He wants to be convinced that he "deserves" it, and above all, that he deserves it in comparison with others. He wishes to be allowed the belief that the less fortunate also merely experiences his due. Good fortune thus wants to be "legitimate" fortune.[23]

To deny luck and claim all mastery over one's fate is to insist that the world is a just place, and that our places in it are due to our own choices, talents, and effort. Of course, the inherent fairness of the world order is an easier sell to those at the top than to those at the bottom. Sorting out how much of our successes (or failures) is properly attributable to luck and how much to skill is essential not only for tempering our valorization of heroes like the Red Baron, Serena Williams, Bill Gates, or Nick Hanauer, but for very practical, legal concerns as well. Indeed, these concerns can strike close to home.

# Buying Hope on Credit

Walter Watkins of Columbia County, Pennsylvania (this author's home county) was hosting small-stakes Texas Hold'em poker games in his garage, with Diane Dent serving as dealer. In 2008, the game was infiltrated by an undercover Pennsylvania state trooper who promptly arrested Watkins and Dent, charging them with violating various state gambling laws. In his decision on the case, Judge Thomas A. James Jr. noted that gambling in PA is not inherently unlawful. Under state case law, what makes for unlawful gambling are three things: consideration (in this case, the ante and betting), reward (the pot), and chance. Everyone conceded that there was betting and a jackpot. James writes, "Thus, the controlling sub-issue is whether Texas Hold'em is a game of skill or a game of chance or, if both, does skill trump chance or vice-versa. Simply, if chance predominates, Texas Hold'em is gambling. If skill predominates, it is not gambling."[24] Poker is not as random as roulette; it is also a game of strategy, which means that there is some element of talent involved in successful play as well. How we can separate out one from the other has been the subject of much analysis. Even Von Neumann and Morgenstern's seminal book on game theory devoted an entire, highly technical, chapter to poker.

Judge James reviewed several popular, academic, and legal works on poker, and concluded that while the house always gets a cut, in general money flows from the weakest players to the strongest players in Texas Hold'em. No one denies that there is an element of luck in poker, but James maintained that poker is chiefly a game of skill in which each player has sufficient information to make an informed judgment and the opportunity to exercise those judgments. He concluded that as far as Pennsylvania law is concerned, poker is not gambling. The case against Watkins and Dent was dismissed.

James's ruling was reversed on appeal.[25] The reversal had nothing to do with the facts of the case, something that all parties agreed on. Rather, the appeals court looked at the same evidence and came to the opposite conclusion about the interpretation of the law. While the outcome of poker may be partly dependent on skill, the Superior Court argued that no amount of skill will turn a deuce into an ace, and there is too much luck of the draw for skillful play to be the main factor in winning. So the appeals court determined 2–1 that poker is predominately a game of chance. The dissenting judge rejected that conclusion, maintaining that the Commonwealth had failed to meet its burden of proof in showing that poker was truly a game of chance (although he did not come right out and declare it to be a matter of skill, as did Judge James). In Judge James's view, his initial ruling was overturned for political, not legal, reasons: the state government in Harrisburg would like to keep legal gambling owned by the state, and the Superior Court was sympathetic to that goal.[26] Ultimately, the DA cut a deal and both Watkins and Dent did twenty hours of community service. It is safe to say, though, that there is not yet a definitive legal ruling in the case of *Luck v. Skill*.

Gambling is essentially decision making under uncertainty, wagering in conditions of incomplete information. The less information available to inform judgment, the greater the subjective risk.[27] Needless to say, gamblers have been extremely inventive in finding ways to increase the information available prior to betting. The first of these was the development of probability theory itself, as we saw in Chapter 1. More recently, professional gamblers have developed ever more ingenious ways to beat the house.

Take blackjack. In this game it is player versus the dealer, and they are each dealt two cards, with the dealer getting one face up and one face down. The player with the closest to twenty-one points, without going over, wins. If a player is dissatisfied with a low point score on their two cards, they can ask for another card, but going over twenty-one is a bust, and the opponent automatically wins. Casino rules require the dealer to stand, or refuse additional cards, with seventeen and to draw below seventeen. The way to beat blackjack is to realize two things. The first is if the dealer has a very low card showing (say, a 6), the odds are good that she will be required by the rules to draw more than one card, which increases the chance that the dealer will go bust. If the dealer has a face card showing, it is much less likely that she will have to draw more than one card (if any), and so the odds of going bust are not as high. The second relevant fact is that the cards being dealt are not completely unpredictable—seeing the dealer's cards and seeing the cards in your own hand provides data about which cards are still in the deck. Every card that is dealt changes the probability of which cards remain. Each state of the game thus has a "memory" of the previous game state. A series of connected events each with a memory of the previous event is known as a Markov Chain. As the dealer works through the deck, more and more information about the remaining cards is provided to the players. At a certain point, a savvy player has enough information from the Markov Chain to make decent predictions about the remaining cards, and adjusts his bets accordingly.

Even games that seem truly random, like roulette, have been beaten. The final position of the ball in roulette is highly sensitive to both the initial state of the wheel and the interacting variables of the angular momentum of the ball and the deflectors. In other words, roulette is a nonlinear, chaotic system. While math alone won't conquer roulette, science might. People have snuck computers into casinos to help them time the velocity of the ball when it dropped off the rim of the wheel and the rate at which the wheel was decelerating; these facts helped predict which deflector the ball would hit and thus which pocket it was likely to drop into. One trio of players using this method won £1.3 million in London's Ritz casino. There are many similar examples such as automated computer betting that seeks arbitrage situations when different betting houses offer varying odds on a sports event or data-mining horse racing statistics to develop predictive models. All these tactics have had substantial success, to the extent that there are entire gambling syndicates that profit by sophisticated wagering.[28] In such cases it is clear that there is a real component of skill, and that professional gamblers do much more than trust to chance.

# A Skill Equation?

Implicit in the tales of personal success of Richthofen, Gates, and Hanauer, or the legal wrangling over the legality of a garage poker club, is something like the following:

- skill + luck = performance

In fact, Nobel laureate Daniel Kahneman states that his favorite equation is success = talent + luck ([Kahneman 2011] p. 177).[29] To be sure, this is yet another questionably formal luck equation, but it encapsulates such a popular idea that it is worth taking seriously for a bit. Let's see how well it holds up.

Is one's performance mostly luck with a little skill (as the PA Superior Court thought about poker), or is it mostly skill with a little luck (as one might think of the Red Baron)? We should expect the contribution of each to vary with the task at hand, with winning at slots wholly driven by luck and victory at chess being entirely skill. Apart from seat-of-our-pants pronouncements, how can we systematically separate out the contributions from skill and luck to see which one is the driving force in performance? If the probability theory of luck works at all to separate luck from skill, it will work in highly quantitative domains. If it fails there, then there is no hope it will sort out the role of luck in our ordinary, messy, nonquantitative lives.

As a first step, note that the following are equivalent to the equation above.

- skill = performance – luck
- luck = performance – skill

If we assume the basic idea that skill + luck = performance, there are then two ways to proceed:

Strategy 1: given a performance level, determine luck and solve for skill

Strategy 2: given a performance level, determine skill and solve for luck

Strategy 1 is definitely the most popular.[30] Suppose we set the skill level to zero. Then *luck = performance – zero*, or just *luck = performance*. Given the probability theory of luck that we are assuming, this means that the outcome or performance is no different from what would be predicted by chance alone. For example, if a mind reader claims to be able to tell whether you are thinking of red, blue, yellow, or green, and gets it right one out of four times, that's no evidence at all in favor of their claims of telepathy. Correctly calling the color 25 percent of the time is exactly what we should expect from random guessing. In other words, the performance = luck. Skill isn't adding anything, and we can safely assume that it is zero; that is, the mind reader doesn't really have any telepathic skills. Real skill is going to be the statistically significant variation above chance success.

In the social sciences, the standard for statistical significance is somewhat arbitrarily set to 5 percent. That is, if there is a less than one out of twenty chance that an event randomly occurred, then that's a fine reason to look for some real cause elsewhere. If the mind reader correctly calls the color three of four times, that might be a streak of good luck, but if she gets it right 75 percent of the time consistently, over many trials, then we can reasonably think that it is not just luck and that something else is at work here. Maybe the mind reader is being subtly tipped off (a la Clever Hans), maybe she is cheating, maybe she really is telepathic. If the performance is greater than what we should expect from luck alone— by a statistically significant amount and eliminating extraneous variables like the possibility of cheating—we are left with the amount attributable to skill.

One tricky matter is that even when there is some success above chance, that may not be skill. Probability does not imply that the random guessing out of four colors always and only provides one out of four hits. This is easy to see with coin tossing: you expect 50 percent heads and 50 percent tails, and in the infinite long run, that's the result. However, if someone flips ten times, and gets six heads, it's wrong to attribute five heads to luck and one to skill. True randomness produces "Poisson clumping"—in the coin-tossing example, this would mean that there will be bursts of heads and runs of tails. The long run will give us a 50–50 split, but the short run will not. In fact, out of ten tosses it is not very likely that it will be exactly five heads and five tails, much less that heads and tails will alternate.

Consider the following map (Figure 2.1). Each dot represents an instance of cancer diagnosed in the past year.

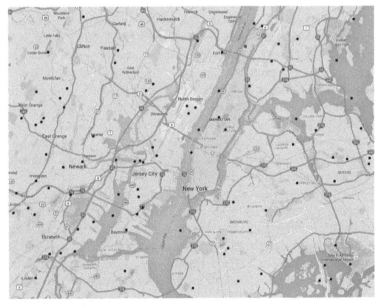

FIGURE 2.1 Cancer map.

The first thing that you probably notice is that there is much more cancer in New Jersey than in New York. In fact, there is a lot more around Jersey City, Bayonne, and Elizabeth. Why? Poor working conditions? Poverty? The presence of petrochemical refineries? There must be some sort of causal explanation. Or consider the job chart in Figure 2.2. In this illustration, each dot means that 10 percent of the people doing that job are women. For example, three dots in Customer Service mean 30 percent of the people with that job are women. The high percentage of women who are secretaries or low-paid food prep workers, and the relative paucity who are lawyers or software developers is no doubt a clear sign of sexist discrimination, right?

Both charts have exactly the same random pattern of dots. The map doesn't really represent cancer clusters, but once told that it does, our brains automatically start searching available heuristics about New Jersey and New York to come up with an explanation. The same is true of the job plot. Again, it is just random dots overlaid an arbitrary list of common jobs, accompanied by some story about the meaning of those dots; it shows nothing at all about discrimination. The real moral of the story is that even when the dots really do represent cancer or women in

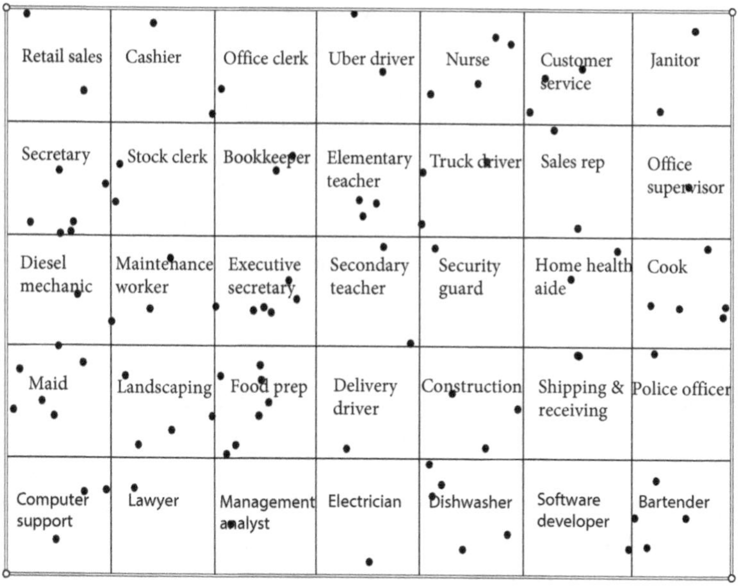

| Retail sales | Cashier | Office clerk | Uber driver | Nurse | Customer service | Janitor |
|---|---|---|---|---|---|---|
| Secretary | Stock clerk | Bookkeeper | Elementary teacher | Truck driver | Sales rep | Office supervisor |
| Diesel mechanic | Maintenance worker | Executive secretary | Secondary teacher | Security guard | Home health aide | Cook |
| Maid | Landscaping | Food prep | Delivery driver | Construction | Shipping & receiving | Police officer |
| Computer support | Lawyer | Management analyst | Electrician | Dishwasher | Software developer | Bartender |

FIGURE 2.2 Job distributions.

the workforce, there may be no deeper significance to their distribution. It is easy to forget that genuine randomness leads to Poisson clumping, and as a result find what seem like patterns in meaningless data. We see patterns in random data as conforming to stereotypes about sexism or New Jersey in the same way that we see faces in the fronts of automobiles, or think that a grilled cheese sandwich looks like the Virgin Mary.

Pulling a true signal from the statistical noise is a subtle matter to be approached cautiously, and a probability theory of luck needs to ensure that a random burst of success above the mean does not count as skillful performance. Perhaps it too is just luck. Separating the relative contributions of skill and luck to success (and failure) have been mostly explored and developed in very quantitative domains with extensive data sets or very calculable outcomes, such as sports, gambling, and commodities trading. Michael J. Mauboussin, a securities analyst, has applied coin-flipping models to assess the role of luck in American football, stocks, and other areas. His approach is to ask what outcomes we should expect to see if they were completely random and compare that with the actual observed outcomes.

A classic football saying is "any given Sunday"—meaning that any team could beat any other team; pro teams are so close in talent that whichever wins is mostly luck. If we take that seriously, then who wins and who loses on any given Sunday is essentially a coin toss. The NFL has thirty-two teams, each of which plays sixteen games. If we're just flipping coins to give the winner, we should expect that the most common season record will be eight wins and eight losses. Toss a few thousand coins and that's the result about 20 percent of the time. Nevertheless, some teams will be luckier, with more wins, and some will be unluckier with more losses. Some teams will go 9–7, fewer teams will finish 10–6, and so on. Winning (or losing) multiple coin-toss games in a row is another form of Poisson clumping, and indicative of true randomness. Mauboussin ran thousands of these coin-tossing simulations (i.e. Monte Carlo simulations) to see how football seasons with wholly random wins and losses would turn out. He then plotted the results for all thirty-two teams on a curve, with extreme outlier teams who went 0–16 on the left and lucky undefeated outliers on the right who went 16–0. The end result was a very peaked bell curve. That is the pure luck scenario.

What if football games are 100 percent decided by skill, and there's no luck at all? If we assume that NFL outcomes are completely decided by skill, then we can rank all thirty-two teams in order from best to worst, and presume that in a head-to-head matchup, the better team always beats the weaker team. Using the NFL's own scheduling algorithm, Mauboussin simulated 5,000 seasons, and found that the distribution yields a very flat curve, with slight dips at the ends for the very best and the very worst teams. The "all luck" hypothesis gives a peaked bell curve. The "all skill" hypothesis yields a flat curve. What's the real-world distribution of wins and losses in the NFL? The actual NFL record from 2007 to 2011 shows a curve somewhere in between the two. Here is his graph (Figure 2.3), with "blended" representing the combination of the models representing skill and luck that best fits the actual empirical results.[31]

The blended model—the closest statistical fit to the observed results—is almost exactly halfway between the "all skill" and "all luck" curves. The recipe for pro football seems to be 48 percent luck and 52 percent skill. Based on this analysis, Mauboussin concludes that NFL wins are slightly more skill than luck (and losses are due slightly more to inferior talent than bad luck), but barely.

## Blending the records

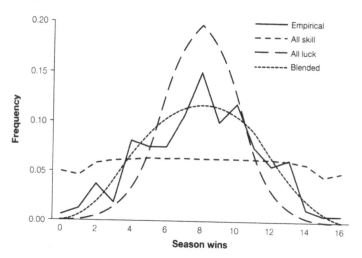

**FIGURE 2.3** Blending the records. Reproduced with permission of Michael Mauboussin.

# Problems with Probability

Statistical methods like Mauboussin's are a valuable way to distinguish chance from skill. Do they really capture luck, though? Some parts of life are easy to measure: whether the Broncos won on Sunday, whether your flush took the pot in poker, whether a stockbroker can reliably beat the market. Not only are they straightforward and objectively quantifiable, but receptive to analysis with mathematical tools. In these matters, probability is the guide to life.[32] But there are cases where these tools break down.

The first difficulty is what's known as the *reference class problem*, and was alluded to earlier. This is something that comes up in all kinds of contexts. For example, how likely is it that the airplane you are on will crash? To determine this, we could look at the likelihood that any plane will crash, that is, the total safety record of all the airlines collectively. Or we could examine the safety record of the airline you are flying right now. Maybe the specific details of your plane and pilot should be weighed as well. The probability of a crash will vary greatly depending on how broadly or narrowly we set the context. The reference class problem is a wholly general conundrum for probability, and one too for a probability theory of luck. If you are on a flight that has a rough landing in a monsoon, it is reasonable to think that it was luck that you didn't crash (reference class = planes flying in monsoons). When you merely land safely, it doesn't seem much like luck; it's just what you should expect from modern air travel (reference class = all commercial flights). These could be the very same flight. So which is it? A big attraction of a probability theory of luck is that it is mathematical, that we can calculate our luck and get a precise measurement. However, as the flight example shows, we can get more than one result, depending on what background assumptions are being made. What's worse is that there's no natural way to decide which background assumptions are the most reasonable. Is it a matter of luck that you are having pumpernickel toast for breakfast? If the comparison class is "all the breakfasts in the world," then it does seem rather unlikely and so a matter of luck. If the comparison is "all the available breakfasts in your kitchen" then pumpernickel toast is a probable choice, and not lucky at all.

Why not just go for the narrowest interpretation—*this* specific plane and pilot flying in a monsoon, *this* very location for breakfast? The problem is that if we do that, we run the risk that every event is (nearly) probability 1.

That is, specify the details and background conditions of an event very, very specifically and narrowly. Given those factors, the chance that the event will occur is effectively certain. What's the chance that Hank Aaron will hit a home run if he swings his bat at such-and-such trajectory and velocity, and the pitch is moving at such-and-such speed, spin, and vector intercept with his bat? If we can specify things with that kind of high resolution, then we'll know whether Aaron either definitely does or definitely does not hit a home run, as least as precisely as we can given the limits imposed by chaos theory. That's not really what we want. Rather, what we want to know is the chance that he will hit a home run in his next at-bat, given his base rate of hitting homers this season. Maybe we want to throw in Aaron's success rate against the pitcher currently on the mound. The probability changes as we add and subtract information. So if Aaron does hit a homer, was it luck? Or to what degree was it luck? We get different answers depending on our reference class assumptions, a very unsatisfying result.

The second challenge for the probability theory of luck is what we might call the *problem of noisy signals*. Consider a very improbable event over which someone has little control and only a tiny chance of success. One example is golfer hitting a hole-in-one. According to *Golf Digest*, the chance of a professional golfer hitting an ace on a given hole is 2500 to 1. An amateur golfer has only a 12,500 to 1 chance.[33] Even frequent players can go their whole lives without hitting a hole-in-one (this author's father, a lifelong player who lives on a golf course, has never done so in over sixty years of trying). Mike Crean of Denver, Colorado, once aced a 517-yard par 5, and Elise McLean of Chico, California, hit one at the age of 102. How could we even begin to calculate the odds of those performances? Or of Tiger Woods's first ace at the tender age of six?

These events are nearly always one-offs, and such outliers on the curve of golfing shots that the parsing of skill and luck seems arbitrary. A pro is five times more likely to hit an ace than an amateur. Nevertheless, if both a pro and an amateur ace the same hole (an incredibly unlikely event for them both) it is misplaced precision to insist that the pro's shot was five times more skillful than the amateur's. Any ace—either from a pro or an amateur—is set against a backdrop of massive failure. Out of thousands of shots that are not holes-in-one, occasionally, unexpectedly, without discernible reason, one lands in the cup. No matter who hit the shot, it seems capricious to exactly parcel out the proper measure of skill and luck in the ace, like imposing artificially precise boundaries on vague terms, or positively identifying a song in a sea of static.

Nassim Nicholas Taleb is well known for insisting that hole-in-one-type events are *black swans*, rare, uncertain events that are unpredictable in principle, other than the very general prediction that they will occur from time to time.[34] A sudden fiscal calamity like a stock market crash in an otherwise stable market (2008), or a massive war flaring up over apparently negligible issues (the First World War), or a wholly unexpected world-altering scientific discovery (penicillin), or a garden-variety thriller rocketing to the top of the bestseller lists (*The Da Vinci Code*), or a populist demagogue with no record of public service getting elected president of the United States are all examples of what Taleb regards as black swans. He considers traditional probability theory as having as much application to the empirical world and everyday life as Platonic solids do to the true geometry of nature. Nature is fractal in design, with recursive hooks and spirals instead of perfect pyramids, cubes, and spheres. The stylized formalism of the probability theory of luck deals poorly with noisy signals like golfing aces, much like a boxer who abides by the Marquess of Queensberry rules hits the ground hard following nunchucks to the crotch. These massive-impact events come out of left field, and it is only after the fact that we construct post-hoc explanations to make them appear more predictable than they really were. "Well, of course a great golfer like Tiger Woods knocked a hole-in-one when he was six," we comfortably opine in hindsight. We can tell ourselves that an ace by an amateur is five times as lucky as one from a pro, but really, they were both a matter of uncontrollable, unpredictable luck.

Taleb's point is that chance in the real world is nonlinear and that we are good at predicting future events only in rigid and highly constrained scenarios like sports and gambling. The approach to luck we have been considering all chapter does best when we have a very calculable, deterministic data set governed by fixed rules. Mauboussin's intriguing analysis of luck in the NFL is possible only because there are a finite number of teams that play an unchanging number of games in a season, games that they either definitely win or lose. Because he has those fixed parameters, he can run Monte Carlo simulations, construct hypothetical performance curves, and compare them with actual performances. But suppose that the number of football teams varied each week, or that the number of games in a year range, from one to a thousand and this fluctuates every year, or that in addition to winning and losing, there are all kinds of in-between possibilities, or even that the rules of the game are prone to spontaneous change. Faced with this crazy mixed-up NFL, there's no way a Mauboussin-style treatment of luck vs. skill can get off the ground. It is like tossing those ping pong balls into Yosemite Falls and trying to predict where each one will wind up. Yet that's much closer to the reality of our everyday lives than rule-bound, precisely quantifiable sport.

Recall the Red Baron, Bill Gates, and Nick Hanauer, who were ready to admit the big role that luck played in their success, or Serena Williams and Stuart Varney, who insisted that their achievements were due to effort and skill alone. There is no prospect of a statistical approach to separating out the contributions of luck from those of skill for, say, Hanauer's investment success. Hanauer kept in touch with some people and forgot others, or pursued some relationships but not others, or invested at this time instead of earlier or later, while all around him other investors are doing similar things, but with other people, companies, and securities. On top of that the laws and customs governing capital investments are in flux, and the market itself swings wildly on the political news of the day. Entrepreneurship is like the crazy mixed-up NFL—we can't just tell a computer to run 5,000 simulations of Hanauer's life and see how often he is a billionaire. With our regular, quotidian NFL we get a new football season every fall with the same gridiron and rules of the game; but our lives happen only once, and they each come with a unique set of circumstances in constantly evolving socioeconomic conditions. What's the chance that Hanauer's life (or any of our lives) turns out the way it did if everything is luck? If everything is skill? There's just no way to plot these curves in a meaningful way and compare them with the actual distribution.

Mathematicians and scientists have loved the probability theory of luck because it is calculable; luck can be captured by numbers and worked out with formulas and graphs. Even in complex cases where the numbers seem very hard to sleuth out, one might keep the faith that *in principle* probability can tell us about the role of luck. It's just that good data is hard (or even impossible) to get. Much more challenging is that luck, unlike chance, is *normative*. Chance is the property of the number-crunchers, but things go awry when it is used to explain how much credit someone deserves for how things have turned out for them, or the degree to which their performance is due to their own merit. Luck is either good or bad and this fact is outside the purview of statistics. Of course, the probability theory of luck also requires that a putatively lucky event also be of some significance, or importance to someone. A teetotaler isn't lucky when the local beer store starts stocking Rochefort 10, although a beer connoisseur is, so one might suspect that this varying significance exhausts whatever component of luck is normative or evaluative. However, the normativity of luck goes beyond just whether one's luck is good or bad. It is also used to work out merit, credit, and desert. When we try to rely on stats alone to determine those things, we run into some serious difficulties, problems that a significance condition doesn't help with either. The last criticism of the probability theory of luck to be considered in this chapter is this *problem of normativity*.

Imagine a basketball free-throw shooter sinks the ball. Was his shot luck, skill, or some combination of the two? In addition, how much credit for the shot does the shooter merit? One natural idea is that the shooter deserves just as much credit as is attributable to skill. So if the shooter's success is 90 percent due to skill then the remaining 10 percent is the result of luck. Since you only deserve credit for what comes from skill, in this case the shooter is entitled to credit for 90 percent of a successful shot. Likewise, deviations from hitting 9/10 are luck—over 90 percent is good luck, under 90 percent is bad luck. Suppose Los Angeles Clippers point guard Jamal Crawford is a 90 percent free-throw shooter (almost exactly his 2016 record). That is, let's just stipulate that Crawford's true skill level is 9/10, or, in other words, when it comes to free throws, Crawford's expected performance is 90 percent. If he shoots better than 90 percent, he is enjoying some good luck, as it exceeds what is creditable to him from skill. If Crawford is shooting worse than 90 percent, then it is bad luck since it is below his skill level. We can even quantify it: if Crawford sinks 83 percent of his throws in a year, then he has bad luck to the tune of missing 7 percent.[35]

It would be very pleasant if such a statistical understanding of credit and skill worked out. Unfortunately, it doesn't, and in a very bothersome way—it leads to a contradiction. Here's how it goes. Let's imagine that next season Crawford shoots 100 free-throw attempts, and 83 go in. Since he is a true 90 percent shooter, that means that .9 of his successful shots was the result of skill, and .1 was due to luck. Thus out of the 83 shots he made, 74.7 (= 83 × .9) are due to skill and 8.3 (= 83 − 74.7) are due to good luck. On the other hand, since Crawford is shooting below his 90 percent expected performance, he also has bad luck. How much bad luck? Well, given his skill level, he should have had seven more baskets. So his bad luck weighs in at −7 baskets. From this we can conclude that overall Crawford has been lucky, in the amount of 1.3 baskets (= 8.3 − 7). We've quantified

Crawford's luck, figured out how to assign the proper amount to skill, and determined precisely how much credit he deserves for sinking those eighty-three baskets. So what's the problem? The problem is that shooting 83 baskets out of 100 attempts is below his expected performance level of 90 baskets. Shooting below his expected performance is bad luck—he did his best but still had a below average season. Now we have derived a contradiction. Crawford's overall performance in shooting 83 of 100 attempts was both lucky and unlucky. Whatever is going on here, Crawford might be lucky, or he might be unlucky, but he definitely is not both at once for the same thing.

Maybe the problem is some kind of illicit double counting. Of the 83 shots Crawford made, we are saying that 74.7 are creditable to skill and 8.3 are the result of good luck. Of the seventeen shots that he missed, we are saying that ten are due to his skill level (we expect him to miss those since he's a 90 percent shooter) and seven are the result of bad luck. It looks like there's a double application of that 90 percent figure: once to determine the number of successful shots he should make, and another time to determine the percentage of successful shots for which he deserves credit. Perhaps we should just claim that the eighty-three successful shots and ten of the missed shots were all due to his skill level. The remaining seven missed shots were the result of bad luck. That way no contradiction arises.

While that works out technically, it still leads to some unpalatable results. It means, for instance, that those eighty-three shots Crawford made are 100 percent the result of his skill, and he merits complete credit for achieving them. Even though he's just a 90 percent shooter, he deserves 100 percent of the credit for any free throw he makes, up to 90/100. But that can't be right. It implies that we can only calculate luck over some large set of events, not the percentage of luck in any particular event. One example that highlights this absurdity is the hole-in-one. If a pro golfer hits an ace, it is 100 percent due to their skill and they are entitled to all of the merit and credit—as long as they don't hit an ace more often than 1 out of 2500 attempts (the professional average), there is no luck involved at all. "Wow Rory, that was a lucky shot to ace that par 4." "Thanks, but actually it was all skill." That just doesn't seem right. Statistics gives us the properties of groups and ensembles, not the properties of individuals and specific events. In addition, very little of life is systematically repeatable like basketball free throws. If the presence and amount of luck can only be gauged when there is a measure of skill determined after many attempts, then not much can be ascribed to luck. Was a person's life an unlucky one? Life is the ultimate one-off event, so the question makes little sense.

It is a vexed matter as to whether it is really sensible to distinguish skill from luck, even when it is a one-time-only occurrence, when there is no history of success and failure to fix an expected performance. Imagine two people are playing five-card stud. Here is the state after each has four cards.

Player 1 has: 2♠, 3♦, Q♣, K♦
Player 2 has: 5♥, 6♥, 7♥, 8♥
There are forty-four cards left in the deck.

Player 1 has nothing, and at best will draw a pair. This will happen with 2♦, 2♥, 2♣, 3♣, 3♥, 3♠, Q♦, Q♥, Q♠, K♣, K♥, K♠. One of these will happen with an objective probability of 12/44. Since Player 1 knows none of Player 2's cards, as far as she is concerned, the chance of getting a pair (subjective probability) is 12/48. Not very likely. From Player 1's perspective, things look dim, and at best she is going to check or call.

Player 2 sees he has an open-ended straight draw as well as a flush draw. In fact, he will achieve one of those with any of the cards 4♣, 4♦, 4♥, 4♠, 9♣, 9♦, 9♥, 9♠, A♥, 2♥, 3♥, 10♥, J♥, Q♥, K♥. One of these will happen with a subjective probability of 15/48. Plus, he has a bunch of pair draws: twelve of them. While Player 2 doesn't imagine that a mere pair will clinch a win, nevertheless a pair in straight five-card poker is a decent hand. Overall the subjective chance that he gets a straight, flush, or pair is greater than 50 percent (27/48 > .5), as is the objective chance (27/44 > .5).

Now suppose that Player 2 is a complete naïf and is betting blindly, randomly, or just based on fleeting hunches. Still, he wins. Even though it was probable that he wins, it still looks like luck because he did not intentionally win. Player 2 may have been intending to win, but intending to do something and successfully doing it is not equivalent to intentionally doing that thing. You can intend to win the lottery—indeed, the whole point of playing the lottery is to win it and you have every intention of winning. So you do everything you can to win, namely, you buy a ticket. Suppose you do win. Surely you did not *intentionally win the lottery*; it was still luck. Likewise, intending to win at poker, and then winning at poker even when it is probable that you do so may not be intentionally winning (winning as a result of skillful play). The win is still luck, even though it was intended and objectively likely.

On the other hand, imagine that while new to the game, Player 2 keeps careful track of the cards and changing odds, and bets strong before the final card. Now it's much more reasonable to see Player 2's victory as partly or even substantially the result of his skillful play. While there is no track record to establish Player 2's skill level (as there was in the case of Jamal Crawford shooting free throws), Player 2's victory in this case looks much more meritorious and praiseworthy.

On the third hand, let's say that here is what happens on the fifth and final card, which is dealt face up.

Player 1 draws K♣. He now has a high pair and feels fairly good; this is a lot better than having nothing (which Player 2 had after 4 cards).

Player 2 draws 9♥. He now has a straight flush, the highest and least likely hand in poker.

Was Player 2 lucky to win in this scenario? He certainly wasn't thinking he would win *that* way. The chances he'd draw a straight flush were only 2/44. Seeing what Player 1 ended up with after the fifth card, Player 2 needed to complete either a straight or a flush to win. The objective likelihood of losing given that requirement was high: only a 15/47 chance of pulling it off. It is no longer clear what role skill has to play here, if any, or how much luck there is in the win. Intuitions are so convoluted at this point that the simple formulas for computing skill sit in silence.

The scholars of the Early Modern period developed probability theory to eradicate luck, to conquer and raze it with weapons of math destruction. However, in a chaotic world of nonlinear interactions, one where the entire universe itself is computationally incapable of solving a simple board game like Go by brute force, the beatific oasis of ultimate predictability has proven to be a mirage. A more modest proposal is that probability contributes to a *theory* of luck and that along with a requirement that an improbable event matter to some person, we are able to assess the degree to which they are lucky or unlucky. One requirement for a satisfactory probability theory of luck is that it can effectively distinguish between merely lucky results and those properly attributable to skill. As we have seen, it cannot.[36]

Luck doesn't just matter when it comes or playing cards or throwing dice. It is integral to understanding how much we deserve the failures of our own lives, to figuring out whether we are Fortuna's victims or can only blame ourselves. Some high-achieving people are ready to concede the importance of luck in their success whereas others concur with E. B. White that "luck is not something you can mention in the presence of self-made men."[37] If having a theory of luck is going to do anything useful for us, it will at least pry apart the contributions of luck and skill and allow us to measure the contributions of each. Yet even given the most optimistic assumptions, it can do so only under the inflexibly artificial constraints we find in sports and games. More realistically, we cannot merely read off praiseworthiness or blameworthiness from looking at the numbers; probability is being tasked with too much. We need to investigate other approaches.

# 3 FRAGILITY AND CONTROL

*"The essential part of every invention is the work of chance, but most men never encounter this chance."*
**—FRIEDRICH NIETZSCHE, *DAYBREAK* §363 (1881)**

Gottfried Leibniz may be best known for inventing calculus, which he did simultaneously with and independently of Isaac Newton. The pair were embroiled in a long-running dispute over priority, with most scholars giving Newton the prize in a photo finish, although we still use Leibniz's mathematical notation instead of his rival's. Leibniz was a man for all seasons, though, and his protean mind ranged from combinatorics to abstract metaphysics, to physics, technology, theology, and even library science. The first edition of his collected works runs to over 4600 pages, and even it is incomplete.[1] One of the issues Leibniz tackled was the problem of evil, a theological conundrum ever since the unsatisfying treatment of it in the Book of Job.

The problem itself is easy to state. God is supposed to be omnipotent, omniscient, and omnibenevolent, and yet the world is filled with suffering—human and animal, young and old, rich and poor, men and women, sinners and saints—all experience some tincture of pain. We are all at times lonely, afraid, anguished, and regretful; we each are subject to being bruised, cut, burned, and diseased. God in his infinite wisdom knows about our pain and, given his unlimited power, could easily alleviate or prevent it. Still suffering rolls in like the sea while we do our best to hold it back, like wielding a pushbroom against the tides. Which means that God just isn't doing anything about it. That's a real mystery, because God is ostensibly perfectly good, the very kind of being who would recognize that misery is a terrible thing and *want* to do something about it. The purely holy cannot be implicated in evil. Does God have excellent, but subtle, reasons for allowing all the suffering? Is he not perfectly good after all? Does this prove there is no God as traditionally conceived? Needless to say, philosophers and theologians have explored the nooks and crannies of each of these avenues.

# Invisible Cities of the Possible

Leibniz's approach was ingenious and unorthodox. Imagine God existing in the void, prior to the creation of the world. In his mind he can survey every possible way that the universe might be, from the very general, like the physical constants and laws of nature, to the very finely detailed, like the percentage of dandelions in your lawn and the precise pitch of your voice. All of these things are in a sense up for grabs, since God could select one speed of light or another, one number of grains of sand on the beach instead of a different amount. Another way to think of it is to visualize an infinite array of distinct, entire universes, each one slightly different from the next. God sits in front of these possible worlds like a child at a candy store, wanting to pick the sweetest treat. Some of the possible realities are clearly better than others, from worlds filled with totalitarian dystopias to those more like Star Trek's peaceful Federation of Planets. Suppose that all these imaginary realities are strictly ordered from worst to best, as in Figure 3.1.

The perfect God only has to survey them all and choose the best of the lot as the one to make real. The best of all the possible worlds needn't be wholly without suffering; it just needs to be the best way the world could possibly be, so that if one kind of suffering were eliminated we would instead get a host of even greater miseries. A world without peril is also a world without heroism, charity, and selflessness, and that may be worse than what we have now. So Leibniz's solution to the problem of evil is that of all the possible ways reality could be, God picked the very best option. One obvious concern is that no matter how good the world is, surely we can imagine that it could be just a little bit better. And that world could be

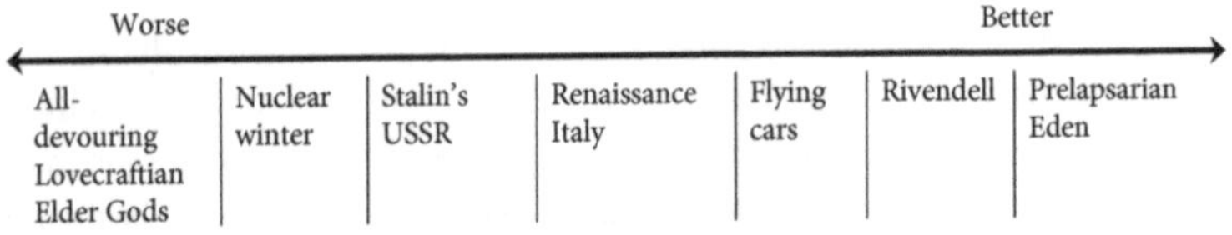

| Worse | | | | | | Better |
|---|---|---|---|---|---|---|
| All-devouring Lovecraftian Elder Gods | Nuclear winter | Stalin's USSR | Renaissance Italy | Flying cars | Rivendell | Prelapsarian Eden |

FIGURE 3.1 Rank ordering possible worlds.

just a little bit better, ad infinitum. If there really is an infinity of possible worlds placed in order by their moral excellence, then for any world w, w+1 is a better world. That would mean there is no "best" configuration for reality, any more than there is a biggest number.[2]

Imagine God at Cantor's Candy Shop. Cantor has an infinitely long shelf of candy, ordered by deliciousness—each type of candy on the shelf is a little better than the one to the left and not quite as good as the one to the right. God naturally wants to pick the best candy, so he starts moving along the shelf. Of course, any place that he stops, there's an even better confection next up. God starts running down the length of the shelf. He stops at a really scrumptious raspberry champagne truffle, but the piece next to it is even yummier. He starts running again, but no matter how fast he moves, God will never get to the end of the selections, never find the absolute best, most delicious candy. Here's the problem: God does at some point buy some candy from Cantor. He does create a world, namely, ours. How is that possible?

Leibniz knew about this objection, and as a result rejected the idea of an infinite continuum of worlds. He endorsed The Principle of Sufficient Reason: there's a reason for everything.[3] There has to be *some* reason why God created the world that we have instead of some other world. He didn't just throw up his hands and declare, "Me-dammit, I'm making *this* one!" In fact, supposing that God did do that, he would be paying an infinitely high opportunity cost, which is not much of a recommendation for divine rationality.

If there were an infinity of possible worlds, each one better than the last, God couldn't have a reason to create *any* world at all, since he would never get to the last, best world on the list. Since he did create this world, he must have had his reasons. "If there were no best among all possible worlds, God would not have created one."[4] Like the candy, he picked this one because—contrary to appearances, perhaps—it is in fact the best. The perennial question as to why God doesn't intervene to stop suffering, or save people from calamities gets an easy answer: this is *already* the best of all possible worlds. If God had to fix some things along the way, that would mean that it wasn't already the best, which of course means that God wouldn't have created it.

Basically no one had a better idea than Leibniz when it came to the problem of evil, so it seemed like as good a solution as any. Until 1755. On November 1, 1755, one of the worst earthquakes in history struck in the Atlantic Ocean off the coast of Portugal. With an estimated 8.5–9.0

Richter magnitude, it destroyed the coastal towns and cities with seismic effects that were felt all the way to Brazil. In Lisbon, it cracked open fifteen-foot wide fissures in the city center, blasted the downtown with a devastating tsunami, and touched off a subsequent fire that raged for six days. Eighty-five percent of the buildings in Lisbon were destroyed, thousands of citizens died, and its great cultural heritage—palaces, libraries, churches, fine art, royal archives—was wiped off the face of the Earth. The earthquake was bad enough, but the fact that it happened on All Saints Day in such a redoubt of Roman Catholicism as Portugal, well, that could only mean one thing. There couldn't merely be some natural (if unknown) cause for the earthquake; there had to be intentionality behind it, some kind of divine message or judgment on the citizens of Lisbon. Here's a sample of the common response, from the Jesuit priest Gabriel Malagrida.

Learn, O Lisbon, that the destroyer of our houses, palaces, churches and convents, the cause of the death of so many people and of the flames that devoured such vast treasures, are your abominable sins, and not comets, stars, vapours, and exhalations, and similar natural phenomena ... It is scandalous to pretend the earthquake was just a natural event, for if that be true, there is no need to repent and to try to avert the wrath of God, and not even the Devil himself could invent a false idea more likely to lead us all to irreparable ruin.[5]

God's voice had sounded in the deep, but why would he visit such pain on the faithful? Maybe some sinners needed correction, but why would he crush those attending the holy day mass with the falling stones of their own churches? Equally troubling was that the brothels, located in a different part of town, were spared. This disconnect was the problem of evil made manifest and, like the Holocaust in the twentieth century, the Lisbon earthquake was a cataract of suffering that made a Leibnizian theodicy seem facile and hollow. Everyday evils might be written off as essential elements of some obscure divine plan, but this was beyond any comprehensible justification.

The French Enlightenment writer Voltaire immediately seized on the Lisbon earthquake as fodder for *Candide*, his scathing satire on Leibniz.[6] Candide and his mentor Dr. Pangloss travel together, enduring every kind of calamity, yet even as things get worse and worse, it doesn't dent their confidence that all is for the best. They get to Lisbon just in time for the earthquake, whereupon Candide's friend, the Anabaptist Jacques, drowns in the harbor, their ship sinks, and once ashore, Candide is hit by falling masonry. As Candide lay half buried in rubble, he begs Pangloss for a little wine and oil to ease what he thought was his imminent death. Instead Pangloss returns with an armload of Leibnizian clichés and jargon about how this was necessarily the best of all possible worlds, everything has been foreordained by a kind and loving God, and *tout est bien.*

# The Garden of (Logically) Forking Paths

As a solution to the problem of evil the idea that this is the best of all possible worlds has found few modern followers; it is just another ingenious but inadequate attempt to reconcile suffering with a morally perfect God. However, Leibniz's underlying idea of possible worlds had real legs in the realm of logic. Logicians have known for awhile that certain kinds of sentences just don't behave the way they should. Formal rules of inference that work nicely for regular declarative sentences in the indicative mood go haywire with subjunctives and contrary-to-fact conditionals (i.e., counterfactuals). For example, in classical logic, indicative conditionals are transitive:

1   If the ice hotel is open, then it is really cold out.
2   If it is really cold out, then it is probably winter.
3   Therefore, if the ice hotel is open, then it is probably winter.

This is familiar if A then B, if B then C, thus if A then C logic, and makes perfect sense. But look what happens when we have counterfactuals instead.

1   If there had been a traffic jam on the highway, then John would have taken an alternate route to save time.
2   If John had been in a car wreck on the highway, then there would have been a traffic jam.
3   Therefore, if John had been in a car wreck on the highway, then he would have taken an alternate route to save time.

Here it is obvious that the conclusion doesn't—can't—follow. John can't be simultaneously in a car wreck on the highway and driving on a more efficient alternate route. The problem is that it looks entirely reasonable to suppose that John would have taken another route to avoid a traffic jam on the highway. And it's just as plausible to suppose that if he had been in a car wreck on the highway that there would have been a traffic jam. In other words, the premises are true but the conclusion can't be. Something must have gone wrong with the underlying logic. Yet it's the same perfectly valid logic of transitivity used in the ice hotel example. It looks like counterfactuals simply refuse to obey transitivity, and we need a different logical understanding of how they work.

A closely related issue is how we can make sense of sentences involving possibility and necessity. We know what would make this sentence true: "Rex is human," and we know what would make it false. We identify Rex and see what his properties are—maybe he's a human, maybe Rex is a dog or something else. How about this one? "Rex is necessarily human." What would make that one true? Just finding Rex and noting that he is in fact a human being is no help in determining whether Rex is *necessarily* human. The "necessarily" is adding something here, but what? Or "the base of this triangle is three inches long" is contingent in a way that "this triangle has three sides" is not. What exactly makes the latter a matter of necessity and not the former?

Writers are obviously interested in exploring the possible—who would win if the Hulk fought Spiderman? What if someone went back in time to prevent the JFK assassination? What if rabbits could talk? Suppose that a resourceful Swiss family was marooned on a remote island; what would happen? How could we understand ourselves if we discovered that aliens had visited prehistoric humans and left a monolith on the moon? Not only do fiction writers weave worlds out of the fabric of possibilities, but so do buttoned-down historians.

Historians are interested in not just the real history of the world, but also in counterfactual histories, accounts of what would have been or might have happened if certain key events had gone a different way. For example, in the early thirteenth century, Genghis Khan's Mongol conquerors were battle hardened from sieges in China and central Asia. Horse masters and bowmen, they possessed speed, well-organized discipline, and sophisticated weaponry. Above all, they inspired terror. Genghis Khan's strategy was systematic massacre: if a city resisted his armies, then once it fell (and they always did), he executed all the inhabitants. The death tolls, according to contemporary chroniclers, were staggering—in the millions. The Mongols reduced the population of China by 30 percent, and they stomped out the Islamic caliphate, literally by tying the caliph in a sack and trampling him to death with horses. The caliphate has never been restored. Even cities that surrendered to avoid total annihilation were looted and razed, and their citizens carted off as slaves. In 1242, a Mongol army led by the feared general Sabotai had slaughtered their way through Eastern Europe, dispatching the Christian armies in Poland and Hungary. They soon were camped within a few hundred miles of Vienna, the last gateway into the West.

Historian Cecelia Holland has argued that the city-hating nomadic Mongols would have faced few obstacles in pressing on to Paris, Rome, and beyond, wiping out European civilization in its entirety. Had they done so, there would have been no Reformation, no Renaissance, no democratic revolutions, and no scientific humanism, no Luther, Gutenberg, or Da Vinci. So what stopped them? The death of a single man. Ögedei Khan was the son and heir of Genghis and ruler of the Mongol Empire. When the hard-partying khan died after an all-night drinking bout with one of his court officials, news was sent out that Sabotai and his troops were legally bound to return home to elect a new khan. The Mongols promptly decamped for China and never returned. In Holland's words, the West survived "by blind luck."[7]

It's true, or at least likely to be true, that Ögedei's death saved Europe from destruction. It is certainly possible that, had he lived, the history of Europe would have been wildly different from what it was. The problem is that it's very hard to see what facts in the actual world *make* those claims true. How can what is tell us anything about the way things would, could, or should have been? The actual does not inform us about the possible or the necessary, but plods forward with blinkered tunnel vision. Prominent logicians such as Saul Kripke and Robert Stalnaker have pushed for understanding counterfactuals, possibility, and necessity on Leibnizian grounds, working out their formal semantics in terms of possible worlds.

It is not the actual world that makes counterfactual histories true, but what the facts are in *other* possible worlds and how our world is related to those others. Our world, the actual one, floats in a sea of possibilities, all of which are other ways reality might have been. Some of these other possible worlds are very similar to our own; if there had been one small change in how things went in our world, one small fact was different, then that other world would be real. One small change in the facts of our world—like Ögedei Khan hadn't died in December of 1241—and Western Europe is conquered by the Mongols. In this sense the fall of Europe in the thirteenth century is *modally close* to our world. It is not a very different world from our own; it is easy to get there from here. Other ways the world might have been are further removed from our own; a great deal more would have to change for that other version of reality to be the actual one. For example, for there to be talking rabbits would mean dramatic alterations in the evolutionary tree of life that would have included not only striking changes in the development of rabbit brain capacity and vocal cords, but sweeping effects on predator-prey relationships and the ecosystem as a whole. When the rabbits are smarter than wolves and can talk to each other, then it is a whole new ballgame. Even further away than talking rabbits are worlds where there are creatures profoundly unrelated to life on Earth, or where the laws of nature themselves are different. A world where the Hulk and Spiderman battle it out is a possible world, but quite far from our own.[8]

Some worlds are impossible ones, worlds with married bachelors, Euclidean triangles with angles that sum to 200°, circles and squares with the same area, and so on. The opposite is when there are truths that hold in every possible world, when no matter how much we imagine the facts to be different, some things always turn out the same. This is how necessary truths are commonly understood: truth in all possible worlds. The truths of mathematics and logic are usually taken to be necessarily true. Tautologies also fit into this group.

- *Que sera, sera.*
- Whatever happens, happens.
- It is what it is.
- Enough is enough.
- Business is business.
- Boys will be boys.
- Things are always in the last place you look.
- People want what they want.
- You should be yourself.
- Orthodoxy has the good luck to be everywhere. (John Locke)

Those are true in every possible world, and are the most irrefutable types of clichés. Sentences that are necessarily false are true in no worlds at all.

Possible worlds radiate out from the actual world along every dimension that could vary from actuality, and there is an intrinsic metric of the closeness of possible worlds that measures how "close" or how "far" from the real world a possibility is. In one direction from the actual world, there is a traffic jam on the highway, leading to John taking an alternate route that avoids the accident. In a different direction from actuality, it is John who is in a car wreck on the highway that jams up traffic. Now it's easy to see why counterfactuals aren't transitive: when one premise is properly evaluated in one world and the next premise is properly evaluated in a different world, they are talking past each other. There isn't a legitimate way to derive the conclusion. It's analogous to equivocation: someone who reasons that "I'm prepared to have myself a merry little Christmas, but I refuse to make the Yuletide gay. I don't think sexual preference should have anything to do with enjoying the holiday" conflates two different meanings of "gay." Assuming that counterfactuals are transitive conflates two different possible worlds.

# A Modal Theory of Luck

Like Leibniz's theodicy, basically no one has had any better ideas about how to understand necessity, possibility, and counterfactuals (call these *modal notions*), so using possible worlds to explain them has become quite entrenched. All of this conceptual machinery gives us a new way to understand the nature of luck. Recall Cecelia Holland's comment that the civilizations of the West were saved by "blind luck." In a close possible world, Ögedei Khan lived, the Mongols swept across Europe, and the history of the world was radically different. You are lucky because if there had been just one small difference in 1241 (even holding all the other facts of the time the same) you might not even exist and if you did your life would almost certainly be diminished from what it is. A flourishing life is *modally fragile*—there are nearby possible worlds in which it does not exist, where one dies in a freak accident, or has an aneurism at a young age, or ekes out survival in a refugee camp. Even if someone's life is wonderful from start to finish, it is still like a pane of glass that survives for a hundred years. The glass is fragile because one small difference in reality and it breaks; in nearby worlds it is nothing but shards and dust.

The opposite of fragility is robustness. As we move farther and farther away from our raft of the actual world into the infinite ocean of possibilities, a fact which still holds or an event which still occurs is a *modally robust* one. Things could change a lot before that particular fact doesn't hold. Unlike the glass, the image here is a diamond. For example, the laws of nature are modally robust. We are far away from the actual world before the speed of light is different, or the strong nuclear force is something else. Move away from reality without bound, and the logically and metaphysically necessary truths are still true. 1+1 will always = 2, composite objects will always have proper parts, and every object will still be identical with itself. At least you can count on those things.

Under the modal theory of luck, an event is lucky when it is significant and fragile. When things could have easily gone wrong and they didn't, you are lucky. When things could have easily gone right and they didn't, you are unlucky. Something is a matter of non-luck when it is insignificant or modally robust. Philosopher Duncan Pritchard is the most enthusiastic supporter of the modal theory, and he notes that it has the advantage of explaining degrees of luck.[9] A basketball team that wins with a three-pointer at the buzzer is very lucky (the ball rimmed out in nearby worlds), less lucky if the team wins with a two point shot at the buzzer, even less lucky if they win with an easy lay-up, even less lucky than that if they win by a large margin. If the Lakers beat the Bulls 87–52, the world would have had to change a good deal before the Lakers lost. The Lakers didn't win by luck. Oxford scientist Richard Dawkins offers this lovely example employing a modal understanding of luck, presenting our own lives as fragile islands in the vastness of unborn possibilities:

> We are going to die, and that makes us the lucky ones. Most people are never going to die because they are never going to be born. The potential people who could have been here in my place but who will in fact never see the light of day outnumber the sand grains of Arabia. Certainly those unborn ghosts include greater poets than Keats, scientists greater than Newton. We know this because the set of possible people allowed by our DNA so massively outnumbers the set of actual people. In the teeth of these stupefying odds it is you and I, in our ordinariness, that are here. We privileged few, who won the lottery of birth against all odds, how dare we whine at our inevitable return to that prior state from which the vast majority have never stirred?[10]

The modal theory really is a new innovation when it comes to understanding luck. At first it doesn't look different from the probability view (which has already been discussed) and certainly they do frequently give the same results. That's actually a good thing, since competing theories ought to save the same phenomena and give diverse results only in anomalous, outlier, or controversial cases. The modal and probability theories provide very different explanations, though. You're lucky to win the lottery on the probability view because it was of great importance to you that you win and it was so vastly unlikely that you would do so. For the modal view you are lucky to win because winning mattered to you but your win failed to occur in close possible worlds; had you picked one different number, or had a single ball in the lottery hopper rotated an extra 20 degrees, or a myriad of other small changes in the world occurred, then you would have lost. While the two theories offer distinct explanations of why winning the lottery is lucky, they are in agreement that it is in fact lucky. So you might suspect that they are just two different ways of saying the same thing.

But they aren't. Here's an example where the modal theory peels away from the probability view. Imagine you decide to play Russian Roulette and luckily for you, you are a winner. Or was it luck? According to the modal account you are quite lucky to win; a tiny change in the world, such as if the barrel had rotated just one more chamber, would have meant losing. Victory in Russian Roulette is modally fragile; it is easy to lose. On the probability account, though, you are *not* lucky to win. The chance of winning is 5/6— it is very likely that you will win Russian Roulette, and so not a matter of luck at all. The difference between the modal and probability approaches is more obvious if you imagine playing Russian Roulette with a very large cylinder—one that holds a googolplex of bullets, say. If all slots but one are empty, then you are fantastically likely to win at Russian Roulette; for the probability view of luck it is plain that there is less luck involved in the win than in literally anything else you might do. Everything else is more probable than losing googolplex Russian Roulette. Yet if a chamber adjacent to the one chosen contains the bullet, then it would have been just as easy to lose as it was in the six-cylinder example. The same small change in the world would have brought about a loss, and so under the modal account the win was still very lucky.

Here's another example of how the modal and probability theories of luck can give different results. Consider losing a fair lottery. You go to the Kwik-E-Mart and buy a Powerball ticket, and just like all the other times, you lose. Since it was vastly probable that you would lose, under the probability account your loss is not a matter of (bad) luck; indeed, it is just what you should expect to happen. However, according to the modal view, your lottery loss really is bad luck—your win was modally close. Just a tiny change in the world (if you had only picked 56 for the last number!) and the prize would have been yours. The possible world in which you win is very close to the actual one. The fact that winning the lottery is modally close but probabilistically remote very likely explains why people play. No one is going to bet on long odds that are also modally distant, like betting that a randomly picked philosopher will win gold in the 100m sprint at the next Olympics. How much would the actual world have to change before that's a good wager? But plenty of people are ready to bet on long odds where they win in close possible worlds, like Powerball.

These examples show that the modal theory may have a leg up on the probability view. Much of what we consider a matter of luck is when we just miss out on something else. The idea of near success or near failure isn't exactly captured by statistical chance, but by this modal sense of some events being on the edge of a knife, where one tiny slip would have meant a very different outcome.

## Transworld 2000

Leibniz (in Figure 3.1) presented an image of the moral goodness of all worlds well-ordered along a ruler of relative righteousness. Integral to the modal theory of luck is a similar idea of a metric of worlds. Luck—good or bad—depends on what happens in nearby worlds; that's what makes an event a modally fragile one. Distant possible worlds remote from our own have no bearing on luck, since robust facts or events are exactly what's not a matter of luck. So there must be an objective measure by which we can determine which possible worlds are near our own and which are distant. Pritchard orders possible worlds by their similarity to the actual world. The more ways that another reality is different from our own, the more dissimilar it is, the more distant that possibility. A possible world that varies from reality in only a few ways, or by one event or fact is a world that is close to our own. However, the notion of a metric of close and distant worlds may not make a lot of sense, which is an arduous challenge for the modal theory of luck. To illustrate the objection, let's imagine a science fiction version of logically possible worlds.

You're strolling through the town park, enjoying the beautiful early fall weather, when you see the most unusual vehicle you have ever seen. Parked on the grass is something that looks roughly like a DeLorean, but it has no wheels and appears to be made out of quicksilver. In fact, you have a hard time focusing on it, and you have the weird sense of a hall of mirrors. The door lifts and a wide-eyed, harried looking person clambers out. She looks around. "Good ... ok," she says, and blows out her breath in a relieved sort of way. She spots you looking at her machine, and gives you an appraising glance. "You like it? It's all yours." The traveler walks away chuckling quietly.

You cautiously walk over to the machine, and look inside. You see what resembles some kind of futuristic car cockpit. What the heck, you think. You climb inside, and settle into a deep leather seat. The door automatically closes, and you feel the air lock hermetically seal. In front of you is a large, dark computer screen instead of a windshield. Taped to the dashboard is a one-page cheatsheet.

*Welcome to the Transworld 2000. We hope that you are pleased with your purchase. Distance among possible worlds is controlled by the dial in front of the navigational screen* (you see a large black rheostat). *Turn to "1 iota" for the minimum distance. "1 iota" represents the minimum change from actuality, one fact or event that is changed in the smallest way that has a causal effect. 1 iota will give you access to the infinity of possible worlds that are the closest to reality. If you choose 2 iotas, that will be two facts changed about the actual world, and provide an even greater variety of alternatives. If you set the dial to maximum iotas* (you look at the dial, and see that this option is marked in police-siren red) *even the laws of nature will be different. There may even be no laws.* CAUTION: you might not be able to return from such realities. Please note that this selection voids your Transworld 2000 warranty. *Once you have chosen the iota distance, use the mouse to select your new reality.*

Well, you think, here goes nothing. Better start cautiously. You turn the knob to 1 iota and press the button next to it labeled GO. Immediately the computer screen in front of you is filled with small glowing orbs. It looks like the Hubble took a picture of a vast black universe filled with bioluminescent tapioca balls. The balls flow off the edge of your screen in all directions, and as you take the mouse and scroll and scroll, you swiftly realize that you will never come to the end. All the shimmering globes look absolutely indistinguishable. There's no way for you to tell one from the other; each radiant sphere is an entire universe with just one fact changed from our own. You randomly click on one of the worlds. Soundlessly, the gullwing hatch of the Transworld 2000 pops open.

You step outside into the very same park you were walking through when you encountered the traveler. Ok, nothing really looks different. Same kids on the swings, same dog chasing a Frisbee, same weather, same smell of grilled hot dogs. Not too troubling. Then you look closely and realize that the swing set is on the other side of the slides from what it was before. It had been on the right, and now it is on the left of the slides. That's the one change in the world? Pretty small beer. Then you start to realize that if the swing set is in a different location, that means that the one iota change had to have been in the past, not the present. The change was whatever led to the swing set's being on the left of the slides. You have no idea what that could be, or, rather, you have many ideas, but don't know which one is right. The park designer made a different decision, the ground on the right of the slides was too rocky and uneven, the kids moved the swings as a prank, the workmen read the blueprint wrong and installed the swings in the wrong spot, a random neural firing caused the installer to have a left/right confusion; there are any number of possible facts that might have changed at some point in the past and led to the swing set being in this other location.

It dawns on you that the instant one iota about the world changes, that immediately sets off a series of other changes, an unpredictable, nonlinear, branching path into the future, like a single drop of blood falling into a bottle of milk. For one event now to be different, that means that there was some event in the past that caused the current event to be different—unless there is some kind of spontaneous, random causation at work. Just as soon as we're ready to accept that there has to be some event or events in the past that were different in order for there to be a difference now, then we are identifying the one iota of change as in the past, not the present. What's more, one change in reality doesn't mean "one change from our specific temporal location in reality." We are simply at one point in time among many, just as we are at one location among many equally real locations. One change in all of reality might have happened at any point in time and still be a world incredibly similar to our own; it is just our world with one alteration.

You return to the Transworld 2000, figuring that you might as see what else is out there. You leave the knob set to 1 iota, and press GO. Again the screen is flooded with an infinite depth of identical luminous marbles, each representing a fully realized reality varying from our own by one fact. You click on one of the spheres.

Suppose that the one iota of difference between that alternate possible world and our own is that Ögedei Khan got slightly less drunk on December 11, 1241, and survived the night. Or the one iota of difference is that some wayward pollen tickled the nose of Lee Harvey Oswald, causing him to sneeze just as he pulled the trigger in the Texas Book Depository. Or Pontius Pilate decided to kick the irritating "King of the Jews" out of town instead of giving in to the mob and crucifying him. Or the fateful Norman arrow missed King Harold Godwinson by a few inches, and lightly grazed his ear instead of burrowing into his eye, and as a result he was able to successfully defend England at the Battle of Hastings. Or imagine the six-mile-wide Chicxulub impactor zoomed harmlessly past the Earth 66 million years ago, instead of plowing into the Yucatan peninsula and exterminating the dinosaurs. All of those worlds seem like they should be modally distant from our own, that they represent great alterations from our own reality. Yet they aren't distant at all: one iota of change, one miniscule event in reality, and those worlds become real.

Feeling reckless, you settle back in the Transworld 2000. "Screw it," you think, and crank the black knob until the indicator is buried in the red warning zone. Maximum iotas. You press GO, and click on the first glowing sphere you see. The gullwing door lifts, and for a brief second you see nothing but absolute blackness. The air rushes out of the machine like a last breath, and you have a peculiar feeling of being stretched in a way that seems impossible, like five-dimensional yoga. Your final thought is "rut-roh." It's unlikely that you figured out the change before the massive black hole tore your body apart into its atomic components, but here it is: the gravitational constant of the universe was just a little different from what it is in the actual world. If gravity is just a bit stronger then the expansion force from the Big Bang can't sufficiently overcome the powerful attractive force of gravity. As a result, all the matter in the universe clumps up into giant black holes, making stars, planets, life, and anything else physically impossible. You had the bad luck to wind up in that world. Of course, you also might have picked a world where the gravitational constant was a bit weaker and the universe rapidly expanded into a thermodynamically entropic thin soup of lifeless fundamental particles. Mess around with the laws of nature, and all bets are off.

Is even the "everything is stuffed into colossal black holes" world modally distant from our own? That's not an easy question to definitively answer. Could the laws of nature easily have been different from what they are? One hypothesis is that the laws of nature were somehow randomly selected at the instant of the Big Bang. Another is that the laws arise out of (supervene upon) the empirical facts of the universe, and those facts were randomly created at the origin. Or maybe the laws of nature are really metaphysically necessary in a way we don't yet grasp, and the idea of other possible worlds with other laws is somehow incoherent. These things are hotly contested.[11] But it may well be that a very small change in reality (like the initial randomizer settled on a different gravitational constant) would give us the black hole world. In that case, even worlds with alternate laws of nature are not distant ones; one iota of change in the facts and we are there.

It now seems as if nothing is modally remote at all. One iota of distance, or maximum iotas—there's no real distinction to be had. Change reality whatsoever and you can get to anywhere. Instead of there being an ordering of distance among possible worlds, the structure of all realities is flat and shallow. That's a real problem for the modal theory of luck. Recall that the intuitive appeal was that luck has to do with modal fragility. You're lucky when things could have easily gone wrong but they didn't, and you are unlucky when things could have easily gone right, but you just missed out. What's not supposed to be a matter of luck at all is the modally robust: when things go right but it would have been very hard for them to go any other way, then it's neither lucky nor unlucky, but a matter of non-luck. LeBron James isn't lucky to sink a lay-up on an undefended court, although he is lucky to hit a three-pointer from half court while being swarmed by defenders. The modal theory of luck separates *good luck/bad luck* from *non-luck* by relying on the modally fragile/modally robust distinction. The point of the Transworld 2000 thought experiment was to show that the fragile/robust division just doesn't hold up. Every event is fragile because every event is one iota of change away from not happening; therefore, every event is lucky. Now we've arrived full circle. After a tour through Leibniz and logical semantics, the modal theory of luck takes us right back to Menander: "All that we think or say or do is Tuche; we only write our signatures below."

# Lucky Necessities

The argument that the black hole world is just one iota of difference away from reality is just one horn of a dilemma. Einstein once remarked to his assistant that "what I'm really interested in is whether God could have made the world in a different way; that is, whether the necessity of logical simplicity leaves any freedom at all."[12] Einstein wanted to know whether God could have made the laws of nature differently, or whether they flow from some deeper necessity, and the physical constants must be what they are. If that's the way things work, then the black hole world is metaphysically impossible—it's not one iota away, it's more iotas than the maximum setting in the Transworld 2000. This alternative scenario is just as bad for the modal theory of luck. It is perfectly reasonable to say "boy, are we lucky that the gravitational constant is what it is, and not a little bit weaker or a little bit stronger. Life wouldn't even be possible if the whole universe were filled with nothing but giant black holes or was an entropic gruel of uniformly diffuse particles." But the whole strategy of the modal theory was to insist that only modally fragile events could be lucky; modally robust ones weren't eligible to be lucky, they were a matter of non-luck. Here's the dilemma, then: either the black hole world is one iota of difference away from our own and therefore everything is lucky or the black hole world is modally distant but we're still lucky that gravity worked out in a way that permitted our lives. Either way the modal theory just doesn't get things right.

There's even more troubling examples. If there is anything that is truly modally robust, it has to be logically necessary truths. They are going to hold no matter what changes happen; even if the laws of nature are different, the laws of logic and the truths of mathematics are still going to be true. Under the modal theory of luck, at the very least *those* things can't be a matter of luck; that *has* to be the realm of non-luck. Yet the modal theory blows it here as well. Here are two examples.

*The logical bandit.* The logical bandit points a gun at you and tells you that unless you correctly answer a logic puzzle, he's going to steal your wallet. He gives you this poser:

Suppose you go to a diner where the cook is famous for pancakes. Actually, he is famous for burning 50% of the pancake-sides he cooks, and cooking the other 50% perfectly. The statistics: One third of his pancakes are golden on both sides; one third are black on both sides;

and the remaining third are golden on one side and black on the other. You order a pancake. When it comes, the side you can see is golden. What is the chance that the other side is golden?

You are horrible at this sort of thing, and are completely flummoxed by the gun, the puzzle, and the whole situation. You make a wild guess and say "it's 2/3." The logical bandit, who could tell you were just guessing, smiles ruefully and replies, "you're lucky the correct answer is indeed 2/3," and vanishes into the night.[13]

Mathematical facts are of course necessarily true, and so it is a matter of logical necessity that the right answer to the pancake puzzle is 2/3.

*Fermat.* The Pythagorean Theorem is $A^2 + B^2 = C^2$. In 1637 Pierre de Fermat wondered if this formula would work for powers other than two. He decided that the answer was no, and that $A^N + B^N = C^N$ has no solutions for N in the positive integers greater than two. He famously wrote in the margins of his copy of Diophantus's *Arithmetica* that he had discovered a marvelous proof of this theorem, which the margins were too small to contain. Generations of mathematicians attempted to prove or falsify Fermat's last theorem, without success, until Andrew Wiles succeeded in 1995. Since it took 358 years for anyone to prove the theorem, and then only by using branches of mathematics that didn't exist in Fermat's day, no one believes that Fermat himself had really discovered a sound proof. Instead his unknown "proof" is assumed to be partial or flawed, as were all the other attempts for over three centuries. Fermat was lucky that his last theorem was true, despite his flawed proof, because it secured his mathematical immortality. Needless to say, Fermat's last theorem is necessarily true.

It sounds perfectly reasonable to say that "you're lucky the correct answer to the pancake puzzle is 2/3" or "Fermat was lucky that his last theorem was true, despite his flawed proof, because it secured his mathematical immortality." Those things do sound like they are a matter of luck. Not under the modal theory of luck, though. The correct answer to the pancake puzzle is 2/3 in every possible world, as is Fermat's last theorem. The modal theory tells us that luck is fragility, but those facts are as robust and non-fragile as anything can be. Notice this is a problem for the probability treatment of luck too. It is only improbable facts that are supposed to be lucky; the super probable is just what we should expect to be true and isn't lucky at all. The logical bandit and Fermat cases are examples of *lucky necessities*, and neither the modal nor the probability theory gets these right. On the one hand, the modal theory rules all kinds of non-lucky things as lucky, since there is no viable metric of distance among worlds and practically everything is fragile. On the other hand, there are lucky necessities which the modal theory can't allow because they are robust.

# A Control Theory of Luck

Neither probability nor modality do what we'd like them to do. While the nature of luck is so far elusive, those approaches are not the only fish in the sea. There is one more popular understanding of luck that has nothing to do (at least prima facie) with either improbable events or modally fragile ones. Ed Smith, an English professional cricket player turned journalist, writes of the shift in his own thinking as an athlete. He began his career believing that his sporting destiny was wholly under his control, simply a matter of developing the iron will to succeed at all costs. His cricket club even banned any reference to bad luck, as just the sort of weak-minded excuse true champions would do without. That all sounded pretty good until Smith's cricket career abruptly ended as the result of a freak ankle injury. With that implacable turn of Fortuna's wheel, he decided that willpower couldn't really beat bad luck after all. Smith now expresses his disdain for the false promises of self-help books that proclaim you make your own luck, or that through positive thinking you alone are the master of your fate.[14] "Luck," he writes, "is that which is beyond my control."[15] Making your own luck is an oxymoron—you can't control what is perforce beyond your control. And there is a lot that is beyond our control.

Smith is not alone in promoting a control theory of luck,[16] and it sounds promising. For one thing, it really does look like a genuine alternative to the probability and modal theories we've so far considered. It certainly gives a different sort of explanation for what's going on in cases of luck. Again, there is a lot of agreement about what counts as a matter of luck, just a different take on why those events are lucky ones. So how does it differ from the others? The last objection to the modal theory was that it couldn't accommodate lucky necessities; since necessary truths are modally robust, then can't be lucky, and yet there are several instances where they do seem to be lucky. Under the control view, though, those *are* lucky after all. Are we lucky that the gravitational constant of the universe is what it is? Sure: that was definitely beyond our control. Was Fermat lucky that his last theorem turned out to be true? Sure he was: whether it was true was certainly outside of his control. Table 3.1 contains a summary of differences.

**TABLE 3.1** Three theories of luck.

| | Good luck | Bad luck | Not luck |
|---|---|---|---|
| Probability theory | *Winning a fair lottery* (because it was very improbable that you win) | *Losing Russian Roulette* (because your loss was improbable) | *Losing a fair lottery* (because it was very probable that you lose) |
| | | | *Winning Russian Roulette* (because it was very likely that you win) |
| | | | *Lucky necessities* (because necessary truths are probability 1) |
| Modal theory | *Winning a fair lottery* (because your win was modally fragile; that is, you could have easily lost) | *Losing Russian Roulette* (because you could have easily won) | *Lucky necessities* (because they are modally robust) |
| | *Winning Russian Roulette* (because you could have easily lost) | *Losing a fair lottery* (because you could have easily won) | |
| Control theory | *Winning a fair lottery* (because winning is outside of your control) | *Losing Russian Roulette* (because the outcome was outside of anyone's control) | ???? |
| | *Winning Russian Roulette* (because winning is outside of your control) | *Losing a fair lottery* (because lottery outcomes are outside of your control) | |
| | *(Lucky necessities* because necessary truths are outside of anyone's control) | | |

All three theories tell us that winning the lottery is good luck and losing at Russian Roulette is bad luck, although they offer differing explanations as to why. Notice that two out of the three rule that losing a fair lottery is bad luck, a different two of three say that lucky necessities aren't really a matter of luck, and only one view proposes that winning Russian Roulette isn't lucky. The theories are not at all the same—they offer varying explanations and divergent results.

There's one remaining open square of mystery: the category of what would *not* be a matter of luck if we accept the control theory. Presumably an event that is within your control isn't one that just happened by luck. That's all well and good, provided we can make decent sense of just when something is within our control and when it isn't. It's probably not a surprise that there's more to sorting control than meets the eye.

# Séances and Rubber Hands

People seldom recognize when they are in the grip of a popular obsession. At the height of the Rubik's Cube mania in the 1980s, the usually brilliant cognitive scientist Douglas Hofstadter wrote "is [the Cube] just some sort of fad? My personal opinion is that it will last. I think the Cube has some sort of basic, instinctive, 'primordial' appeal … it fits into a niche in our minds that connects to many, many general notions about the world."[17] A year or two after Hofstadter wrote those words, Rubik's Cubes were collecting dust in everyone's closet. In nineteenth-century Europe, the craze was for spiritualism. This was a collision of older faith traditions with the Age of Reason[18] and the Industrial Revolution, yielding a fascination with using empirical evidence for things unseen. Séances, table-turning, Ouija boards, and spirit cabinets were all touted as earthly portals to the invisible world of spirits. Of course, there were many fraudsters who merely performed magic acts dressed up in spiritualist garb to a gullible public. There were also some mediums who truly thought that they were in contact with another world, and saw themselves as the vessels through which the messages of the spirits mysteriously passed. These enthusiasms caught the critical attention of prominent scientists. Benjamin Franklin and Antoine Lavoisier, for example, investigated mesmerism, the contention that there is a magnetic fluid in living bodies that causes all sorts of bizarre phenomena, and concluded that the whole business was the result of imagination and fraud.[19]

The chemist Michael Faraday examined the matter of table-turning, a form of séance in which participants would sit around a small table and lightly place their fingers on the top. The table would then tilt, spin, and tip in different directions, and even move across the room. The direction of tilt was sometimes supposed to indicate different letters, which would then spell out a message from spirits beyond the grave. Faraday performed a variety of experiments during these séances, ruling out various other hypotheses such as electrical or magnetic effects or the rotation of the earth. Finally, Faraday sandwiched four glass rods between two thin pieces of cardboard that he loosely fastened together with rubber bands. Then he fixed the bottom half of the sandwich to the table top. The top piece of cardboard could move along the tops of the glass rollers within the limits of the rubber bands. By means of a couple of pins and "a straight hay-stalk 15 inches long," he rigged up an indicating lever. Séance participants were supposed to put their hands on the table top with only downward pressure; the slightest lateral movement would be indicated by the swinging of the hay-stalk indicator. Of course everyone at the table swore that they did nothing and the spirits were the ones that moved the table. The hay-stalk, however, told a different tale. When everyone was careful to not move their hands and keep the indicator immobile, the table failed to move as well.[20]

The séance-goers may all have been sincere, honest, upright citizens, who genuinely believed that they had nothing to do with the table movement. It turns out that they were lied to by their own brains. In anticipation of the table tipping or spinning, the participants subconsciously began to press their hands in the direction of the expected movement, thus causing the very effect they came to experience. This was first figured out in 1852 by the psychologist William B. Carpenter, and he dubbed it "the ideomotor effect."[21] Dowsing rods are another instance in which subtle, subconscious muscle movements are amplified to noticeable and eerie results. An even more common experience is when a moviegoer watching a hang glider or a race car from first-person point of view leans into the turns. We expect the centrifugal force and move as if it is acting on us, even in an immobile theater seat. The ideomotor effect is an example of when we really do have causal control over some event—we're the ones moving the table, turning the dowsing rod, or leaning into the turns; they aren't due to either natural or occult forces—but we consciously deny that there is any such control.

Not only do we have control when we think we lack it, but we lack control when we think we have it. In a famous experiment, the psychologists Matthew Botvinick and Jonathan Cohen sat subjects down with their left arms resting on a small table. They hid the arm from the subject's view with a screen, and put a realistic-looking rubber left arm and hand on the table in front of the subject. As the subject stared at the rubber hand, the experimenters used paintbrushes to simultaneously stroke the backs of both the subject's real left hand (hidden from view) and the rubber left hand (in plain sight). After a few minutes, the subjects reported feeling the touch of the viewed brush, not the hidden one; their bodily proprioception reached out to incorporate the rubber hand into their own body image. The brain tries to synthesize and make sense of the taps and strokes that it sees and the ones that it feels, and after a bit the brains of the test subjects concluded that the rubber hand must be part of their body. They felt the rubber hand as being their own.[22]

The neuroscientist V. S. Ramachandran has taken these experiments further. It turns out that subjects can project bodily sensations onto inanimate objects that don't even resemble ordinary body parts. Instead of a rubber hand, Ramachandran tapped and stroked the surface of a desk, while simultaneously doing the same to the subject's left hand which was hidden under the desk. Soon they started experiencing the taps and strokes as coming from the desk itself, despite the manifest absurdity of such a thing. The illusion was so compelling that when Ramachandran made a longer stroke on the desk than on the subject's hidden hand, the subject exclaimed that, like Reed Richards of the Fantastic Four, his hand had lengthened or stretched to absurd proportions. Ramachandran then took a hammer and smashed the table, causing a fight-or-flight response as if he had smashed the subject's own real hand. Control subjects not under the influence of the illusion had no such response.[23] Even parts of the body that cannot usually be seen can be projected. In another setup, Ramachandran had subjects watch an experimenter stroke and tap the back of plastic mannequin head with one hand while stroking and tapping the back of the subject's own head in perfect synchrony. In no time the naïve subjects started experiencing the sensations as coming from the mannequin's head instead of their own.[24]

What's uncanny about these experiences is that the subjects know perfectly well that they don't have a rubber hand, and yet powerfully feel that they do. In some subjects the "phantom head" effect with the mannequin was so strong that they had the spooky sense of being temporarily decapitated![25] If there is anything you can be sure of (within the limits of radical skepticism), it is that your head is still attached. In these examples, people don't feel that they have control over body parts that they clearly do control; they don't even recognize those body parts as being their own. The wonderful thing about these cases is that they are simple experiments anyone could try at home, not instances of rare medical disorders.[26] The upshot is that we are very poor judges of what we control and what we do not; our intuitions or feelings about control are unreliable and easily manipulated. If a theory of luck based on a lack of control is to have any traction, we need a much better understanding of what control really is. We can't rely on our feelings to tell us whether we lack control.

Given that our instinctive judgments about whether we have control over something can't be trusted, what does "being in control" amount to? Surprisingly, most scholars who have thought about control tend to just gloss over the nature of control on their way to more pressing matters such as "conscious control" or "rational control" or "voluntary control" and the like.[27] About the only thing that everyone agrees on is that control has something to do with causal influence. Of course, that's about as helpful as saying that scotch has something to do with alcohol. Sure it does, but so do beer, wine, and the rest of the liquor cabinet. Every kind of accident involves causal influence but not control—wrecking your car caused some things to happen, but you certainly weren't in control. It's common to add a condition of intention: if you have control over whether your forehand went cross-court, then your intentions to hit it cross-court were in some way causally related to the ball's actually going cross-court. What about the séance-goers? They went to the séance intending to be participants in table-tipping, and they caused the table-tipping. If you think that's still not enough to say they were in control of the table's motion, then we probably need to add a requirement of *conscious* intention. Even that runs into the problem of *causal deviance*. Suppose you're playing tennis, consciously intend to hit a winner, and do hit a winner; in other words the winning shot is the causal result of that conscious intention. Can we be sure that you were in control of hitting that winner? Sadly, no. If the ball accidentally clipped the netcord and barely fell in for an unreturnable shot, we cannot plausibly say that your ball control won the day. It was still luck.

# Wimbledon 2012

When we think of control, we often turn to mastery—if anyone has control over an outcome or event, it is surely someone who is an expert in that particular arena. Maybe a closer look at expert action will help sort out the difference between luck and control. A highly trained cardiac surgeon isn't lucky when a routine operation goes well, precisely because she was in control the entire time. A juggler isn't lucky not to drop the balls; he's done it a thousand times and has complete command over them. Keith Jarrett isn't lucky to hit the right chord and it is not just luck that Dale Earnhardt, Jr. was able to easily merge into busy traffic. They are in control. Yet even in the case of experts, even ignoring the causal deviance problem, it is not always easy to tell when their successes are the result of control or the result of luck. That's not welcome news for the control theory, since it aims to parse just that difference. Here's a troublesome example.

In the second round of the 2012 Wimbledon tournament, Rafael Nadal played Lukas Rosol. Nadal was ranked #2 in the world, and was the second seed in Wimbledon. Rosol was ranked #100 in the world, and everyone expected Nadal to thrash him. Even Rosol himself only hoped "just to play three good sets [and] don't lose 6–0, 6–1, 6–1." Instead Rosol soundly beat Nadal in what was the greatest upset at Wimbledon in the last quarter century (6–7 (9), 6–4, 6–4, 2–6, 6–4). Was Nadal unlucky to lose, or, conversely, was Rosol lucky to win? Instinctively, Rosol was incredibly lucky to beat the far superior Nadal, but that is not easy to show under the control theory of luck.

Under the control view, Nadal would be unlucky to lose if his loss was outside his control. According to the United States Tennis Association, the five controls of the ball are depth, height, direction, speed, and spin, and certainly Nadal was able to repeatedly and effectively choose those. In addition, he was able to direct points, implement strategic shot selection, and pursue tactical advantages. Out of the 276 points of the match, Nadal committed only sixteen unforced errors.[28] In other words, Nadal played like the world-class tennis champion he is, not like a weekend hacker spraying his shots with limited command of the ball. Nor was his loss due to a series of fluke accidents; by any sensible measure, Nadal's performance on the court was under his control.

The control theory states that Nadal's loss was a matter of luck just in case that loss was beyond, or significantly beyond, his control. But it surely wasn't. By comparison, if a casual tennis player were to play Nadal, his inevitable and rapid loss would most certainly be beyond his control. There is nothing a weekend warrior could do to beat Nadal, and Nadal's crushing victory would hardly be a matter of luck. However, his loss to Rosol is intuitively a matter of bad luck, even though that loss was not reasonably beyond his control. The control theory gets it wrong.

Was Rosol lucky to win? He was not in control of Nadal's return shot selection, speed, spin, or strategy, although he *was* able to dictate most of the points in the match and able to keep Nadal on the defensive. So one could reasonably hold that under the control account of luck, Rosol's victory was not a matter of luck—he simply delivered a superior performance and more control than Nadal. Thus under the control account, Rosol was not lucky to win and Nadal was not unlucky to lose. *That* can't be right. Obviously Rosol's outstanding performance was within the range of his skill as a tennis player, but he was deviating far above his mean performance level. He was lucky to be "playing in the trees" the day of his match against Nadal. The best match of his life might have shown up at any time over the course of his career and Rosol is lucky it happened the day he played Nadal at Wimbledon.

One might object that Rosol has no control over the level of his performance, no control over when he has an outstanding day on the court, and this lack of control means his success was indeed due to luck. However, such an objection makes the demands for control unreasonably, even impossibly, high. Rosol and Nadal always try their best in major tournaments. As top athletes with superb mastery of the game and no unusual interference (no one was sick, injured, etc.), they are in control of their performance. No one has control of when their performance at a task deviates substantially from their mean performance; otherwise everyone would give their best possible performance every time. A golfer who *could* hit an eagle on a par 5 *will* hit an eagle every time. Then the eagle becomes the mean performance. Put another way: it is impossible to always play above average. Being in control cannot require doing the mathematically impossible.

Now, one might argue that if Nadal were truly in control of the match, then he would have won; genuine control entails success. If that's the standard, though, then it makes the demand for control so strict that practically nothing will qualify.[29] Exactly what do you have such control over that you are *perfectly successful*? As Samuel Johnson noted, "Faults and defects every work of man must have."[30] If true control requires infallibility, then nearly all successes are lucky ones. Instead of fending off Fortuna, again we fall back to the fatalism of attributing everything to luck. Let's lower the bar. Surely someone who usually succeeds in a task or is very likely to succeed can plausibly be said to be in control.

The idea that being in control of something means probable or frequent success in doing that thing runs aground with baseball. Ty Cobb, for example, is one of the best hitters in the history of baseball, and one of the first four players to be elected to the Baseball Hall of Fame. Cobb continues to hold the major league record for the best career batting average, batting .366. Nevertheless, he still didn't usually succeed—despite being the best hitter in history, he failed to get a hit nearly two-thirds of the time. Every time he was at the plate it was improbable for him to get a hit, and so whether Cobb gets a hit in any particular at-bat is significantly beyond his control. Not only is hitting not a basic action that might be within his direct control (like moving his arm, say), but Cobb cannot control which pitches he received, what distractions might affect his concentration, or the play of the opposing fielders. No batter can plausibly be said to have control over whether he hits the ball. All this means that when Cobb does get a hit, it is always luck. Take it to the next logical step: no one in baseball history ever batted over .500 for a season or even in a streak. Hitting is unusual, uncommon, and not sufficiently within any batter's control, which means that every hit in the history of the game is attributable to luck.

"Control" can't be understood as either infallible success or probable success without giving wonky results about luck. What if by control we just mean *greater than average success*? Ty Cobb wasn't lucky to get a hit because he was much likelier to do so than the average person, and that's really all we mean by saying that he was in control. His typical success in making contact with a professionally thrown baseball was much higher than average—stick a weekend softball player at the plate in front of a Nolan Ryan heater and it's just luck if he makes contact at all. On the other hand, pros can do that with predictable regularity, even if they can't get a hit most of the time.

The "greater than average success" idea might salvage Cobb as being in control when he gets a hit, but it too has some untenable consequences. For example, suppose there is some task where the average person fails 99 percent of the time, but you only fail at the task 98 percent of the time. Are you in control? An example might be the difference between an amateur golfer and a professional golfer getting a hole-in-one, as discussed in the last chapter. Even though the pro was five times as likely to hit the ace, it is so ridiculously rare and unlikely that it is absurd to say that the pro was in control of the shot. Or suppose that a professional gambler is just a tiny bit better at predicting horse races than a novice. Even when the gambler is right, it is nonsense to suppose that she was in control of the outcome. "Greater than average success" only ensures barely emerging out of the bubbling mudpot of randomness, not *control*.

We started by asking what events a control theory of luck would decree as not being a matter of luck at all, and found the whole topic as clear as mud. All in all, the control theory of luck struggles to get things right. We can't count on our naïve judgments about control since, as the ideomotor and rubber hand illusion examples show, we need a theoretical understanding instead. Yet giving a satisfactory analysis turns out to be quite difficult. Rosol was lucky to beat the far superior Nadal at Wimbledon, even though there is a clear sense in which neither player lacked control. When the standards for control are raised high enough to give the result that Rosol really was lucky to win (since Nadal's control did not guarantee his victory), then we risk making every event a lucky one. If we lower the benchmark for control to merely probable success, it gives the result that the best baseball hitter in history was just lucky every time he made contact with the ball. When we try making control a matter of greater than average success, we run into scenarios where someone is considered in control when their skill level is just barely better than randomness.

The control theory was also advertised as an authentic alternative to the modal and probability views. When we try to figure out just what "control" is supposed to be, it risks collapsing into one of the rival theories. If what it is for you to be control of some outcome or event is that you have a *greater than average chance* of bringing about the event or you can *probably* cause it to happen, that's just another way of stating the probability view. Being in control means having a certain probability of causing an effect, and a lack of control/low probability of causing an effect indicates luck. If instead we interpret "control" to mean that you are in control just in case it would be very difficult for you to fail, then the view turns into the modal theory. "Control" is no more than a modally robust ability to bring about an event, and luck = lack of control = a modally fragile ability to cause the event. So not only will a competent control theory have to get around the Rosol/Nadal and Cobb problems, but it will have to find a way to carve out a niche in conceptual space that shows control to be more—or other—than a cumbersome way to state a probability or modal theory of luck.

But wait, there's more!

# Synchronic and Diachronic Luck

It's easy to find listicles like "The Top 25 Buzzer-Beaters & Game-Winners in NBA Playoff History" or "Top 10 Clutch Shots of the Last 20 Years" or "The 50 Best Game Winning Plays in Sports History." Each vignette in these lists has the same structure: the game is almost over and the score is so close that either team could win. Then a conquering hero makes a bold move that cements their team's victory, practically standing arms akimbo with his sword sticking out of a deceased dragon. For example, Wikipedia dispassionately characterizes Michael Jordan's final goal in game 6 of the 1998 NBA Finals as a "game-winning shot [that] has been immortalized around the world." This sort of hero narrative is bothersome. What about all those other players who put points on the board? Their contributions were every bit as essential to winning. If Jordan's teammates hadn't driven the score to 86–85, one point away from a tie with the Utah Jazz, then his two-pointer at the end would have meant nothing. What makes him more important or admirable than the others? The only possible answer could be that he was the anointed, lucky one because it was his last-second shot that put the team over the edge. The same shot at any other point in the game would have been routine—a contribution, but a quotidian one. But to clinch victory at the last second? That's what's special, that's what's lucky.

Something is diachronic when it takes place over time, and synchronic when it happens all at one time. Judgments of luck turn out to be sensitive to this distinction in surprising and inconsistent ways, and no theory of luck so far examined can make any sense of it. Diachronically, an event is judged to be lucky as a part of a series or streak that takes place over time, but synchronically the same event is not regarded as lucky when it is considered atemporally, independently of its relations to other events. One can be lucky diachronically but not synchronically, and conversely. Call this the problem of diachronic luck. Here are some examples of diachronic luck and how they cause problems for theories of luck.

Take Joe DiMaggio's celebrated streak. His 1941 streak of safely hitting in fifty-six consecutive baseball games is widely considered the most outstanding record in the history of sport.[31] The late Stephen Jay Gould claimed that DiMaggio "beat the hardest taskmaster of all, a woman who makes Nolan Ryan's fastball look like a cantaloupe in slow motion—Lady Luck." DiMaggio was in full agreement, writing, "I have said many times that you have to be lucky to keep a hitting streak going."[32] The mathematicians Samuel Arbesman and Steven Strogatz ran a Monte Carlo simulation on the history of baseball, using a comprehensive baseball statistics database (from 1871 to 2004).[33] They constructed a variety of different mathematical models of alternate possible histories of baseball, taking into account for each player the number of games played, number of at-bats, times walked, being hit by a pitch, sacrifice hits, and so on. Their five models varied the minimum number of plate appearances and a few other variables, and they ran 10,000 computer simulations for each model. These simulations amounted to complete alternative histories of baseball. One of the results was that there was only between a 20 percent and 50 percent chance that anyone would have safely hit in fifty-six or more consecutive games. DiMaggio, who in the actual world did have a fifty-six-game hitting streak, was barely in the top fifty of the most probable players to hold that record. In fact, they write that "while no single player is especially likely to hold the record, it is likely that an extreme streak would have occurred."[34] The probability of someone or other having a long hitting streak is high, but the probability of DiMaggio in particular having the record is low.

So, given the Arbesman and Strogatz analysis, it was very unlikely that DiMaggio would hit in fifty-six consecutive games, and so he was hugely lucky to have the streak. In fact, the longer the streak went on, the luckier he was to keep it up. Was DiMaggio unlucky on July 17, 1941, the date that his streak ended? He thought so. "When my streak came to an end, it was again a matter of luck—this time bad luck."[35] In that game, Indians third baseman Ken Keltner made two terrific backhanded stops to prevent DiMaggio from hitting successfully in what would have been the fifty-seventh game of the streak. The day after the streak ended, DiMaggio began another hitting streak that lasted seventeen games. Surely it was terrible luck that Keltner made such good plays and prevented DiMaggio from getting a hit in game 57. If he had, then instead of being fifty-six games long, DiMaggio's hitting streak would have been a stunning seventy-four games in a row. It's worth noting that safely hitting 73 of 74 games in a row is also still a record. Viewed as an element of a series that takes place over time (the diachronic perspective), DiMaggio was right: he had bad luck against the Indians in game 57. Had he managed to get even one hit that game, then he would have the untouchable mega streak of hitting in 74 games in a row.

Considered in isolation from any location in time or relation to other hits (the synchronic perspective), it was not bad luck that DiMaggio failed to connect. In fact, it's exactly what we should all expect. Baseball players rarely hit; a Hall-of-Fame hitter might only get a base hit a third of his at-bats. As was argued earlier, on all three theories of luck it is simply luck when a baseball player gets a hit—it is always improbable, modally frail, and not really within their control. Even during his streak DiMaggio missed most of the time (batting .409). The fact that he failed to hit in game 57 was a wholly ordinary, routine part of baseball. If it were any other game, no one would think DiMaggio was uncommonly unlucky; it is only because of its location between his two streaks that it seems that way. So, did DiMaggio suffer from bad luck in game 57, was it not even an issue of luck, or what? The answer seems to be that there's no way to assess his luck without adopting a particular point of view. At best we have only a perspectival assessment: DiMaggio was diachronically unlucky (which the theories of luck under consideration cannot accommodate) but synchronically his performance was not a matter of bad luck at all (both intuitively and according to the three theories of luck).

Or consider a streak in which a player is diachronically lucky but viewed synchronically his performance is not due to luck. Micheal Williams, a point guard for the NBA Timberwolves, holds the NBA record for a free-throw streak: over a period of nine months in 1993 he sunk ninety-seven free throws before missing.[36] Since his career free-throw percentage was .868, on the probability account no individual free throw was lucky—Williams was very likely to sink it. On the modal account it is difficult to judge how distant the closest possible world is in which Williams misses any particular free throw. Unlike baseball, where each pitch is different and more generally the playing conditions vary, free throws have replicable conditions. Players shoot from the same spot, and no one else interferes with or controls the ball prior to their shot. So it may be that the world would have to be considerably different for Williams to miss a free throw that he made in the actual world. On the control account Williams has significant control over the basketball— he is a pro ballplayer and is shooting without interference or unusual distractions. So it seems that all three theories of luck are in agreement: Williams is not lucky when he hits any particular free throw. Nor is he unlucky; successfully sinking a free throw just isn't a matter of luck at all. His success seems properly assignable to skill, not luck.

Nevertheless, Williams was lucky to hit the seventy-ninth shot in a row, the one that broke Calvin Murphy's old record, since that was the shot that cemented his place in the record books. As NBA Hall of Famer Rick Berry writes, "All great free-throw shooters must possess technique, confidence, routine and a little luck." Calvin Murphy agreed, complaining at the time that "what really bugs me is Micheal Williams breaking my consecutive streak and now he's shooting 83 percent. That tells me he was lucky." Williams was lucky to make the record-breaking shot, despite the fact that he was in control of the ball, very likely to make it, and apart from the streak it was more-or-less an indistinguishable shot from any other free throw.

Maybe it's just something about sports. We like myth-making, with tales of heroes overcoming the odds and performing great deeds that elevate them to glory. Perhaps we're making too much out of our all-too-human penchant to spin out a narrative that transmutes a leaden tale of a grown man hitting a ball with a stick into the gold of legend. As a result, it is easy to suspect that all this is trying too hard to suss out something important about luck. Yet the exact same issue arises in non-sporting contexts with wholly random events than have nothing to do with skill or personal achievement.

Suppose you are playing an old-fashioned mechanical slot machine (new ones are digital, computer-controlled, and randomized). Pull the lever, and three reels spin around independently of each other, each with the same probability to land on a lemon, cherry, apple, lime, grape, watermelon, etc. A common setup is to have sixteen different images per reel. The reels do not stop all at once; the one on the furthest left stops first, then the middle reel, then the one on the right. You pull the lever. The first reel lands on a cherry. That's not luck; you don't care. It is irrelevant what the first symbol is. Then the second reel also stops on a cherry. You're still not feeling too lucky, because there's no payout for two cherries. Now you are certainly crossing your fingers for the third reel, hoping for a visit from Lady Luck. When it stops, it too lands on a cherry. Jackpot! You were very lucky that the third reel came up cherry.

Told in that manner, it is perfectly sensible that the first cherry was not a matter of luck at all, the second cherry also not luck (or maybe a tiny bit lucky), but the third cherry was tremendously lucky. Viewed as an element of a diachronic series, the final cherry was lucky, since it secured the jackpot. However, the spins of the reels are independent trials and are not causally connected to each other. Furthermore, each wheel had to land on the same symbol in order to win; it was no more necessary that the third reel land on cherry than it was for the first two. Given that the third reel was cherry, the first two had to be as well. Viewed synchronically, no one wheel seems any luckier than any other. They all had to cooperate together to yield a payout.

Consider how our three theories of luck fare. The probability that the final symbol would be a cherry was no lower than the chance the first symbol was. The chance that all three would hit on the same fruit was low (.02 percent), so the probability theory gives the correct result that beating a slot machine is lucky. However, whether it is lucky to get a streak of cherries is not the issue: *was getting a cherry on the third reel luckier than getting one on the first or second reel?* On the probability theory the answer is no. The chance was the same for each reel.

We saw earlier that the modal theory relies on drawing a distinction between some events as fragile and some as robust, but that difference didn't hold up very well. The point of the Transworld 2000 thought experiment was to show that nearly every fact is fragile. Let's set all that aside. *Even if* the fragile/robust distinction holds up, the modal view is helpless in the slot machine case. All it takes is a small change in the world (the reel stops a few clicks later or a few before what it did in the actual world) and reel 3 would have not hit on a cherry. Yet the exact same thing is true of reels 1 and 2. The success of reel 3 in producing a cherry is no more modally fragile than the other two reels; therefore a cherry on reel 3 is no luckier than the other two. The control theory lines up with the others. A player has no control over where any of the reels stop spinning. One has no less control over the third reel than over any of the others. Therefore, under the control theory the relative luck assigned to each of the reels is exactly the same. It doesn't matter for our purposes here whether it was lucky or not lucky that a reel hit on cherry. The salient issue is whether it was luckier that the third reel did so.

Synchronically, all the theories get it right: landing on a cherry on reel 3 isn't any luckier than getting one on either of the other two reels. Yet none of the theories are able to accommodate the diachronic judgment that during play the successful spin of the third reel seems vastly luckier than the other two. Hitting a cherry on the third reel seems both luckier than a cherry on the first two reels (viewed diachronically) and also not luckier at all (viewed synchronically). There is a sense of a gestalt switch going on here—first it is a duck, then a rabbit. While the extant theories of luck can accommodate synchronic luck, they cannot explain diachronic luck.

One might argue that hitting cherry on the third reel just plain mattered more than it did for the first two reels. So even if the probability of, modal fragility of, or control over cherry on the third reel was no different from the first two, its importance was, and therefore it really was luckier for the third reel to come up cherry than it was for the first two reels. However, this rejoinder is mistaken, and in fact only highlights the problem of synchronic vs. diachronic luck. The whole idea is that considered synchronically, in isolation of its position in a temporal series, it is no more important that a cherry come up on one reel over any other. It was equally essential for the same fruit to appear on each reel to hit the jackpot. It was just as important, or unimportant, for the first or second reels to come up cherry as it was for the third. Another way to see this is that it doesn't matter at all what fruit shows up on a reel—any reel—when the reel is considered alone, apart from anything that happened before or after. Some fruit or other is going to appear. If it is a cherry, so be it. However, what happens on the third reel does seem to matter more when it is considered diachronically, as an element of a series. Given that there were cherries on the first two reels, it is now of considerable significance that a cherry come up on the third. The fundamental phenomenon is the differing attributions of luck depending on the diachronic or synchronic perspectives.

Lucky streaks and game-winning shots are as much a matter of the perspective on luck that we choose as it is due to their own accomplishment. Of course, the same is true in reverse for our villains. The Mets won Game 6 of the 1986 World Series after Red Sox first baseman Bill Buckner missed fielding a routine ground ball in the tenth inning. Buckner's bad luck rested not only on his fielding error, but on the diachronic perspective. The exact same mistake at any other point in the game would have long since been blown over by the sands of time. Which point of view on luck we adopt isn't a matter of which is truer or better, but of the story we are using luck to tell. Acknowledging the perspectival nature of luck might lead the Jordans of the world to humility and the Buckners of the world to solace; their "luck" is in a sense of our own making.

The modal theory of luck adopts Leibniz's logically possible worlds as radially branching away from actuality, strictly ordered by their similarity to reality. Actual events that could have easily not happened (they happen in close possible worlds) are fragile ones. Fragile events are lucky. Events that could not have easily failed to occur are robust, and they aren't a matter of luck. The modal theory is distinct from the probability view, and seemed to hold promise as a way to understand luck. Yet the idea of close and distant worlds didn't hold up well to scrutiny; all kinds of bizarre possibilities happen when we change just one iota about reality, entailing that nearly everything is lucky after all. Even with logical or mathematical necessities—truths that are robust as anything could possibly be and thus couldn't be lucky according to the modal theory—we find cases of luck. This discovery is as problematic for the modal theory of luck as finding a 2 billion-year-old rabbit fossil would be for evolution by natural selection. If the theory were right, such a thing just couldn't be possible.[37] The control theory of luck tries a new tack, classifying an event as lucky for someone only if that event is outside of their control. If something is within your control, then its occurrence isn't a matter of luck. We're prone to psychological quirks that undermine any confidence that we can just tell when we have control over something by either observation or instinct. What we need is a theory of control that we can fall back on. Working out a sense of control that gets things right also turned out to be a great challenge. And the problem of diachronic luck was a poser for every treatment of luck—probability, modal, and control.

Luck is maddening because it is easy to come up with superficially plausible analyses of what luck really is, but they all seem to fall apart with just a little critical pressure. It is hard to see a path forward to a conceptual understanding of luck that resolves or skirts all the difficulties so far considered; the troubles come from so many different directions and kinds of considerations that it is like a single soldier fighting a war on many fronts. Or, to choose a different metaphor, it feels like we trying to get out of a hole by digging deeper. Perhaps a closer examination of the role luck plays in our lives will help us find our way out. In the next two chapters we will look more closely into why luck seems to matter so much for calculating the credit we deserve for veridical discoveries and the role it plays for understanding our moral culpability and accessibility. Let's approach the problems of luck from different directions and hope that we can thereby triangulate the truth.

# 4 MORAL LUCK

*"Let us sit and mock the good housewife Fortune from her wheel, that her gifts may henceforth be bestowed equally."*
**—WILLIAM SHAKESPEARE**[1]

One fine October day in western Oregon, local woman Cinthya Garcia-Cisneros and her brother had picked up a take-out meal and were driving home to enjoy it. A large pile of raked fall leaves was slopping out of a suburban homeowner's yard and into the street, and Garcia-Cisneros drove through it without much thought. She noticed there was a loud bump when she drove over the leaves, but thought that it was just sticks or packed-down yard waste.

Now imagine two possible endings to this tale:

1 Garcia-Cisneros and her brother got home without further incident; just an unremarkable drive through the autumn countryside.

2 A few hours after arriving home, Garcia-Cisneros saw a news report on the hit-and-run deaths of two young sisters who had been hiding in a leaf pile when struck—and she realized what had really happened.

Garcia-Cisneros wasn't driving recklessly; she wasn't texting, drunk, stoned, speeding, or neglectful. She didn't have malicious intent. She just drove through a heap of leaves in the road. The only difference between these two endings is luck: in version one, the good luck that the bump really was just branches and compacted leaves, and in version two the bad luck that children were hidden in the leaf pile. Harvard psychologists Justin W. Martin and Fiery Cushman gave the case of Garcia-Cisneros to two different groups, with one group getting the version one ending, and the other reading the version two ending. The researchers then asked them whether Garcia-Cisneros deserved punishment, and if so how much. For the harmless ending, 85 percent of respondents said she merited no punishment at all. In the death ending, 94 percent said she did deserve punishment, and recommended an average of 1–3 years in prison,[2] even though the only difference between the two was a matter of luck.

This is a true story. Unfortunately, the second version is what really happened. Initially Garcia-Cisneros was sentenced to three years' probation for felony hit-and-run, although this judgment was later overturned on the grounds that Oregon law doesn't have an "implicit requirement" that a driver return to the scene of a traffic accident after later learning that someone was injured or killed.[3] Essentially, she was convicted for having bad luck. The very morality of driving through those leaves seems to hinge on nothing besides the caprice of fortune. But that's really perplexing. The ethical standing of our actions should have to do with our free and informed choices, the results we can control, the products of our will, or at the very least the rationally expected outcomes of what we do—not luck. When something happens because of luck, it is disconnected from our agency. It just doesn't have anything do with the credit we deserve or the blame we warrant. On the other hand, luck is all important in the case of Garcia-Cisneros. Why *does* luck seem to matter for morality? How can it? When?

# The Kantian Puzzle

Immanuel Kant was short, with a high squeaky voice, and lived his entire life in the unprepossessing port town of Königsberg, Prussia, on the Baltic Sea. A lifelong bachelor, Kant was mostly known to his neighbors for his evening constitutionals, which were so reliably punctual that they would set their clocks when he strolled by. He wasn't the clearest or most mellifluous of writers. Nietzsche described his writing as something to be endured, the result of a "deformed concept-cripple" who cannot make his words dance.[4] Kant may have been aware of his shortcomings, writing in the preface to his most famous book, *The Critique of Pure Reason*, "this work can never be made suitable for popular consumption." Still, out of this less-than-inspiring backdrop, Kant managed to become the most important philosopher of the modern period, and his work on ethics set the stage for the contemporary theory of rights. In his *Groundwork of the Metaphysics of Morals*, a book never out of print since its publication in 1784, Kant writes:

What makes a good will good? It isn't what it brings about, its usefulness in achieving some intended end. Rather, good will is good because of how it wills—i.e. it is good in itself. Taken just in itself it is to be valued incomparably more highly than anything that could be brought about by it in the satisfaction of some preference—or, if you like, the sum total of all preferences! Consider this case: Through bad luck or a miserly endowment from step-motherly nature, this person's will has no power at all to accomplish its purpose; not even the greatest effort on his part would enable it to achieve anything it aims at. But he does still have a good will—not as a mere wish but as the summoning of all the means in his power. The good will of this person would sparkle like a jewel all by itself, as something that had its full worth in itself. Its value wouldn't go up or down depending on how useful or fruitless it was.[5]

You may have the purest and most angelic of wills and do everything you can to follow the moral law, yet you're still punished hard by Murphy's Law (Murphy's Power Law?) and everything goes wrong. According to Kant, you're not to blame. Likewise, if you luck out and the positive results of your actions exceed expectations, you don't deserve any extra praise. We cast our bread upon the waters, but how—or if—it is returned to us is beyond our control. Moral assessability hinges on intent and effort, not on what happens in some unguaranteeable future. Luck might intervene at any point, so our command over what happens in the future is limited at best. The future is an unexplored country; our reputations as pioneers cannot depend on lands into which no one has set foot.[6] What we *do* have control over is our decisions and what we will, which is why, in Kant's view, we are to be assessed on the basis of those things, not outcomes.

In a slogan, *you are properly morally judged only to the extent that what you're judged for depends on factors under your control.*[7] If a lifelong friend steps into an elevator that you are on, gives no notice of you at all and even fails to acknowledge that they know you in the slightest way, well, you might easily feel offended and snubbed. Suppose, however, that your friend is the neurologist Oliver Sacks. Sacks suffered from moderate prosopagnosia, which made him horrible at recognizing pretty much anything, but in particular faces. Sacks once met with a psychotherapist whom he knew well, only to see the man again in the lobby five minutes later and have no idea who he was. He would repeatedly walk past his own home because he failed to identify it, and couldn't even recognize his own reflection in a mirror.[8] Prosopagnosia is not something that can be treated or cured, and Sacks spent a lifetime trying to find a way to compensate for it with nothing to show for his efforts. Your anger or annoyance at being snubbed in the elevator rightly disappears when you understand that your friend has a neurological deficit and can't be blamed for not spotting you. It's not under his control, and so he isn't at fault—that's the Kantian instinct.

This problem of the interplay between the good will (with intent and negligence tossed into that hat) and outcomes is longstanding. Somewhat later the utilitarians insist that the rightness and wrongness of actions just has to do with consequences, but whether someone is blameworthy or praiseworthy for his or her action, that's where good will becomes relevant.

Consider the matter of "friendly fire," in which battlefield troops accidentally kill their own comrades. This was how T. J. "Stonewall" Jackson met his end.[9] Jackson, a Confederate General in the American Civil War, is widely considered one of the most outstanding tactical leaders in US military history. After his successful rout of Union forces at Chancellorsville, Jackson and his staff were riding at night back to camp, only to be mistaken as enemy soldiers by the 18th North Carolina Infantry. Jackson's party tried to identify themselves, but the Carolina infantry was convinced it was a Yankee trick and started shooting. Jackson was hit three times and, although his arm was amputated in an attempt to save his life, he contracted pneumonia and died in a week. The Carolina soldiers certainly didn't intend to kill one of their own generals; utilitarians would say that although they did the wrong thing by shooting Jackson, they aren't blameworthy for it. Kant would agree that the 18th North Carolina Infantry isn't properly blamed, but in his view, there are no moral aspersions to be cast at all. The Infantry thought the hated enemy was trying to trick them under cover of darkness, and opened fire in good faith. We might abstractly blame the fog of war, but the Infantry itself did nothing wrong; they, and Stonewall Jackson, were merely the victims of bad luck. Why, then, do we have a lingering sense that the North Carolina Infantry's bad luck made their actions morally worse than if it really had been a Yankee trick and they fired on Union blue instead of Confederate gray?

It wasn't until 1976 when a pair of famous articles from the philosophers Bernard Williams and Thomas Nagel drew proper attention to this inconsistent group of claims, each of which looks really plausible:

1  No one deserves moral judgment for things that aren't their fault.

2  Things that happen because of luck are no one's fault.

3  Bad luck can make someone morally worse.

As Nagel comments, "the importance of luck in human life is no surprise ... it is the place of luck in ethics that is puzzling."[10] Cases like the death of Stonewall Jackson or the driving of Garcia-Cisneros, Nagel calls *outcome luck*. Once you see the recipe, it's easy to put together more examples. Nagel's own include a drunk driver who makes it safely home (an act of negligence that's bad, but not *that* bad) vs. a drunk driver who kills a pedestrian who ran in front of her car (an act of negligence that's clearly worse). To take another example, a would-be assassin who misses his target when the intended victim unexpectedly bends over to tie his shoes did a terrible thing with obvious bad intent. Of course, a successful assassin who doesn't miss did an even worse thing. The unlucky drunk driver can't control when pedestrians run in front of her car, and a would-be assassin has no influence over whether the target decides to tie their shoes. But, as with Garcia-Cisneros, their final moral standing was all down to luck. The lucky drunk driver is *morally better* than the unlucky one; they did something less bad.

Our ordinary judgments are like Figure 4.1.

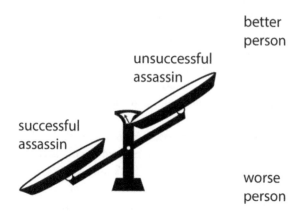

**FIGURE 4.1** A successful assassin is more blameworthy than an unsuccessful one.

**FIGURE 4.2** Equal blameworthiness between successful and unsuccessful.

The problem of moral luck is that the results of drunk driving or attempted assassination are ultimately out of our hands, part of a future that we cannot command. That's exactly why we shouldn't be accountable for them, any more than Sacks should be blamed for inadvertent rudeness when he ignores you in the elevator. If we are really determined to reject the idea that bad luck can make you a morally inferior person or that good luck can make you morally superior, we have to reject Figure 4.1 as correct. A tempting and easy solution is to balance the books, as in Figure 4.2.

There are three ways of interpreting Figure 4.2.

Option 1. Safe drunk driving and attempted assassination are much worse than we usually think. Indeed, they are just as bad as drunkenly hitting a pedestrian and successful assassination. Just bite the Kantian bullet and say that attempted murder that fails only because of luck really is just as bad as successful murder. Or declare that a drunk driver who drives safely acted just as unethically as one who had the bad luck to hit a pedestrian. Drunk driving—safe or not—is still a bad thing, and puts others at risk. So maybe even safe drunk driving is a lot worse than we ordinarily think. Likewise, trying to kill someone is morally awful, even when the attempt fails. Perhaps the right lesson is that a failed effort is worse than we thought, that it is as equally immoral as successful murder. Negligence and bad intent are much more wicked than we thought.

Option 2. Safe drunk driving really is on a par with drunkenly hitting a pedestrian, and a failed assassination attempt truly is equivalent to a successful one. Option 1 has that right. It's not that safe drunk driving and a failed murder attempt are much worse than we think. Rather, drunkenly hitting a pedestrian and successful assassination aren't as bad as we usually think. Actually, they are no worse than safe drunk driving and a failed assassination attempt. Murder's bad, but no worse than attempted murder; luck alone separates one from the other.

driving through empty leaf pile

driving over children in leaf pile

better person

worse person

FIGURE 4.3 Equal blameworthiness in driving case.

Option 3. Safe drunk driving (or unsuccessful assassination) is worse than we usually think it is, but at the same time harmful drunk driving and successful assassination aren't as bad as we typically believe. In other words, we should split the difference between options 1 and 2. All in all, we just need to moderate our intuitions. Kant's got it right and luck doesn't make a person morally better or morally worse.

The problem is that none of these options seem to fit the case of Stonewall Jackson, as the 18th North Carolina Infantry lacked bad intent and it's not easy to charge them with negligence either. In fact, the Confederate leadership seems to have believed that they acted properly in a confused situation, and even promoted one of the officers involved.[11] The same is true of Garcia-Cisneros: while she caused a tragedy, she was neither malicious nor neglectful. She didn't even realize that something terrible had happened until she saw the news. Attempting to adjust our intuitive moral reactions doesn't help. Here would be the chart if we tried (Figure 4.3).

The idea behind Figure 4.3 is that someone who harmlessly drives though an empty mound of fall leaves is just as blameworthy as one who runs over and kills two children—there's no moral difference between them. But that idea can't possibly be right. Garcia-Cisneros wasn't doing something that was kind of wrong already and then made worse by bad luck, like the drunk driver or the would-be assassin. She wasn't doing anything wrong at all. Perhaps even stranger is what the attempt to capture the Kantian intuition means for the friendly fire case.

According to Figure 4.4, there's no moral difference between shooting the enemy in wartime and killing your own brothers-in-arms. That's absurd even for committed pacifists. The 18th North Carolina Infantry followed the rules of war. Like Garcia-Cisneros, they didn't act maliciously, they didn't secretly hate Stonewall Jackson, and they seem negligent only

**FIGURE 4.4** Equal blameworthiness in friendly fire case.

with the benefit of Monday-morning quarterbacking. *Everything* morally suspect about Garcia-Cisneros and the friendly fire soldiers was due to bad luck. If we think about alternative "happy ending" scenarios, where the leaf pile was just a leaf pile, and the Yankees really were playing a trick on the Rebs, there's nothing morally pernicious going on. With the lucky drunk driver we can aver, "Well, she was still doing something bad, she just got away with it and no one was hurt." We can't do that in the Stonewall Jackson and Garcia-Cisneros cases; everything that's morally bad about the real-life scenarios is 100 percent the result of luck. Moral luck isn't going to be sorted out so easily.

But now we're back to square one, and the Kantian puzzle remains. On the one hand is Kant's compelling idea that your moral virtuousness can't have anything to do with something as capricious and out of your control as luck. On the other hand is the sense that causing terrible outcomes does make you a worse person, regardless of your intent, even when you think you're doing the right thing or believe that you've done nothing wrong. Now what?

# The Egg of Columbus

Everything's obvious after the fact. A magician's trick can be completely inexplicable—even disturbing in its apparent violation of nature[12]—but when the secret is revealed it's all so evident that it's hard to see how we missed it the first time. Even great achievements and discoveries can look mundane the morning after. In 1565 the Italian historian and adventurer Girolamo Benzoni tells this story in his book *History of the New World*. When Columbus returned from his epoch-making journeys over the

Atlantic, he was fêted by Europe's gentility. At one soirée with the Spanish nobility, the talk was, naturally, of the Indies. One proud Spaniard told Columbus that even if he never made it to the New World, the prize would not have remained unclaimed for long, since Spain was "full of great men clever in cosmography and literature." Columbus didn't say anything directly, but instead asked for an egg. Sometimes a little demonstration can be worth a great many words. He put the egg on a table and proceeded to offer a wager: that no one but himself could make the egg stand up on end. All the aristocrats gave it a go, and uniformly the egg wobbled back down and refused to stand. Columbus then took it and crushed one end a little against the table. Sure enough, the egg now stood at attention. Columbus looked around, saying nothing, but everyone understood his point. After the deed is done, everyone knows how to do it.[13]

Before his voyage, the Admiral of the Ocean Sea was laughed at, dismissed, and struggled to secure funding for what would surely be a foolhardy trip. As soon as he gets back all the Spanish Lords can't wait to tell him that they had had plenty of brilliant men lined up to discover the New World and Columbus hadn't done anything particularly special. Although the homely illustration of the egg put the nobles in their place, their judgment that "we knew this all along" or "we can see that the discovery was inevitable" is nearly irresistible. Forecasting events before they happen is a tough business, but after they happen we tend to look back and see them as easily predictable.

Once we know what to look for, hindsight bias pops up everywhere.[14] An outsider politician is elected and now we can see the obvious evidence of voter distrust in the establishment. An unfaithful spouse is caught and her husband castigates himself for missing the now-clear warning signs. An underperforming quarterback plays brilliantly and the coach congratulates himself on knowing that the player had it in him to turn things around. Hindsight bias is the difference between our estimates of the probability of an event before it happens, and our estimates of how likely it was for the same event to occur when seen in hindsight. It leads to a kind of tunnel vision, where we latch onto the easiest or most salient explanation for an event and stop looking. What's the chance of a poor harvest next year? That's not easy to answer, although farmers and commodities brokers are keenly interested in figuring it out; agriculture is multicausally sensitive to all kinds of inputs that themselves are chaotic. What was the chance of last year's poor harvest? We should have all seen that coming, what with global warming (or El Niño, the drought, the locusts, immigrants, or whatever your hobbyhorse).

Luck is tightly connected with hindsight bias, as the matter of soul mates illustrates. In a country where there is partisan rancor on practically every topic, there is widespread agreement on one thing: that people have soul mates. According to a nationwide Gallup survey, "An overwhelming majority (94%) of never-married singles agree that 'when you marry you want your spouse to be your soul mate, first and foremost.'"[15] A Rutgers University study found:

Among single men and women [ages 20–29], a large majority (88%) also agree that "there is a special person, a soul mate, waiting for you somewhere out there." And never-married singles are highly confident that they will be successful in locating that soul mate; a substantial majority (87%) agree that they will find that special someone when they are ready to get married.

These are astonishing numbers. More people believe they have and will find a soul mate than believe that the earth revolves around the sun.[16]

Given the vast number of human beings, and the very small fraction of them that you will even meet in your lifetime, what is the objective chance of finding the one person who is perfectly matched to you, whose appearance, interests, education, sense of humor, political and religious views, personal habits, manners, fashion sense, musical tastes, moral outlook, and so on match your ideal better than anyone else on Earth? Vanishingly small.[17] So if you do in fact meet your soul mate, then it must be destiny.

Obviously, the retrospective judgment that your partner is your soul mate is another instance of hindsight bias. In looking back to all of the contingent events that led to a relationship—selection of college, having this friend or that, attending a specific party or event, having consumed enough but not too much liquid courage—we trace out the bright line connecting them all and see in it the machinations of fate. If all those choice points had turned out otherwise, then you would have a different partner, and would see an altered historical pathway leading to that person. No matter who your partner is, you can build a narrative of inexorability that led to your union, an inevitability that only providence can explain.

A familiar alternative to the drumbeat of destiny is to see it all as a matter of coincidence and luck.[18] Everything needed to meet your "soul mate" and successfully form a relationship is just a wildly improbable string of chance events. Here's another way to see the point. Suppose that there is a 25 percent chance of attending the college you did, a 25 percent chance of attending the party where you met your spouse, a 25 percent of your friend introducing the two of you, a 25 percent chance you didn't make a fool of yourself, etc. What is the collective chance that all those things happened? Multiply the individual probabilities, and it is a low number indeed. Again this is hindsight bias: it relies on the post hoc judgment that there is a terribly small chance of being with your soul mate and revises all the past data to fit. There may be a very high probability that you will regard your partner as your soul mate, whomever that person may be.

We decide that a current state of affairs is vitally important ("I married my soul mate!") and retroactively judge all the steps in the past that led to it as lucky ones. We're at step Z and look back to everything that happened since step A and see that winding drunkard's walk as a series of lucky events. But if we had started in the past at step A and imagined a future of marrying that same person at step Z, we wouldn't think that getting from A to Z was a matter of luck. As the photographer Ansel Adams put it, "I have often had a retrospective vision where everything in my past life seems to fall with significance into logical sequence."[19] Of course— that is the natural human tendency; whether that logical sequence is then viewed as fate or luck is just two sides of the same coin.

Hindsight bias is a solid contender to explain the psychology of moral luck. We hear about Garcia-Cisneros crushing two little girls to death and think, "she heard big bumps when she drove over those leaves and didn't even think to pull over and see what it was? Everyone knows children play in leaves. I can't believe she wouldn't have at least swerved around that pile." And her culpability and guilt feels palpable. Or we read about Stonewall Jackson's party frantically attempting to identify themselves, only to be met with Major John D. Barry of the 18th North Carolina Infantry defiantly shouting, "It's a damned Yankee trick! Fire!" We think—shoot first and ask questions later? There was no way to confirm whether it really was Jackson and his men before opening fire? Barry looks trigger-happy and foolish, if not downright derelict in his duty. Something went wrong, and we *want* an identifiable target to blame. We want Garcia-Cisneros and the 18th North Carolina Infantry to be negligent, we want to tell ourselves that the results of their actions were foreseeable outcomes, that a reasonable person would have done otherwise, and other bromides.[20] Those people should have known better, and we know this because in hindsight the clear linear connection between their actions and the terrible outcomes is blindingly obvious. Of course, in the moment it was anything but.

When something awful happens, we're compelled to find something or someone to blame. If an earthquake destroys our hometown of Lisbon, we blame ourselves for impiety and sin. When Serena Williams hits an unforced error, we accuse her of poor shot selection. Our enthusiasm for blame seems connected to our fervor for suffering. In his 1887 book *The Genealogy of Morals*, Nietzsche catalogued the bizarre cruelties that human beings inflict on each other in every context from war to weddings, and concluded that "to see suffering does you good, to make suffer, better still—that is a hard proposition, but an ancient, powerful, human-all-too-human proposition to which even the apes might subscribe ... in punishment there is so much that is festive!"[21] While it goes against a pleasant self-narrative of increasing tolerance and liberality, Nietzsche is surely right. It's a rare person who doesn't feel a visceral satisfaction in seeing a tight end get absolutely clotheslined by a defensive tackle. Who doesn't enjoy the catharsis of a villain's bloody end in a thriller? Call of Duty, professional wrestling, Itchy and Scratchy, The Avengers—there's no end to the number of acceptable channels for our love of violence.

You might think that it's not suffering that we enjoy, but justice. When it is the enemy (player, soldier, team, criminal, outgroup), then misery inflicted on them is just righteous smiting. In one of his action movies, Arnold Schwarzenegger's character is confronted by his wife, who is stunned to discover that he is a secret agent. She asks if he has killed anyone and Schwarzenegger's explanation/defense is simply, "Yeah ... but they were all bad." Unfortunately, it is equally self-serving to think that we punish people only because they were already bad. One of the big stories of post–Second World War psychology is that ordinary citizens are all too eager to punish first and then demonize their victims as deserving of malevolent treatment; the punishment wasn't truly in response to their failings.[22] One of the subjects in the Milgram obedience studies insisted that his putative victim was "so stupid and stubborn that he deserved to get shocked." It's after the war starts that the enemy becomes kikes, gooks, imperialists, crusaders, or ragheads. They were all bad.

Equally surprising is the fact that we love to correct and punish others, *even when we are convinced that they are not to blame*. A toddler who throws her food on the floor has no idea that she is doing something wrong, and may be acting out of impish, but certainly not malicious, intent. Not exactly blameworthy, but her parents will still correct her nonetheless. A dog who defecates in the house gets punished for it, despite not realizing this is unacceptable behavior. Nietzsche reasonably argues that punishment has the function of instilling a memory and a sense of responsibility; the toddler or the dog may not "deserve" punishment, but they will learn to adjust their behavior to avoid it in the future.

All of this suggests another explanation of moral luck. The first idea was that with 20–20 hindsight we overestimate how likely it was that someone could have foreseen their actions leading to horrible consequences. So hindsight bias explains why we find culpability even for outcomes that included a big fat dose of bad luck, like Garcia-Cisneros driving over that leaf pile. Here's an alternative explanation of the psychology of moral luck: we want to hold people absolutely responsible for the results of their actions, even when they are not properly blamed, even when those results were due to luck, so they can learn a lesson that will influence their future behavior.[23] The lucky drunk driver will think twice about getting behind the wheel after a few drinks when he has already been punished for it in the past, despite the fact that he drove safely home and harmed no one. And presumably the 18th North Carolina Infantry was more circumspect the next time they ran across a nighttime band of travelers.

The idea that moral luck has something to do with modifying future behavior fits nicely with this datum too: you might punish a toddler for throwing her food, but not for a sneezing fit that knocked her food on the floor. In the former case, we assume the toddler has *some* control over the outcome, in the latter case she has no control at all. Punishing a toddler for messy sneezes isn't going to lead to anything positive. Of course, none of this tells us a thing about whether we *ought* to punish others for their accidental behavior or bad luck consequences. It only helps explain why we do.

# The Accidental Nazi and the Museum of Medical Oddities

Like a jealous dog, luck noses its way in between our actions and their intended outcomes, leaving us alarmed and dismayed when things work out badly. And, to stay with the simile, we wind up accused of the hound's misbehavior. The good part is that while these intrigues of luck may reflect badly on us, they don't affect who we are. Garcia-Cisneros's character was unaltered by the bad luck of children playing in the leaves; whether she is a loyal, fair, patient, self-reliant, generous, or civil person has nothing to do with one unfortunate and unpredictable event. One swallow does not make a summer, and in those cases of outcome luck, the moral self seems untouched. It would be more disturbing if the puzzle of moral luck arose at the deep level of our personal agency, our own character and will.

Prepared to be more disturbed. Who we are and the people we become are commonly shaped by our circumstances, and those circumstances are easily the result of luck, as the following case dramatically illustrates.

In 1929, a nineteen-year-old Jew named Josef Yufe left his hometown in Romania for the Caribbean, looking to escape both widespread anti-Semitism and the strict religious expectations of his orthodox father.[24] On the way he met a young German Catholic woman named Liesel, who fell for his good looks. They lived together for four years in the British Crown Colony of Trinidad, and had three children, including the identical twin boys Oskar and Jack, born in January 1933. Six months after their birth, Liesel, sick of Josef's womanizing and excessive love of rum, decided she'd had enough. They separated and Liesel returned to Germany, apparently still hoping that Josef would turn things around and come join her. For Josef the ladies' man, it was more out of sight out of mind; in her absence he married a beauty queen, Miss Trinidad. He never went back to Europe.

It's really the story of Oskar and Jack that matters here. When their parents split, so did the boys. Oskar went to Germany with his mother, just in time for the advent of the Third Reich, which was epically poor timing for a boy with a Jewish father. It was immediately clear that any trace of Jewish ancestry had to be forgotten, and Oskar was advised never to say "Jew" again. He understood what was expected in his new life. When his school's vice principal asked him about his last name: "Yufe? Doesn't that mean Jew?" Oskar swiftly replied, "no, it's a French name, pronounced Yufé [Yu-fay]." Oskar's grandmother, trying to stay ahead of the curve, subsequently changed his last name and had him baptized Christian. Oskar became an enthusiastic member of the Hitler Youth, convinced by the message of the Führer and inspired by German nationalism. Although he was still a boy when the war ended, it's not hard to picture Oskar's life trajectory if the war had gone on longer or if the Axis powers had won.

Jack stayed behind in Trinidad with his father, making friends with the local black children, becoming a British citizen, and being raised Jewish. Just as Oskar disavowed his Jewish side, Jack did what he could to lessen the stigma of a German mother. He became a British patriot, joining the Sea Scouts (a first step toward entering the British Navy) and even earned an award from King George VI as a teenager. By the time the war ended, Jack had fully embraced his Jewish heritage. He moved to Israel, enlisted in the Israeli Navy, and married a woman he met at the Kibbutz Ma'ale Ha'Cramisha. Proud of his faith, Jack took to wearing a Star of David around his neck. It is hard to imagine twin brothers taking more divergent paths in life.

When the twins reunited in the 1950s, their meetings were initially tense and, unsurprisingly, they viewed each other with wary curiosity. Although they discovered that they had many habits in common such as wrapping tape around pens and pencils for a better grip, underlining heavily when reading books and magazines, an outsized taste for butter, the same manner of scratching their heads, and a short temper, they did not share cultural, familial, political, or religious backgrounds, or even a language. While Oskar and Jack did eventually develop an ongoing relationship with each other, they were acutely aware of the dramatic role circumstantial luck played in their lives. With a haunting insight into the precarious nature of the self, Oskar once acknowledged to Jack that "if we had been switched, I would have been the Jew and you would have been the Nazi."

Earlier thinkers knew luck played a role in forming our characters, although they failed to see how strange it is that luck should infect morality. Machiavelli, for example, contrasted the role of *virtù* and *fortuna* in the success of statesmen and legislators, celebrating those who, through their own virtues, could capitalize on those situations that good luck had provided. One of his commentators remarked that "the career of any individual in a given society is conditioned by the particular circumstances of that society, which, not being of his making, are part of his *fortuna*."[25] All that really means is that Machiavelli recognized the important role of circumstantial luck in setting the parameters of our futures. What you do with that luck is, for Machiavelli, where *virtù* comes in. Yet he never spots what Nagel did: to the extent that our moral characters—our habitual virtues and vices—are the result of luck, they aren't the result of *us*. Luck formed who Oskar and Jack turned out to be; it wasn't just some external stimulus that they might respond to out of their own intrinsic and unchanging natures. Their very characters were forged in the fires of Tuche.

Oskar and Jack are an extreme case of circumstantial luck—and wonderful for that reason—but theirs is not a rare example. The legitimate son of the king rises to the throne in splendor but the bastard son lives in secret shame. An impoverished student walks uphill through the snow to Mediocre State University, while a different student with no more talent drives her BMW to Gilded Ivy College. Steve Reich's Grammy Award-winning composition *Different Trains* is about this sort of luck: it contrasts train travel in the United States in the 1940s, and the romance of traveling coast to coast with Pullman porters, with European trains in the 1940s, which were packed with Holocaust victims on their way to concentration camps.[26] As Donald Trump remarked, "You were born into the greatest country in the world. You don't think that's lucky?"[27] *Different Trains* evokes that very feeling: it *is* luck to be riding the scenic California Zephyr to the seaside instead of the windowless Sonderzüge to the gas chambers at Treblinka.

With outcome luck it was difficult to see how we could square the ache to blame Garcia-Cisneros or Major Barry with the fact that the results of their actions were so clearly outside of their control. The temptation is hindsight bias—we try to retrospectively drum up some kind of reason to think that they really were negligent or careless after all. Either that, or we decide to hold them accountable anyway, even if we concede they are blameless. Those ways of coping are much less psychologically appealing in the circumstantial luck cases. How much can we hold accountable a patriotic Hitler Youth for the man he becomes? A Nazi had no more power over his upbringing than Anne Frank had over hers. We might punish the lucky drunk driver in the hopes that he learns not to take that chance again, but to punish the ordinary Nazi so he learns—what? Never to grow up in Hitler's Germany again? To develop hypertrophic moral courage and next time join the Resistance? The individual moral choices of Jack and Oskar aren't at issue with circumstantial moral luck. Rather, it enters in at the larger perspective of their personal well-being, prospects for living well and doing good in the world, their own ideas about virtue, patriotism, and how to divide the good guys from the bad guys. Those were determined by their divergently lucky upbringings.

Luck interjects itself between our plans and their outcomes, decides whether we are a Jew or a Nazi, and even fixes our material composition.

It would be nice to think that we are disembodied creatures of light and pure reason who make all the choices of our lives with perfect knowledge and omnipotent freedom. *Then* we could rightly be judged, *then* we could truly own the misfortunes or good results of those selections and be held accountable. It only takes a trip to Philadelphia to appreciate Fortuna's final power over the kinds of people we become and the value of our lives. Even more than circumstances, the book of our lives is written with the alphabet of nucleotide bases in double-helix sentences, sentences that may contain typos.

The College of Physicians in Philadelphia maintains an imposing red brick Beaux-Arts museum filled with a most disturbing collection of medical oddities, pathologies, and bizarre anomalies. In one case is the skeleton of a 7'6" pituitary giant, side-by-side with a 3'6" dwarf. Other cases hold rows upon rows of human skulls, some honeycombed by tertiary syphilis, others pierced by bullets. There are glass jars of vast distended colons, a two-headed baby, assorted tumors, and the connected livers of the Siamese twins Chang and Eng all pickled in formaldehyde. On display is a woman who was buried in an alkaline environment and spontaneously turned into soap. The museum contains a large array of antique medical instruments that look suitable for Dr. Frankenstein's laboratory, and they have a cabinet filled with 2,000 objects removed from people's throats.

The holdings of the Mütter Museum reflect the immense range of the possibilities for the human genome and the ways in which our biology fixes the courses of our lives. At one extreme is Harry Eastlack, who suffered from an extremely rare and disabling genetic disease called Fibrodysplasia Ossificans Progressiva (FOP). In FOP the bone repair mechanism goes berserk and turns all the connective tissues of the body—muscles, ligaments, tendons—into bone. Joints become fused and great plates and ribbons of bone form where there should be soft tissues. Tendrils of bone wired Eastlack's jaw shut and bony lattices branched across his rock-like rib cage to weld his upper arms to his torso. By the end of his life at nearly age forty, Eastlack could barely move his lips, so completely encased as he was in a second complete skeleton. Ordinarily, after the disintegration of the tender fleshy parts, the bones collapse into a pile that must be articulated by specialists to re-form the shape of the body. Not so for Harry Eastlack; his skeleton stands like a suit of armor in the museum, without much need for curatorial intervention. Eastlack's genes dictated the main story of his life, which was a tale beyond his authorship and outside of his control. His was a bad luck story that had nothing to do with outcomes or circumstances, but with his very make-up.

At the opposite extreme from Harry Eastlack is Albert Einstein, a man whose name is synonymous with genius, and whose mighty brain is on display at the Mütter, sashimi-sliced and layered onto microscope slides. Although Einstein had requested cremation, his physician just couldn't bring himself to commit Einstein's brain to the flames, hoping that future generations of study could unlock the secrets of his intellect. That project has not yet borne fruit, although the slides themselves are something like holy relics of pilgrimage. Einstein, of course, had no more say over his scientific aptitude than Eastlack had over his physical constitution. Both men made the most of what they had to work with.

Einstein and Eastlack represent the winners and the losers in the genetic lottery, and a walk through the Mütter Museum feels like a tour of lucky outcomes, both good and bad. We are all born into some kind of society which carves the channels of our lives, molding our characters and helping fix the degree to which we flourish, as we saw with circumstantial luck. We are also born with specific genetic gifts and detriments over which we have no influence or choice. Richard Overton, for example, was a Second World War veteran who recently died at nearly 113 years old.[28] As an African-American born in 1906, he lived three times as long as his life expectancy at birth; on top of that, his health habits included daily whiskey and cigars. Clearly good constitutional luck has a lot more to do with his longevity than anything else. At the other end of the spectrum, Down Syndrome children are more prone to practically every kind of disease, in addition to cognitive impairment and a shortened lifespan. Certainly being born with an extra copy of chromosome 21 is unpredictable, uncontrollably bad constitutional luck.

The psychological explanations of why we feel the need to blame and punish in the outcome luck cases didn't hold up well with circumstantial luck, and they are even less useful with constitutive luck. We can praise Einstein all day long for his creativity, ingeniousness, and work ethic, but not for his native gifts that he had nothing to do with. Shaquille O'Neal may get all the credit for his stylish dunks, but not for his 7'1" height which made them possible. And, of course, it would be cruel and misguided to somehow hold poor Harry Eastlack accountable for the limitations he suffered because of FOP. We might be morally assessable for the outcomes of our specific actions—even when infected by luck—but not the global outcomes of our lives even when clearly they too are as just as much a matter of luck. That's a splinter in the eye of ethical insight without obvious tools to remove it. Shakespeare's suggestion that we mock Fortune so "that her gifts may be henceforth bestowed equally" is insufficiently prosaic, but maybe something could be done to even out the role of circumstantial and constitutive luck.

## Equalizing Fortune

There's plenty of overlap between the social and genetic lotteries, and not many things fall purely into one camp or the other. Consider height. In prehistoric and ancient times, being genetically programmed to grow to seven feet high was a real advantage. Large size made it easier to fight off the predators and take down prey. In warfare it was also a plus; there's good reason that the smart money was on Goliath instead of David, even though David got a lucky shot in at the end. At the Tower of London is a medieval suit of platemail made for a man 6'8"—imagine the terrifying might of this warrior charging with a two-handed claymore. After a while humans developed tools to augment any stature and didn't really need to be huge to avoid predation or to hunt. Size wasn't even an advantage in war, since a runt with a rifle could easily best an armored giant wielding a broadsword.

In modernity great height comes with a raft of disadvantages. Being a little taller than average leads to greater income and a better mate selection, but more than one standard deviation in height does not. It's hard to find clothes that fit, you hit your head on doorways, and forget about sitting in restaurant booths. Riding in planes, trains, and automobiles ranges from very uncomfortable to impossible. In general the world just isn't built for your size, and being extremely tall has no real upside. At least, that's how things were until James Naismith decided it would be fun to tack a peach basket to a wall 10' above the floor and toss a soccer ball through it. Once pro basketball took off in popularity, suddenly towering height became a huge advantage that translates directly to personal prosperity and success. Here we have a biologically determined (genetics + nutrition) quality that moved from advantageous to detrimental and back to advantageous based solely on changes in society.

There are other instances of biological traits whose value fluctuates along with social conditions. For example, human bodies evolved to not feel full for about twenty minutes after a meal, a fine adaptation in the Pleistocene when abundant food was only an occasional treat and overeating once in a while helped pack on fat that could be used by the body during leaner times. Now that there are loads of high-calorie foods about, the old programming leads to obesity. Being fat used to be regarded as an indicator of wealth, since it proved the corpulent didn't have to do manual labor in the fields or the mills and weren't affected by the last famine. Many thought that the excess weight would help to resist infectious or wasting diseases as well. In the nineteenth Century, it was believed to be so important to fatten up that patent medicines were developed to help (Figure 4.5). Furthermore, for many societies excess weight was considered a sign of conviviality and social harmony, and they celebrated the jolly fat man over the sad thin waif. Think Falstaff instead of Hamlet, or Fezziwig instead of Scrooge.

In the modern West, of course, obesity is recognized as a risk factor for diabetes, hypertension, and heart disease. Not only is being fat no

**FIGURE 4.5** Grove's Chill Tonic. Public domain image.

longer regarded as a sign of health, but the overweight are seen as morally inferior, as gluttons who lack self-control.[29] This contemporary Western attitude is a far cry from the Efik tribe of Nigeria where even today future brides spend long periods of time in the Fattening Room, where they bulk up to become the ideally plump wife. We may have evolved to overeat, but whether those excess pounds are seen as a symptom of the diseases of obesity and food addiction or regarded as a symbol of beauty and prosperity has to do with social norms alone.

Should we venerate the brides who are just the right size, or the basketball players who are the best at sinking three-pointers? They are the ones who are best rewarded, with their choice of high-quality mates, or with wealth. As a society we do what we can to ensure that their lives are good ones, with financial and social success well above average. The narrative we want to believe is that their achievements are a wholly personal matter of effort, talent, and hard work. It's a matter of personal choice and determination to practice on the court day after day, or to maintain attractiveness, so *of course* those people deserve the rewards. Constitutive and circumstantial luck complicates this narrative, though—Harry Eastlack was never going to play for the Lakers, no matter how hard he worked.

Talent deserves reward. Nonetheless there's no intrinsic connection to any specific reward, and that fact matters greatly when we think about fair distribution. Some people with very specialized abilities lead fabulous lives of wealth and public adoration and others don't. For example, here's a list of champions with substantial achievements where some translate into wealth and others do not:

1 Paul Hunn is the Guinness world-record belching champion. He can burp at 110 decibels, which is as loud as a rock concert.

2 Katy Perry is a widely enjoyed pop singer-songwriter, with several hit songs.

3 Joey Chestnut is the reigning world-champion competitive eater. He has eaten seventy-four hot dogs and buns in ten minutes, drunk a gallon of milk in forty-one seconds, and pounded down 10.5 lbs. of macaroni and cheese in seven minutes.

4 Usain (Lightning) Bolt is the fastest man in the world, with records in the 100m and 200m races.

5   German adult model Beshine has the largest fake breasts in the world. A gradual series of breast enlargements has stretched her chest to a 32Z with 10,000cc implants.

6   Thomas Blackthorne spent six years building up the strength of his tongue, and now can lift 24 pounds, using a hook pierced through his tongue.

7   Chris Kyle is the deadliest military sniper in US history, with 255 kills.

8   Mathematician Marion Tinsley was the greatest checkers player in history, and lost only seven games (two of them to the Chinook computer program) in his entire forty-five-year career.

All of these achievements took effort, practice, and dedication. Many took courage, intelligence, and effective planning. Even the examples that sound bizarre or stupid are tinged with admirability. They may be talents, but they are not all *wealth-talents*; that is, they aren't necessarily going to make their practitioners rich. They aren't even accomplishments that are necessarily going to improve their lives, or provide stability for their families, or lead to reproductive success. But some of them are: Katy Perry is the highest-paid entertainer in the world, and has a net worth of $330 million. Our society is arranged so that Perry's talents lead to enormous success; in a world without telecommunications she would be reduced to being a popular local singer, no matter how great her skill or devotion. Most people know Bolt's name, but not Beshine, Blackthorne, or Hunn because the Olympics do not showcase their abilities. Competitive checkers never captured the public imagination like the World Series of Poker, so Tinsley never got to cash in. The circumstances that allow one to flourish but not another are a matter of luck.

The outcome of our lives is a matter of personal responsibility only to the extent that those outcomes are the result of our choices. Yet choices depend on opportunities, and opportunities do not take place in a vacuum. They are wholly the result of what society provides. A zaftig Rubens nude—a celebrated body type at the time—would never make it on a twenty-first-century Milanese catwalk, and Joey Chestnut would be impossible in times of scarcity. Interestingly, Chris Kyle was sensitive to these factors, writing, "You need skill to be a sniper, but you also need opportunity. And luck."[30] Kyle mentions the role of luck more than two dozen times in his book *American Sniper*. Kyle's shooting skills wouldn't lead to a best-selling book and popular movie without a long war in which to practice his trade, a background factor well beyond personal choice. More than anything else, the greatest success-talent of all looks to be luck.

It is fitting to admire virtue, those good traits made habitual within a steady character. It is not fitting, though, to admire luck. For sure, we envy the lottery winner, but we don't esteem her because her success had nothing to do with *her*. No one wins the lottery because of their fine personal qualities; it isn't skill, cleverness, or a strong work ethic that claims Powerball. It is sheer luck alone. There's no injustice in the distribution of luck when pretty much everyone has an equal chance at it. The lottery is like this: tickets are so cheap that even the poor can afford one. People may choose not to play, but everyone can take a shot if they wish, and every player is on equal footing. So it's not unfair or unjust when one person wins the lottery and many lose.

The problem with the social lottery is that not everyone has an equal chance—we are each given different aptitudes and abilities, and whether these are wealth-talents depends wholly on the cultural milieu into which we are born. With Powerball you can play or not play and you can pick one set of numbers or another. However, you have no kind of choice over either your abilities or the society into which you are born. In some societies being tall or overweight pays off, in other societies it does not, and you get the one you get; there was never a true alternative. It's not like you could have opted not to be born, or had a chance at a different society. Oskar Yufe had bad luck in the social lottery, and it seems unfair that he couldn't have the good luck of his twin brother.

Maybe, just maybe, we should take steps to make the distribution of luck more egalitarian. Perhaps societies could do something to diminish the role of luck in success, so that it is more personal initiative, determination, and effort that leads to success, not luck. How do we level the playing field? Bad luck is a largely unpredictable, unevenly distributed risk. The best way to ameliorate riskiness is some kind of insurance. There're things we can do to cut down on risk in other areas— we can put a lightning rod on the peak of our house, we can buy a car with three-point seat belts and air bags, we can try to eat healthily and get some exercise. Yet even fitness instructors get heart attacks, and the most cautious driver in a Volvo can wipe out on black ice. So we buy insurance.

Most people won't use their insurance, or they underuse it: the amount of money they (and their employers) pay for insurance is greater than the amount returned by the insurance company. It works that way by design. Insurance-buying is made behind a partial veil of ignorance. We all toss our money into a risk pool, knowing we probably won't get it back—in fact hoping that we won't get it back (who wants cancer just so insurance pays out?). Some people will be heavy insurance recipients because they have uncommonly bad luck, but even after those payouts, there will still be some profit left in the kitty so that the insurers can pay their employees and keep the lights on. In short, the lucky people pay out money for something they don't need, because they wind up not making insurance claims, and that money goes to the unlucky people who are thereby compensated for their misfortunes. Mostly everyone thinks this is a pretty good system, even if there are complaints about the specifics of implementation.

Medical insurance is one way to counteract drawing the short straw in the genetic lottery. About half of all women born with mutated BRCA1 or BRCA2 tumor-suppressor genes develop breast cancer and almost that many top it off with ovarian cancer as well. Having insurance that pays for testing and prophylactic medication or surgery helps them to lead statistically average lives. Developing insurance that compensates for losing the social lottery in all the myriad ways that have already been discussed is a plausible way of giving more people a chance to succeed, not just the people who were lucky that their talents turned out to be wealth-talents, or are natives of a society values their traits, or were born into a loving and prosperous family. The present line of reasoning is the luck egalitarian argument for the welfare state.[31] Public assistance to the less fortunate is just another kind of insurance, a risk pool into which we pay with our taxes.

If there is one thing that philosophers like, it is turning reasoning upside down. Here's a bit of argumentative judo from philosopher Susan Hurley.[32] All of this luck egalitarian/insurance/welfare stuff assumes that equality is the natural state, and it is deviations away from equality that need justification. If equality is the natural state of things, then it is precisely what we should expect; it's the default state of the world. In that case, *no* one is responsible for *non*difference. However, that doesn't entail that *anyone* is responsible for *difference*.

It is tempting to reason

| From: | It is a matter of luck that A and B are unequal. |
| To: | It would not be a matter of luck if A and B were equal. |

But it is the same pattern of inference as this less attractive move:

| From: | It is a matter of luck that A and B are equal. |
| To: | It would not be a matter of luck if A and B were unequal. |

Equalities can be the result of luck just as much as inequalities. If the lives of Jack and Oskar Yufe turn out exactly the same in terms of personal flourishing, happiness, moral virtue and number of cars in their respective driveways, that could be a lucky outcome just as much as the fact that their lives turned out to be radically different was due to luck. If our goal is to neutralize luck in that case, we would have to *increase* inequality, not decrease it.

Here's a way to think about it. Imagine Antiluck, a costumed superhero. Armed with his trusty neutralizer gun, he battles the villains Tuche and Fortuna. The goddesses of luck bring fortune and misfortune into people's lives, they may give two people equivalent lives or radically disparate ones, all by the power of their lucky touch. When Antiluck blasts away with the neutralizer, all the effects of luck are dissipated. The lucky lose their mojo, the unlucky have more of a spring in their step, unlucky inequalities disappear, but so do lucky equalities. Neither equality nor inequality is the natural condition; there is no inherent connection between equality and neutralizing luck. Overcoming luck does not mean we necessarily wind up with an even playing field—having a level playing field could also be lucky.

# Privilege

One flashpoint in the culture wars is the idea of social privilege. On one side are charges that white people, men, and heterosexuals are privileged when authorities treat them with respect and dignity. Cops are supposedly courteous to a white driver when they would harass or beat a black one, and landlords and bank officers reputedly give more grief to black applicants than white ones. A successful white male is told "you didn't build that," and told to check his privilege. On the other side are angry denunciations along the lines of "I built everything I have with my own two hands and no one helped me," and "I'm dirt broke but you tell me I'm privileged?" Then the first side accuses the other of White Fragility and moral blindness, and the second side rejoins that the first is simultaneously infantilizing blacks (or women or gays) and unappreciative of the plight of the white (or male or straight) working poor. Then it degenerates into further insults and everyone has a nice time like that.

The concept of social privilege (whether in its white, male, or heterosexual variants) is a useful tool only if it can improve our understanding of the allotment of social goods and benefits and to what degree that dispersal is fair or just. If it can't do that, then it should probably be abandoned. "Privilege" isn't a eureka-moment discovery; it's a theoretical notion that has value only to the extent that it is illuminating. It turns out that the very idea of social privilege rests on the bedrock of luck. That's probably discomfiting, as by this point it should be clear that luck is a soft, shifting, and porous ground.

The most basic idea behind being privileged or underprivileged is that of possessing certain benefits or advantages. It is an advantage to acquire wealth, easily procure a car loan, purchase a home in a neighborhood of one's choosing, and not be pulled over by the police. Merely having such benefits when others lack them tells us nothing at all about who deserves what. You might become wealthy through hard work and merit, gain a car loan because of an excellent and diligently maintained credit score, have the fairly earned resources to live where you want, and not be pulled over because of careful and legal driving habits. All those advantages might be earned or the result of aptitude and effort. A better idea is that privilege is *un*earned, that somehow a privileged person is simply lucky to have benefits that others do not—the trust fund baby who never has to work a day in her life, or the child of famous actors who has an easy entrée into the world of celebrity. That kind of luck is moral luck, particularly constitutive or circumstantial moral luck.

A lucky trust fund baby might be privileged, but that doesn't really capture what's typically meant by white privilege or gender privilege. Those things are supposed to be systematic, with laws and general social norms granting unearned benefits to dominant groups. People who think the idea of privilege is a helpful one think that's unjust: dominant groups shouldn't be getting better treatment than minority groups. Keeping down the minorities and giving everything to the majority is the whole problem—that's the opposite of equality and justice for all.[33]

The simple view that *giving unearned benefits to majority groups is unjust* is straight-out false. For example, demonstrably law-abiding citizens are the dominant group, and they have the benefit of not being sent to prison. The law-abiding may not have done anything, or even intentionally refrained from doing anything, to earn that privilege; they could be wholly ignorant of the laws. Furthermore, law-abidingness could be due to circumstantial luck—perhaps most people haven't been in a position where they were seriously tempted to break the law. In such cases it's incorrect to think of the law-abiding as having *earned* the privilege of not going to prison. They didn't do anything or even try to do anything. As a result, it's wrong to conclude that laws granting unearned privileges or benefits (like remaining free) to dominant groups (like the law-abiding) are invariably unjust.

Even a system of granting substantial, life-altering benefits to some persons but not others on the basis of luck is not obviously unethical. Consider a national lottery. You might argue that such lotteries are unjust in that some players are gambling addicts, and that the poor disproportionally squander their money on the lottery. On the other hand, we tend to allow people to do things that are unhealthy, might lead to addiction, or are otherwise dubious, like smoking and excessive drinking. Plus there is a questionable paternalism in having the government control the spending of the poor for their own good. In any case, let's assume that a national lottery is minimally just and fairly administered, and that all citizens are free to participate or not as they choose. A lottery winner is privileged to the extent that he received a significant benefit, it was unearned and due to luck not skill or merit, and was made possible by a system that allows and grants such advantages. But there was nothing wrong with winning; it was not unjust. Lottery winners are envied, not accused.

If "privilege" is to make any sense, we need to add something. The best contender to get a more satisfactory account of privilege is to add that the system of distributing benefits is corrupt or unjust. Consider, for example, the 72-year-rule of Louis XIV, in which Louis declared himself absolute monarch by divine right, asserted "*l'état, c'est moi*," and the wealth of France was concentrated in the hands of a few hereditary aristocrats. Under the *ancien régime* the granting of trade monopolies, the liberty of worship, and the membership of the powerful advisory councils was decided by the king alone. In a very direct way, the path of your life and well-being depended on the capricious decisions of one man and the chance relationships one might have with him or his proxies. In eighteenth-century France, your fate was not only heavily indebted to circumstantial luck, but the dispersal of that luck was due to a fundamentally unfair method based on patronage and cronyism.

So this looks like the most plausible account of privilege: it is the *unjust systematic differential distribution of unearned or unmerited advantages or benefits*. Surprisingly, given the best, most charitable interpretation of privilege, there's not one thing wrong with having it. What's bad is *lacking* privilege. Here's why. If everyone deserves to be treated with dignity and respect, but only some groups are so treated due to systematic bigotry, it does not follow that members of the "privileged" groups do not deserve their decent treatment. By hypothesis, everyone deserves it, only some are receiving it. The scholar Lewis Gordon points out that everyone looks for safety, food, clothing, shelter, self-improvement through education, and a positive sense of self. We all desire and are entitled to these goods as fundamental human rights and so possessing them is not unjust. That means privilege is not unjust, only a lack of privilege is. Gordon's reasoning is why we need to understand privilege in terms of luck, not as possession of stolen goods. Whites aren't privileged because they possess benefits or advantages unfairly stolen from blacks (since, if Gordon is right then all— both whites and blacks—ought to have such benefits), but because whites were born lucky.[34]

The privileged ones are fortunate to be born white in a racist society that disproportionally benefits whites, or male in a sexist society that advantages men at the expense of women, and so on. The privileged are lucky; they may deserve their decent treatment in a general moral sense, although of course they are not *especially* deserving. The underprivileged are unlucky and suffer moral harm and costs to their well-being due to the bad luck of being born black in a racist society, female in a sexist society, homosexual in a homophobic culture, into a Shiite family in a Sunni society, Jewish in an anti-Semite culture, and so on. Privilege just amounts to good circumstantial moral luck, and lack of privilege is no more than bad circumstantial moral luck. The takeaway point is that the whole debate over privilege relies entirely on the notion of luck.

What's more, behind all these reflections on privilege is the luck egalitarian instinct: in a just society the dispensations of Fortuna would be more or less evenly distributed. As we saw earlier, getting to that conclusion requires more than just pointing out the role of luck. Equality itself could be a matter of luck and eliminating luck would then mean increasing inequality. The idea of privilege might rest on moral luck, but it's a shaky foundation.

The discussion of moral luck so far has been mostly sui generis, in isolation of the ruminations on luck in previous chapters. As we are about to see, when we place moral luck in the broader context of general theories of luck, even more puzzles arise. There is an unexpected challenge to the cogency of moral luck arising from—of all places—metaphysics.

# Essential Origins

Aristotle is the greatest thinker in the history of thinking. He made important contributions to every subject one could study in ancient times, from anatomy to zoology, from aesthetics to theology. He had serious interests in poetry, physics, philosophy, psychology, and politics, and that's just the "Ps." Aristotle was a peripatetic encyclopedia who invented logic, pioneered empirical science, and named Antarctica. His understanding of formal logic was unsurpassed for 2300 years, and his formulation of virtue ethics may still be the best.

One of his interests was in the distinction between those properties that are essential to an object and those which are merely accidental to it. A kitchen, for example, is essentially a room where meals are prepared. A room where no meals are made could be a bedroom, living room bathroom, and so on, but definitely not a kitchen. Aristotle thought that kitchens have many accidental properties as well; not accidental in the sense of "they happened randomly" or "whoops," but that they are *changeable.* You repaint the kitchen from brown to gray and it's still a kitchen. The kitchen has to be some color or other, but not any particular one. You get some new appliances and it's still a kitchen. Put in an island or some new lights, and it's still a kitchen. What you can't do is strip the room to the bare walls, put in a bed and a dresser and pretend it's still a kitchen. Nor can you tear down the building entirely without also destroying the kitchen. Some of the kitchen's properties are essential to its existence, and it can't survive their loss. Others are contingent, "accidental" qualities that can come and go.

In the Middle Ages, Thomas Aquinas liked Aristotle's way of distinguishing those properties essential to a thing and the qualities that were mere accidents, and he thought it would be a handy way to explain a Christian mystery. The mystery was transubstantiation. In the sacrament of the Eucharist, the priest gives bread and wine to the worshippers, which somehow turns into the body and blood of Christ. The devout then eat the dead god. Theophagia was a familiar ritual from prehistory; Neolithic worshippers ate the grain of the harvest that represented the fertility/harvest deity whose death saved the community from hunger and who would be reborn in the spring. A more recent version of this idea is in the medieval English folksong "John Barleycorn" in which the barley grain is personified. John Barleycorn is buried, slain, beaten, and ground, only to be reborn as whiskey and in that form triumphs over his tormentors. While modern Protestants interpret the bread and wine of communion as mere symbols of the body and blood of Jesus, Aquinas took it to be a matter of literal transformation. How could wine literally become blood, though? How is that supposed to work? His idea was that the essential properties of the consumed substances remain from beginning to end and what changes are the accidental properties. You eat and drink one thing in the ceremony, but the miracle is in the alteration of the contingent, accidental features of those substances from wine into blood and bread into flesh.

It's not always obvious which properties of a thing are essential ones and which are not. In fact, it is seldom obvious. Water has the property of being essentially $H_2O$; many things can be wet, drinkable, and good for washing, but if they are not $H_2O$, they are not water. It took a long time to sleuth that one out. Among other things, we had to invent chemistry first. Similarly, until the development of atomic physics, we didn't know that an essential property of gold is that it has seventy-nine protons. The shape of a bit of gold is an accidental property—it might be a coin, a ring, or a nugget, but it stays gold so long as it retains its atomic structure. A piece of the world with more than seventy-nine protons or with fewer just can't be gold. Some qualities are open to argument. Is it an essential property of whales that they are mammals, or is our Linnaean taxonomy itself a matter of convention, and "being a mammal" is not essential at all, but contingent on our scheme of classification? We needn't dive into those deep waters here.

What matters for luck is a claim first made by the American logician Saul Kripke, namely, that the origins of a thing are essential to it. A cherry bookcase could not have started out as steel; that would have been altogether different bookcase. Queen Elizabeth could not have been the product of a different sperm and egg. For that very person to exist, it had to be the result of the specific gametes that made her. Superman couldn't have been the son of Thomas and Martha Wayne any more than Batman could have been the child of Jor-El and Lara. Since you have your parents essentially, all the childhood fantasies of imagining what your life would be like if you had different parents are nothing but impossible dreams. Children born to other mothers and fathers are certainly not *you*. They are other kids. Likewise, a black child couldn't have been born to white parents, and an xy-chromosome boy could not have been born an xx-chromosome girl.

Given origin essentialism, it's tough to make good sense out of constitutive and circumstantial moral luck. Moral luck is a nonstarter if we adopt either the probability theory or the modal theory of luck. Most of the paradigm cases of moral luck turn out not to be matters of luck at all, and it is merely coincidence if any of the residual cases survive. Consider first the probability theory, according to which an event is unlucky for a person if and only if it was improbable that the event occurred and it was significant for that person. Very likely events are neither lucky nor unlucky; they are the expected path of life. One kind of loss in the social lottery—emphasized by those who think social privilege is real and an example of bad moral luck—is being born black in racist society that favors light skin, or being born female in a sexist society that favors males, or being homosexual in a homophobic society.[35] Under the probability and modal theories of luck, these turn out not to be cases of luck at all, and thus not cases of bad luck or of bad moral luck.

Take a specific example, say, Frederick Douglass. In his stirring autobiography, Douglass discusses his life as a slave in the American south, surreptitiously learning to read and write, his successful escape from bondage, and his life as an abolitionist and renowned orator. Douglass was a loser in the genetic or social lotteries only if the terrible events of his life can be marked down to bad luck. Well, are any of the following events improbable ones?

A   Douglass was born to black parents.

B   Douglass was born into a slave-holding state in 1818.

C   Talbot County, Maryland in 1818 was a largely racist society.

D   Douglass suffered discrimination because of his racist society.

E   The evolution of Douglass's character, his interpersonal relationships, and his place in society were shaped by that discrimination.

F   Douglass's well-being and life prospects were harmed or reduced as a result of racism.

Given the essentiality of origins, (A) is metaphysically necessary. God did not roll dice to choose Douglass's parents; he couldn't have been born to any other parents than the ones he in fact has. (A) is probability 1. The probability of (B) is also near certainty. Parents very rarely have a choice as to which society their children will be born in, and certainly

Douglass's parents had no choice at all. He was born into slavery, never knew his father, and was separated from his mother at an early age. There's no reasonable doubt that (C) is highly likely as well. There were numerous slave owners and plantations there, slavery was legal under state and federal law, and blacks were routinely seen as inferior. Even a brief review of his autobiography reveals how (D), (E), and (F) were foregone conclusions in the life of a slave, and Douglass details the privations and whippings he had to endure. None of the dreadful facts of Douglass's life were improbable, and since the probability theory of luck insists that lucky events be unlikely ones, Douglass was in no way the victim of bad luck.

Much the same reasoning holds with the modal theory of luck. Recall that an event is lucky under the modal theory only if it fails to occur in nearby possible worlds; that is, slight changes in the actual world would have prevented the event from occurring. Events are lucky when they are modally fragile, and not a matter of luck when they are modally robust. Since it is metaphysically necessary for Douglass to have had the parents he did, it is as modally robust a proposition as possible. Likewise, we may reasonably imagine that the world would have been substantially different for Douglass to have been born into a different society from the one he was in the actual world. So much would have been altered for Douglass's parents to have moved to another country prior to his birth that it beggars the imagination. A world in which 1818 Maryland wasn't racist, or a black slave didn't suffer in some way as a result of that discrimination, is remote from our actual world. All the facts (A)–(F) of Douglass's life are modally robust ones—his world could have changed a good deal and they still would have been true. Again, this means that none of those facts are lucky ones. It turns out that moral luck fares no better with the modal theory than it did with the probability theory.

Under both the probability and modal theories, Douglass was not the victim of bad luck. There wasn't any luck at all involved. Obviously, everyone can still argue that slavery was wrong, that racist society needed to change, Douglass suffered unjustly, and all of that, but not based on luck egalitarianism. Since the idea of privilege is grounded in moral luck, he was also not morally underprivileged.

All the same reasoning shows that losers in the genetic lottery aren't unlucky either—at least not by the lights of the probability and modal theories of luck. Consider Zelda Fitzgerald, who was born with the genetics for developing schizophrenia, developed the disease in adolescence, and suffered in the predictable ways as a consequence. Was it improbable that she became schizophrenic? No, not given her genetic make-up—it was highly probable that she would develop the disease. Was it improbable that Fitzgerald had the genetic make-up that she did? It is improbable that any particular child will be born with schizophrenia, as the disease is uncommon in the general population, just as it is improbable that any particular passenger will be killed in a plane crash. Plane crashes are rare. However, given that one is in a plane crash, death is very probable. Likewise, given that one is Fitzgerald, with her essential genetic nature, schizophrenia is very probable. And, of course, given that she is schizophrenic, the negative impact on her life is very probable as well.

Things are no different with the modal theory of luck. If we agree that had Fitzgerald's genetic coding been different that it would not have been Fitzgerald but someone else; then in every world in which she exists, Fitzgerald regrettably has the genes that encode for schizophrenia. Given that she has those genes, it is modally robust that she develops the disease at some point; it is only in distant worlds that she never gets it. Much about the actual world would had to have to be changed for Fitzgerald to never suffer from schizophrenia; the world would have to be vastly unlike how it actually is for Fitzgerald to be schizophrenic and not have her life impeded or her life prospects damaged in any way. All of the relevant facts about Fitzgerald are modally robust; on the modal theory of luck she is not the victim of bad luck. Luck is a non-issue for Fitzgerald.

The present chapter has tried to drive home the idea that luck and morality may be an uneasy mix, but mixed together they are. We seem to be morally culpable for things that happen as the result of luck, and Fortuna weaves the warp and woof of our lives out of circumstantial and constitutive luck. It's these reflections that underwrite the more political notions of luck egalitarianism and privilege. As powerfully compelling as those ideas are, they begin to fray when we start to think about what luck really comes to. As we've just seen, moral luck is nonexistent if we accept either one of the popular probability or modal theories. Which means that there is one contestant left standing: the control theory of luck.

The facts of Frederick Douglass's birth and upbringing were out of his control; as a slave, nearly all the circumstances of his life were. Likewise, Zelda Fitzgerald had no control over whether she became schizophrenic. So, we can say that in this sense both of them suffered from bad luck. Before getting too complacent about just signing on for the control theory of luck, recall from the last chapter that the view faced some problematic objections, not the least of which was that it ran a serious risk of just morphing into either the probability or modal view after all. If "you are in control of some outcome" just means "you are probably able to bring that outcome about" or "it would be difficult for you to fail to bring it about if you tried," then the control theory of luck doesn't offer anything new. It's just a lick of fresh paint on a car that's rusting apart, a plague mask on a corpse. That's bad news for the possibility of moral luck, and leaves us foundering to understand the meaning of the random or unexpected in our lives.

We've been examining the relationship of luck to morality in the context of the theories of luck discussed in earlier chapters, and found that luck and morality are intertwined in various ways that aren't easy to sort out either psychologically or philosophically. Looking to theories of luck was of limited help at best, because it turns out that two of the three theories of luck considered can't even be applied to moral luck, and the third theory might just be a variant of the first two. But forget all that. Let's suppose that we *can* find a legitimate conceptual niche for the control theory, and that it turns out to be just the panacea we need for moral luck. Before pulling out the noisemakers and party hats, we'd better see if the control theory works in other areas where we'd like to grasp the machinations of luck.[36] If it doesn't, then that's a blow to the idea that luck is a complex, but univocal phenomenon, like having a theory of gravity that works on Earth but nowhere else. In the next chapter, we'll take a look at how luck affects the discoveries we make, and our very knowledge itself.

# 5 KNOWLEDGE AND SERENDIPITY

*"Even in our counsels and deliberations there must, certainly, be something of chance and good-luck mixed with human prudence; for all that our wisdom can do alone is no great matter; the more piercing, quick, and apprehensive it is, the weaker it finds itself, and is by so much more apt to mistrust itself."*
**—MICHEL DE MONTAIGNE, *ESSAYS*, CHAPTER XXIII (1580)**

*"It is always by favour of nature that one knows something."*
**—LUDWIG WITTGENSTEIN (*ON CERTAINTY* §505)**

We want to do good in the world. At least, we don't want to make things worse. Moral action is a kind of personal achievement, something we do from character or effort. We have already seen the various ways in which moral luck can interfere, turning permissible actions into wrong ones and changing nobility of purpose into horrible mistakes. Fortuna's hand lays heavy on our constitution and our circumstances to the point that teasing out what is properly creditable to our own abilities is deeply vexed. Not only do we pursue the good, but we pursue the true as well, and achieving either of those goals by the exercise of our own abilities is a high aim. It should come as no surprise that luck plays havoc with our knowledge just as it does with morality. Let's try to brush out the dreadlock weave of outcomes, circumstances, abilities, and luck when it comes to gaining truth.

## Finding Meno

In the 2003 Disney/Pixar animated film *Finding Nemo*, Nemo is a young clownfish living in Australia's Great Barrier Reef who is separated from his overprotective father, Marlin. Marlin's fears are realized when Nemo is captured by scuba divers who take him for a pet in a dentist's saltwater aquarium. The main plot of the film is the father's quest to find Nemo and bring him home. One of the first allies that Marlin makes in the hunt for his son is Dory, a regal blue tang. Dory is comic relief; she has such severe short-term memory loss that she is incapable of remembering the thread of a conversation, and flits from topic to topic. Dory is cheerful and upbeat, but seemingly not much use as a detective. After the divers capture Nemo, one of them accidentally knocks his diving mask off the boat into the irretrievably deep waters below. The mask had the diver's address written inside. In a later scene, it is Dory who sees the address inside the mask: "42 Wallaby Lane, Sydney," their only real clue as to where Nemo might be.

To her astonishment, Dory manages to remember the address long enough to tell Marlin, and the story moves forward. Dory lives in such a state of perpetual confusion that at the end of the film she encounters Nemo, back in the ocean after having escaped the dentist's aquarium, and she doesn't even recognize the significance of meeting him, despite the fact that finding him was the whole point of her journey all along. Dory is the most untrustworthy of testifiers, perpetually mixing things up, confabulating explanations to paper over the holes in her memory. When she does manage to hang on to a bit of reality, it is by accident—a random bright neural connection in the darkness of her mind. There is no reason for either her or Marlin to have any confidence that she knows what she is talking about. She gets "42 Wallaby Lane, Sydney" right, but against the backdrop of constant forgetfulness and slip-ups, it's hardly a piece of knowledge. Similarly, in the documentary film *Prisoner of Consciousness*, the well-studied British amnesiac Clive Wearing was shown various photographs and asked to identify their subjects. He correctly recognized his alma mater Cambridge University in one photo, but since he also mistook Queen Elizabeth II for a member of his choir (Wearing was a conductor), his sporadic accuracy looks like no more than chance.[1]

Dory got the address right. She and Marlin successfully pursued Nemo to Sydney, so what does it matter whether she *knew* where they were going or not? They got to the right place nonetheless. Why would having knowledge be more valuable than merely getting it right fortuitously? Plato asks this very question in his dialogue *Meno*. Socrates imagines a traveler asking a stranger for the directions to Larissa, a town some 200 miles distant from Athens. Would it be better if the stranger knew the way to Larissa, or just had a lucky guess about how to get there? Socrates's interlocutor Meno suggests that knowing the way is better, because if you know, then you'll always be right, but with a lucky guess, sometimes you'll be right and sometimes not.

Socrates points out that a lucky guess is always just as accurate as knowledge. If you have the truth, then you have the truth, even if it is by guessing. A lucky guess isn't right less often, it is right *exactly* as often as actually knowing the answer. Dory correctly led the way to Sydney even though she didn't know that was right. What is she missing out on, if anything? Socrates mentions that the statues carved by the sculptor Daedalus were so famously lifelike that, unless chained down, they would get up and walk away. He suggests that perhaps knowledge is something like that; the cause of a bit of knowledge chains down the truth so it doesn't give us the slip. It's not much use having the truth if it gets up and walks away.

Guessing rightly is a perfectly reliable way of getting hold of the truth, but guessing in general is not. You can't count on it in the way that you can count on knowledge. Suppose you have an old plastic coffee maker that makes a 1980s Mr. Coffee look like a brand-new Gaggia.[2] Still, you're desperate for java and make a cup. Somehow the old wreck spits and spews and manages to make the perfect cup of joe. It's every bit as good as something made by a barista in a Torino caffè. It's a crazy fluke for sure, and the next time you use that machine it will probably produce coffee-flavored crude oil. What makes your current cup of coffee worse than one made from an excellent machine? Nothing; we're supposing it is just as good. You can't count on the machine, though.

What makes Dory's guess about directions worse than asking a knowledgeable source? In this instance, nothing. However, Dory herself is not as virtuous as she would be if she knew the way. Actually knowing something is an achievement for which you deserve some credit, having the truth by luck is not. It's like the difference between earning wealth by hard work and ingenuity vs. inheriting it. You might be just as rich either way, but you only deserve respect for the former. You are a more admirable person if you are a knower rather than not, even if your knowledge isn't any more accurate than a luckily true belief.

Although Dory got the address right this time, you can't rely on her in the future. That's something that a knowledgeable person has going for them: they are reliable. It's not very easy for the truth to just walk away. One way to put this idea is that knowledge is the proper norm of assertion. You shouldn't make an assertion, that is, tell someone that something is a fact, unless you actually know that it is a fact. If you don't have knowledge, but just a hunch or a suspicion, you should be a lot more cautious about acting on it or telling other people that it's what they should believe. The same is true for practical instructions. You shouldn't show anyone how to run the chainsaw if you don't know how. You shouldn't do surgery if you flunked anatomy. And you shouldn't be giving anyone directions to Larissa if you don't know where it is or how to get there. Of course, if Dory had abided by the "norm of assertion" rule, she would have kept her mouth shut about 42 Wallaby Lane and *Finding Nemo* would have been short and unsatisfying.

Nonetheless, let's assume that we do prefer having knowledge to not. Getting things right by luck is all well and good, but not nearly as good as knowing. If that's right, then we had better figure out what knowledge is, and how we can distinguish between it and lucky guesses. Venomous North American coral snakes have red, yellow, and black bands, but so do nonvenomous milk snakes, just in a different order of coloration. It is obviously important to be able to tell them apart. Even if we're pretty sure about the value of knowledge, that doesn't let us know how to spot it or how we can tell it apart from its less benign kindred. Yellow, red, STOP! is a good traffic-light based mnemonic for coral snakes, but we don't have anything similar for knowledge. As we'll see, when we try to come up with good criteria for knowledge, we run smack into another problem of luck.

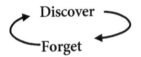

As a species, we're terrible at remembering much of anything. Consider the Golden Buddha of Bangkok. In the Middle Ages, a solid gold statue of Buddha was crafted in Thailand.[3] This wasn't just any solid gold statue, but one that was ten feet tall and weighed five and a half tons. Which is to say, it is one of the most valuable things ever made and the melt value alone is $250 million. When Thailand was threatened by invaders from Burma in the eighteenth century, the Thai King had the statue completely covered in plaster so nobody would pay it any attention, correctly predicting that stealing a super-heavy plaster statue didn't hold much appeal. This strategy worked so well that for the next 200 years everyone forgot they had a massive lump of gold, and the statue was relegated to a tin shack. In the 1950s, the Thai decided that a centuries-old plaster Buddha deserved a little more respect than a dilapidated shed and decided to build a new room off the local temple to house it. When the movers showed up, they unsurprisingly underestimated the weight of the thing, and their ropes broke when they tried to lift it. The plaster coating cracked open when the statue landed, and revealed the glowing yellow metal underneath.

We're even lousy at keeping track of our really good discoveries—the New World being a case in point. Twenty thousand years ago, intrepid explorers from East Asia crossed the Bering Strait land bridge into what is now Alaska, spread out, and neglected to tell anyone back home that they found an entire brand-new continent. The next time anyone from the rest of the world took notice of this massive real estate was 19,000 years later, when Norse sailors made their way to Greenland and Newfoundland. The Vikings encountered the locals, whom they ironically dubbed "barbarians" (*skrælingi*). The two groups were instantly suspicious of each other, their interactions turned violent, and the Norsemen decided the whole adventure was more trouble than it was worth. So, they headed home, where Leif Eriksson, Thorfinn Karlsefni, and Eric the Red disappeared into the mists of legend. It was another 500 years before Columbus and a new wave of discovery.

While not as world-historical as unexpected continents or golden statues, the trickster interference of luck with knowledge has been repeatedly noticed, neglected, and found again. Like so many of these things, the original problem comes out of Plato. Plato's dialogue *Theaetetus* relates how Socrates was at a wrestling match at the Athenian palaestra when he is introduced to Theaetetus, a young man praised for his intellect (although not his looks, which were compared to Socrates's own unattractive mug). Socrates naturally begins to probe Theaetetus's presumed sagacity, taking up the question of *what is knowledge?* The nature of knowledge turns out to be just as thorny as its value.

Everyone thinks they are right. That wouldn't even be a problem if people weren't constantly disagreeing with each other about who has the true god, right political leader, best sports team, or any one of a million other pettier issues. One way to broker disagreement is the classic relativist strategy of declaring everyone to be winner, going back to Protagoras's doctrine of *homo mensura* (man is the measure of all things). One person's trash is another's treasure, beauty is in the eye of the beholder, and so on. Socrates and Theaetetus point out that *homo mensura* itself is, by its own lights, true for some and false for others, which Socrates calls "a really exquisite contradiction." If we reject relativism as a Faustian bargain, then we're back with some opinions are objectively true and others as objectively false.[4] All well and good, but how can we tell who actually knows what they are talking about and who is just producing (in Plato's expression) a wind-egg?

It's tempting to declare that objectively true opinions are knowledge, and everything else is not. In *Gulliver's Travels* (1726), Jonathan Swift guessed that Mars had two moons, a guess that turned out to be true. Even if that really was Swift's own opinion, he didn't *know* that Mars had two moons—no one did until the American astronomer Asaph Hall spotted them in 1877. Swift's belief may have been true, but it was only by luck. The idea that knowledge is true belief was on the right track, but there has to be more to it, since a belief that was true by luck surely wasn't knowledge. The proposal offered in *Theaetetus* was that knowledge is true belief coupled with reason. That is, behind your belief has to be reasoning, evidence, explanations, justification, some sort of warrant. You can justifiably believe something false, like the victim of a clever lie. And you can believe the truth without justification, like Swift and moons of Mars. You can even be justified in believing something you refuse to accept, like a Holocaust denier. The gold ring, though, is getting all three: truth, belief, and justification. That's knowledge, and that's what separates the wise from the layers of wind-eggs. At least it seemed that way for a long time.

The Leif Eriksson of epistemology was the eighth-century Tibetan Buddhist writer Dharmottara, who discovered that even adding the requirement that a true belief was determined correctly, or somehow justified by evidence, doesn't prevent the termite of luck from hollowing out knowledge. He imagines a case where you're in the desert on a blazing hot day, searching for water. You see water in the distance, and make for it eagerly, only to find out that what you saw is only a mirage. When you get to the site, though, you *do* find water hidden under a rock. Did you have genuine knowledge that there was water in that location? You saw water, believed there was water, and in fact there was water. But, says Dharmottara, you didn't really know. It was just luck that there was water under that rock.[5]

In the late fourteenth century, the logician Peter of Mantua rediscovered the same problem. He imagined a scenario where you are running a race and believe on good grounds that Socrates is running next to you. The problem is that all those ancient Greek philosophers kind of look alike, and you've mixed up Socrates and Plato. In fact, it is Plato who is running beside you. The kicker is that you believe that Socrates is running, and you are right—he *is* running, just in Rome in a completely different race. You firmly believe that Socrates is running, have justifiable grounds for that belief, Socrates really is running, and yet you don't know that he is, since it was just luck that he was hoofing it up in Rome.[6]

Classical Sanskrit (the language of Dharmottara) is at best on life support, and Peter of Mantua is so obscured by the detritus of history that he doesn't even rate an entry in *The Stanford Encyclopedia of Philosophy*. To the extent that their ideas are remembered at all, it is by the most specialized of scholarly scribblers. The problem of luck undermining our conception of knowledge was discovered yet again in the twentieth century by Bertrand Russell. Only this time, like the Thai with their golden Buddha, Russell plastered over his great idea and didn't realize its true value. Russell discusses an example of someone, call her Dora, who checks the time by looking at a usually reliable clock.[7] That seems like a perfectly legitimate way of finding out the time, and Dora believes that it is 3:00 as a result. And Dora's right—it *is* 3:00. She was just unaware that the clock's battery had died and it was stopped at 3:00. As the saying goes, a stopped clock is right twice a day, and Dora had the good luck to glance at it at just the right time. She believed it was 3:00, it truly was 3:00, she had excellent reasons for thinking it so, and still she didn't know it.

Russell had other things on his mind and never pursued the problem of epistemic luck. It fell to Edmund Gettier in 1963 to be epistemology's Columbus. Like Don Christopher, it was Gettier's discovery that proved to be the lasting one. Gettier's three-page paper in the journal *Analysis* has been cited thousands of times, and was the sole publication of the author's long career.[8] Gettier offered two counterexamples to the justified-true-belief analysis of knowledge. Here's a Gettier-style case.[9] Imagine you have a colleague, Mr. Nogot. You have excellent reasons to believe that Nogot owns a Ford. He loves Fords, talks about Fords, and you have seen him driving a Ford. As a result, you believe "there's someone in my office who owns a Ford." Unknown to you, another colleague, Ms. Havit, just bought a new Ford Focus. Also unknown to you, Nogot's Ford F-150 has been repossessed because of nonpayment. Once again, it is true that someone in your office owns a Ford, you believe it, and you have good grounds for believing it. Still you don't know; the justification for your belief did not connect it to the truth. It was luck that made the connection.

Gettier problems show how an individual case of a responsibly formed true belief can be undercut by luck and thereby be prevented from amounting to knowledge. That's unfortunate because, for one thing, we'd *like* to have knowledge. As argued in *Meno*, knowledge looks like a better deal than mere true belief. It's also disappointing because it shows that the justified-true-belief account of knowledge isn't right (we can satisfy all those conditions and still fail to know). We don't have the nature of knowledge worked out, which means it's back to the drawing board.

Some have argued that Gettier-style puzzles are inescapable,[10] others insist that we just need to add a "no luck" clause to knowledge.[11] Whatever knowledge is, as Duncan Pritchard puts it, "it cannot be a matter of luck that one's belief is true."[12] All post-Gettier attempts to analyze knowledge have had to clear Pritchard's threshold; epistemologists are like drug dogs, ready to sniff out any whiff of illicit luck. The "no luck" idea sounds good, right up until we realize that getting a grip on luck may not be any easier than sorting out knowledge. Socrates asked Theaetetus, "Do you fancy it is a small matter to discover the nature of knowledge? Is it not one of the hardest questions?"[13] As we have seen so far in this book, discovering the nature of luck may be just as tasking.

The Gettier problem is a kind of outcome luck. In the last chapter, we saw that external events could interfere with someone's action in a way that flipped its moral valence like a switch. It is perfectly blameless to drive though a pile of leaves in the road, unless of course children are hidden in it, a fact which is beyond the driver's control and is up to luck. There's nothing wrong with firing on enemy soldiers in wartime, unless you had the bad luck to mistake your own comrades for the enemy. The Gettier problem does something analogous. Dora does know that it is 3:00, unless luck breaks the connection between her evidence and the truth. You do know that someone in your office owns a Ford, or at least you would if Fortuna hadn't made the switcheroo between Nogot and Havit. As a believer you weren't doing anything wrong; it was luck that interfered and screwed things up.

It's tempting to think that the Gettier problem is a scholarly cul-de-sac, an edge case that matters only to specialists. The justified-true-belief analysis of knowledge is like Newtonian mechanics—so close to the truth that it is perfectly serviceable for our day-to-day use. We don't need to consult relativity physics to successfully meet a friend for lunch at noon, even though we are in different inertial reference frames and therefore have different "noons." Those differences are just too fine to matter. Much more disturbing is the possibility that luck is not so much of an impish and occasional threat to a bit of knowledge, but rather a weapon of mass destruction that threatens to lay waste to knowledge altogether. That is the threat of skepticism.

# The Man Who Sold the Eiffel Tower and Other Skeptical Threats

Viktor Lustig (1890?–1947) was by all accounts a suave gentleman who spoke five languages, wore expensive suits, and conducted himself with courtly grace. Lustig styled himself a European "Count" and presented himself as a wealthy immigrant from the Austro-Hungarian Empire. So mysterious that he was described by one Secret Service agent "as elusive as a puff of cigarette smoke and as charming as a young girl's dream," Lustig had forty-seven aliases and dozens of passports. Little is known of his true ancestry; an historian in 2015 was unable to unearth the smallest scrap of evidence that Lustig had ever been born. One thing is certain: in the hierarchy of con artists, Lustig was nobility of the highest degree.

Having mastered the typical trades of being a pickpocket, burglar, and card sharp, Lustig wanted to up his game, and so hired a craftsman to build him a counterfeit machine. Actually, it was more of a counterfeit counterfeit machine. Lustig would sail on transatlantic ocean liners, pretending to be a rich young Austrian. When his wealthy Jazz Age marks asked about the source of his wealth, Lustig would very confidentially show them a "Rumanian money box," his specialist-crafted cedar box filled with complicated brass gears and rollers, which he said used radium to copy banknotes. Lustig was ready with the proof. He would insert a $100 bill, a couple of drops of "processing chemicals," and after a period of twelve hours or so, turn a crank. The machine would then spit out two $100s—the original and a copy (with its serial number carefully altered in advance to match the original). Interest piqued, the marks always attempted to purchase the box from Lustig. After faux-reluctant negotiations, he would agree to sell the machine at the end of the voyage, for some tens of thousands of dollars. Lustig would salt the box with a couple of genuine $100 bills so that it would produce real money for a while, allowing him to high-tail it before the mark got wise.

Lustig's boldest con was selling the Eiffel Tower. In the 1920s, the Eiffel Tower was not the Parisian icon that it is today. Its modern design and bare iron construction was polarizing in a largely medieval city, and the repairs, painting, and general upkeep were a toll on the public coffers. Lustig decided to sell it for scrap. He had stationery printed with the official letterhead of the *Minstère des Postes et des Télégraphes* and hand-couriered letters to the six major scrap metal dealers in Paris, inviting them to a private meeting. Ostensibly too confidential a discussion to be held in the official office, the group met at a grand hotel on the Place de la Concorde. Lustig told the assembled group that the government wanted to receive sealed bids on the project before a public announcement. In reality, he had already picked out his target, a nouveau riche metal dealer aptly named Andre Poisson.

After the official meeting, Lustig pulled Poisson aside, describing his miserable salary and complaining about working for an unappreciative bureaucracy. The Poisson was hooked. He had been a bit doubtful of the whole matter before, but now he was on solid ground. Who but a legitimate French minister would be openly looking for a bribe? That was surely the true explanation of the secrecy and the meeting in a hotel suite. Poisson wrote a check on the spot for the whole shebang—the bribe plus 7000 lbs. of scrap iron. Lustig deposited the check, grabbed one of his many passports, and took the first train to Vienna. Poisson was too humiliated to go to the police so, after a suitable wait, Lustig thought he would return to Paris and sell the Eiffel Tower a second time. Which he did.

The real money, though, was in money. Finally dissatisfied with the fake counterfeiting of the Rumanian money box, Lustig teamed up with the forger Tom Shaw to do some authentic counterfeiting. The $100 notes they produced were so flawless that they fooled the close scrutiny of bank tellers, and they were churned out in such numbers that the federal government worried that they would undermine confidence in the US currency system. The American Numismatic Association has described the Lustig–Shaw forgeries as the "supernotes" of that era. Lustig's printing presses finally ground to a halt after a jealous girlfriend dimed him to the feds, and he was remanded to the Federal House of Detention in New York City. Lustig promptly escaped on a rope woven of torn bed sheets.[14]

Essential to an effective con is giving believable evidence that the whole thing is legit. When Count Lustig was peddling the Rumanian money box, the marks believed that the notes it produced were fake, but Lustig gave them good reasons to think the box itself really did make them. On the one hand was the evidence of the box itself: it was supposed to produce money and it did. Lustig would put in a bill, do the requisite hocus-pocus, and out came the original $100 plus another bill with the exact same serial as the original, both of them so good that any bank teller in town would certify them as genuine. On the other hand was the smooth story Lustig would tell about the genius who invented the machine and was on the run from European law. This gave the necessary stage-set for the performance.

In the case of the Eiffel Tower, Lustig went to great lengths to make everything about the swindle appear credible, from very real controversies over the Tower, to the official stationery, to the fancy meeting place, to the deal-clinching move of soliciting a bribe. The marks were not stupid men; they looked to the evidence, evaluated it, formed their beliefs on that basis, and were just terribly wrong.

You can pay attention to the evidence and try to reason your way to a good decision, but still be nowhere near the truth. The broader issue is general skepticism: How can we ever be sure that our evidence connects us with the truth instead of falsely misleading us? The problem isn't how we can be certain, or how we can know that we know, but *why think that our reasoning and perceptions take us anywhere close to the truth*?

The idea that at any given time we could be badly mistaken about what's real has been troubling since antiquity. In *Theaetetus*, Plato brings up the concern that we cannot reliably distinguish between dreaming and being awake, as each at the time feels compelling and genuine. At almost exactly the same time but 5,000 miles away, the Chinese sage Zhuangzi famously recalled a dream in "he was a butterfly, a butterfly flitting and fluttering about, happy with himself and doing as he pleased. He didn't know that he was Zhuangzi. Suddenly he woke up and there he was, solid and unmistakable Zhuangzi. But he didn't know if he was Zhuangzi who had dreamt he was a butterfly, or a butterfly dreaming that he was Zhuangzi."

The father of modern philosophy, René Descartes, worried about the possibility that we are conned on a massive scale.[15] One of his thought experiments is about an "evil genius" who is perpetually engaged in deceiving us, so that we move from illusion to illusion, never getting things right, no matter how the world seems. Imagine an unholy combination of Count Lustig, Harry Houdini, and Mephistopheles. If there were such an evil genius, we would have no way of detecting it; we could never figure out the con.

With the Rumanian money box, Lustig's marks were convinced that a genuine $100 bill was a fake, produced by the box. After he moved into actual counterfeiting, the marks were convinced that a fake $100 bill was genuine. Both times they were persuaded by the evidence of their senses (the bill looks, feels, and smells genuine), coupled with a background knowledge of the world (there are $100 bills and currency is made by some kind of printing process). Since the money you got from Count Lustig was sometimes real and sometimes phony, and you can't tell the difference, it was merely good luck if your evidence led you to a true belief about the note in your hand.

Descartes's evil genius idea more generally decouples any link between our evidence and reality. There are all kinds of hypotheses that explain your experiences—drugs, dreaming, demons, a world outside of your mind that your perceptions accurately represent—and you can't figure out which one is right based on experience. Closer, more careful scrutiny of our perceptions won't help, much like close study of a mirror won't reveal what is on the other side. Compelling experiences are the very mechanism used by the successful con artist. The skeptical threat is that they can be made so bullet-proof that if we get things right at all, it's just a matter of luck.

A form of epistemic luck also turns up with the skeptical problem of the criterion.[16] Imagine that you are doing business with Count Lustig, and you want to make sure that the $100 bill he just handed you is genuine. You certainly aren't going to take him at his word. There're two basic ways you can proceed. The first is to assume that you already have some genuine examples of $100 bills. You take Lustig's note and compare it with your real currency to see how well it matches up—does it have the watermarks, security threads, the right kind of paper, textured engraving, and so on? So you start with authentic bills and try to work out a reliable method to separate the good bills from the bad ones. That's the approach of particularism.

The other way to decide about Lustig's $100 is to begin by assuming that you already have an excellent method for distinguishing between good bills and bad ones. Perhaps you have one of those testing pens that cashiers use, which uses iodine ink to react with the starches present in photocopier paper but not banknote paper. All you need to do is apply your method and it will start dividing currency into the real and the phony. That's the approach of methodism.

Particularism assumes that you already have some $100 bills you are sure are real. The task to be done is working out the method of detecting fakes. Methodism comes at it from the opposite direction. It assumes that you have a valid testing procedure and you just need to use it to pick out the genuine $100s. You may notice a bit of a problem here. Particularism assumes you can already tell the difference between real bills and phony ones. That's how you know you have some examples of genuine Benjamins. Which is to say, particularism works only by presupposing that you have some reliable method of picking out the true from the false. Methodism, on the other hand, presupposes that you already have some samples of real bills—that's how you're able to decide among different methods to detect counterfeits and figure out what system is the trustworthiest one. So particularism can work only if you already have a reliable method; in other words, methodism is logically prior to particularism. On the other hand, methodism will work only if you already have samples of bills you are positive are genuine; in other words, particularism is logically prior to methodism. We wind up with a vicious circle, as given in Figure 5.1.

The solution to the money wheel is that the Federal Bureau of Engraving and Printing (BEP) makes the money. It is an independent guarantor of which bills are real ones and which are not. That means we can be particularists, stand at the end of printing press in the BEP, and

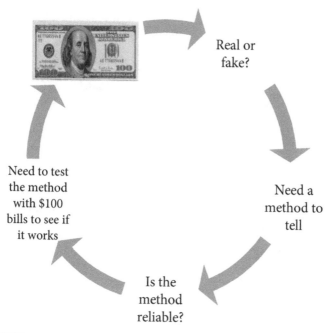

**FIGURE 5.1** The money wheel.

Real or fake?

Need a method to tell

Is the method reliable?

Need to test the method with $100 bills to see if it works

be certain that $100 bills rolling toward us are authentic. The Treasury worried that if there were too many fake Lustig bills in circulation that they would undermine the currency system itself—the bad bills would poison the good ones. Analogously, instead of separating money into piles of real and fake, we want to separate our beliefs into two piles: true and false. As with currency, the bad beliefs tend to poison the good ones, so we need to identify, and throw away, the bad ones.

We don't make the truth like the BEP makes the money, so there is no independent guarantor of what's true. For any belief you care to offer, we can ask whether the belief is true or false. To figure it out we'll need a method of telling the true from the false. Of course, we want a trustworthy method that will reliably give us accurate results. Let's say that we go with the scientific method. That's a reliable method only if it usually separates true claims from false one. The only way to be sure that the scientific method is correctly separating true beliefs from false ones is if we *already* know which are which. But that's the very question we started with!

As Figure 5.2 shows, we are caught in the circle again. This time with no way out. If we pick methodism, we're just assuming without reason that

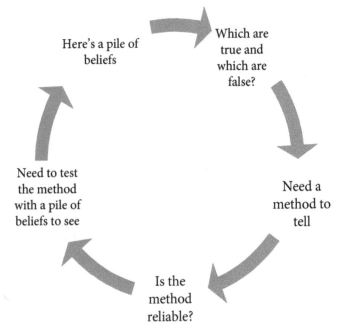

FIGURE 5.2 The wheel of beliefs.

the method we've chosen is trustworthy and can consistently separate the true beliefs from the false ones. Getting the method right would be a lucky guess. If we decide to be particularists, then we are begging the question in the other direction with the unsupported assumption that we have some true beliefs in hand. Since we don't already have a good method for choosing those beliefs, again it is just luck if we wind up starting out with true beliefs instead of false ones. Both classical Cartesian skepticism and the problem of the criterion are battlegrounds in the war on luck.

Global skepticism is outcome luck gone berserk. The inferences from our evidence aren't slyly meddled with as we saw in Gettier-type examples, turning what ought to be knowledge into something less. The skeptical argument is that all of our inferences and even our putative evidence itself will get us to the truth only by accident. If we're particularists and reach into a grab bag of possible beliefs to begin our reasoning and come out with a fistful of truths, it was no more than a lucky door prize. If we're methodists, then it's just the same thing, only starting with methods of reasoning instead of beliefs. Either way we can never be sure of our success. Radical skepticism breaks any ties between our evidence and reality, like a vandal who mixes up all the street signs in a town and leaves the tourists wandering confused. In such a case it is luck alone to get to your destination. Yet we are blameless; we do all that we can to gain knowledge and still fail through no fault of our own.

Let's leave the skeptical problem aside. Circumstantial luck also has an epistemic analogue. Even when proper reasoning and careful observations do yield knowledge, it may be just good luck that we are in a position to acquire it. Luck sees to it whether one becomes a Jew or a Nazi and whether one wins the genetic lottery or loses it. In that way it determines not only the goodness or badness of our lives, but our own moral character as well. Whether the truth about something is even within the scope of what you think is worth considering, that too is fixed by luck. Our capacities as inquirers seem as open to caprice as our capacities for living well and doing good.

It's not hard to find local-scale examples of circumstantial epistemic luck.[17] A few years ago, the zoo in war-torn Gaza saw its sole zebra die. It would have cost $30,000 to bring in a new zebra through the smugglers' tunnels that supply Gaza with most of its goods, a price that was well beyond the reach of a zoo that struggles to keep its animals fed. What they decided to do was fake one. The zookeepers took an ordinary donkey, cut its hair short, and painted on zebra stripes using human hair dye.

Their "locally made" zebra was quite successful, fooling schoolchildren who had never seen a real zebra, and most of the adults as well, although the zoo director conceded that a couple of sharp university students had spotted the fakery.[18]

Suppose that the Gaza "zebra" were adopted by a harem of real zebras. One of the evolutionary advantages of their stripes is motion dazzle—it's tough for predators to pick out any particular target from the harem when what they see is a mass of flickering stripes. No individual stands out. Now imagine you are out on a photo safari and see the zebras grazing on the savannah, painted donkey included. You point to one of the real zebras and correctly identify it as such. Do you know that you are looking at a zebra? You are in Africa getting a good look at a real zebra and believe that it is a zebra. It sure sounds like knowledge. Except for the fact that you could have so easily gotten it wrong. Like a lion confused by all those stripes, you might well have pointed to the painted donkey and called it a zebra. It is just luck that you didn't, and getting the truth by luck isn't the same as knowing it.[19]

In this case it is bad circumstantial luck that undercuts your knowledge. Identifying that zebra should have been knowledge, ought to have been knowledge, and would have been knowledge except for that damn painted donkey. But circumstances conspired against you. Well, painted donkeys are not all over the place. Like Gettier cases, perhaps this is just an anomalous speed bump in the road to genuine knowledge. Unfortunately, there's a way to scale up the problem of circumstantial epistemic luck.

## The Overton Window

No one thinks that every idea should be considered. No one thinks that every argument merits refutation or even evaluation. There are vast realms of beliefs most sincerely held by other human beings—concepts and opinions to which they have pledged their lives and sacred honor—that you summarily dismiss without a pang of guilt. This attitude is perfectly reasonable and even necessary. Physicians don't bother to examine energy chakras or chi. Marxists don't take seriously, as a genuinely possible true story of the world, the contention that capitalism is the most virtuous and efficient means yet devised to lift peasants out of poverty. Biologists take no more notice of creationists than they do the barking of the neighbor's annoying dog, no matter how convinced the dog is that he is saying something worthwhile. Theories are like perceptions; we are overwhelmed with a blooming, buzzing confusion beyond assimilation and have to do some hard winnowing out to have any coherent sense of things.

We don't decide what to pay attention to and what to ignore based on reason, precisely because what we only reason about the things we give our attention to. As soon as Sam Harris or Richard Dawkins takes a look at the latest Papal bull, if only to dismiss it, they have already taken it seriously enough to read, consider, and reject. In other words, they have *already* rationally engaged it, which is the opposite of ignoring. Attending to things brings them within the sphere of reason. So how do we draw the boundary between the ideas we're considering and those that are beyond the pale, if it is not by reason? That's one problem. Possibly more troubling is this: What if the truth falls into the category of ideas we're dismissing as too crazy to take seriously?

Joseph P. Overton was a lawyer working for Mackinac Center for Public Policy, a libertarian think tank in Michigan, when he developed a handy way to characterize the range of ideas that are considered within the limits of reasonable discussion. The window of discourse in a political discussion could range from those that are mostly on the right to mostly on the left, but extremist views are outside that window and not worth considering. Despite sounding like the title of a Robert Ludlum thriller, his proposal has come to be called The Overton Window. Overton originally set his ideas along the political dimension of the degree of government control, as in Table 5.1.

Overton's original plan of setting the range of ideas along the dimension of government control/anarchy is not essential to his fundamental insight. The Overton Window can explain the range of legitimate ideas along any number of different dimensions. The boundaries of the Overton Window are the boundaries of the ideas it is socially acceptable to believe. Beyond that frontier are the nutjobs, cranks, and wacko fringe. In this way it fixes the range of what, within your peer group, is a belief worth considering. People at the top of the window are more likely to turn up their noses at the people at the bottom, and conversely, but they see each other —more or less—as legitimate adversaries to debate. Like a Renaissance nautical map, beyond the borders are monsters.[20]

**TABLE 5.1** The Overton Window.

Complete Statism/ government control

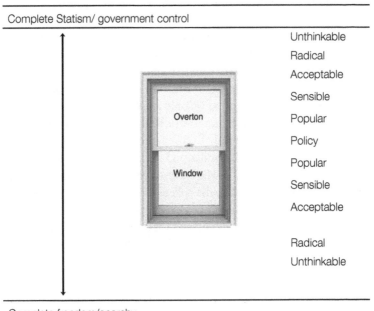

| | Unthinkable |
| --- | --- |
| | Radical |
| | Acceptable |
| | Sensible |
| Overton | Popular |
| | Policy |
| | Popular |
| Window | Sensible |
| | Acceptable |
| | Radical |
| | Unthinkable |

Complete freedom/anarchy

Public debates about homosexuality are a good example of the Overton Window. Consider Table 5.2.

Until recently, the Overton Window for ideas about homosexuality in the West looked something like the gray part of Table 5.2. Policy was that homosexual behavior was legal and accepted, but there were no legal or social protections for couples, which meant that filing joint taxes and collecting alimony wasn't possible, and various other things like hospital visitations, child adoption, and custody were very complicated. At the extreme of ideas loosely tolerated in society was the very liberal idea that homosexuality should be fully normalized and tolerated and the very conservative idea that it should be illegal even if that law is not vigorously enforced. The people closest to the middle—the pro-civil union folks, and those who thought being gay is some kind of bizarre anomaly and possible mental disorder—had to take each other seriously if they wanted to debate gay rights. Both incentivizing homosexuality and punishing gays or compelling them to undergo therapy were ideas only held by fringe extremists.

**TABLE 5.2** The traditional Overton Window for homosexuality.

| | |
|---|---|
| Unthinkable | Compulsory homosexuality/gay marriage |
| Radical | Homosexuality socially or legally incentivized |
| Acceptable | Homosexuality fully normalized and unremarkable |
| Sensible | Gay couples allowed to marry |
| Popular | Gay couples allowed civil unions |
| Policy | Homosexual behavior mostly legal and accepted, but no protections for couples |
| Popular | Homosexuality seen as weird and anomalous, possible mental disorder |
| Sensible | Homosexual behavior technically illegal under antiquated regulations but widely tolerated |
| Acceptable | Homosexual behavior illegal and sporadically prosecuted |
| Radical | Homosexual behavior severely punished or subject to forced psychotherapy and medication |
| Unthinkable | Homosexuals summarily executed |

It wasn't that long ago that the Overton Window was lower. Recall that in the 1950s the British government forced psychotropic medication on the great logician and cryptologist Alan Turing to "cure" his homosexuality. That decision led to his suicide. In the West, the window is now higher, with gay marriage not only sensible or popular, but policy. What happened to Turing is now seen as a horrific crime against a war hero. In Yemen, Saudi Arabia, Iran, Somalia, and several other countries, the window remains so much lower that homosexuality merits the death penalty.[21]

The gray area in Table 5.3 more closely represents the current Overton Window in the West. One might quibble about the details or the exact boundaries, but there's no doubt that 5.3 more closely represents the current state of affairs than 5.2.

Before anyone starts to think that the Overton Window is really a chart of progress, here's a silly example (Table 5.4) to disabuse you of that suspicion.

**TABLE 5.3** The current Overton Window for homosexuality.

| | |
|---|---|
| Unthinkable | Compulsory homosexuality/gay marriage |
| Radical | Homosexuality socially or legally incentivized |
| Popular | Homosexuality fully normalized and unremarkable |
| Policy | Gay couples allowed to marry |
| Popular | Gay couples allowed civil unions |
| Sensible | Homosexual behavior mostly legal and accepted, but no protections for couples |
| Acceptable | Homosexuality seen as weird and anomalous, possible mental disorder |
| Radical | Homosexual behavior technically illegal under antiquated regulations but widely tolerated |
| Radical | Homosexual behavior illegal and sporadically prosecuted |
| Unthinkable | Homosexual behavior severely punished or subject to forced psychotherapy and medication |
| Unthinkable | Homosexuals summarily executed |

**TABLE 5.4** The artichoke Overton Window.

| | |
|---|---|
| Unthinkable | Eating artichokes forbidden under penalty of law |
| Radical | Artichokes are, at best, a bizarre regional food akin to durian fruit or kæstur hákarl (Icelandic fermented shark). |
| Sensible | Artichokes are kind of strange and it is odd to like them |
| Popular | Artichokes are OK |
| Policy | Artichokes are delicious |
| Popular | Artichokes are seriously underrated and everyone should eat more of them |
| Sensible | Artichokes are the Best. Vegetable. Ever. |
| Radical | Artichokes should be in every dish |
| Unthinkable | Artichokes should be our sole source of food |

The United Council of Artichoke Growers has an interest in pushing the window lower, so that anyone who thinks eating artichokes is a strange thing to do is seen as a radical. That's the point of public relations and marketing, whether it is trying to move the window on homosexuality or artichokes—to turn the sensible into the popular, make radical what was once acceptable, and make acceptable what was once radical. It is complex sociological forces only tenuously engaged with evidence-based reasoning that move the Overton Window.

While Overton's interests were in public policy and in understanding the contours of public sentiment, the Overton Window is also a useful way to sort out one's own personal range of what's rationally acceptable. A Hindu Brahman won't even consider the barbecue enthusiasm of a Texas cattleman; it's not an idea that deserves to be entertained, much less given the honor of a refutation. A devotee of the World Naked Bike Ride is not going to earnestly consider the Amish view that buttons are too worldly and showy. When an idea is outside the boundaries delimited by your Overton Window, it is *ignored*. Furthermore, it is properly ignored. No one wants to waste their time taking the beliefs of crackpots and extremists seriously.

The problem is that sometimes—rarely, maybe—the crackpots are right. A proposal that you are legitimately ignoring because it lives in crazytown could in fact turn out to be the truth. In 1934, at the height of the Depression, Walt Disney mortgaged his own house to finance a $1.5 million feature-length *cartoon*. No one at the time thought that cartoons were good for anything other than funny short subjects, and here Disney was spending close to a thousand times the annual income of the average movie patron on one. Everyone, including his wife Lillian and his business partner/brother Roy Disney, tried to talk him out of it, and the rest of the Hollywood movie industry derided his plan as "Disney's Folly." But Disney was right. *Snow White and the Seven Dwarfs* has earned close to a billion inflation-adjusted dollars, Walt Disney won an Oscar, and the American Film Institute named it the greatest American animated film of all time.

One pleasing result is that the notion of the Overton Window promises to explain intractable disagreement. When someone's ideas are outside of your window, you refuse to engage, and they refuse to engage with you for the same reason. If those are narrow windows—the range of acceptable ideas is very small—then there's rapid polarization. "You think artichokes are *weird*? Thou clay-brained guts, thou knotty-pated fool, thou whoreson obscene greasy tallow-catch." "Wait, you think everyone should eat *more* artichokes? From Hell's heart I stab at thee; for hate's sake I spit my last breath at thee." Even small differences get magnified into open war. Of course, it is easy in hindsight to see that tiny doctrinal differences in the Christian theologies of the sixteenth century were not worth decades of war and burning people at the stake. It's much harder to recognize the same social forces and structural similarities in contemporary political debates.

Opening the window a bit wider will help, since both parties would then be receptive in principle to a bigger selection of artichoke-related ideas, and they might therefore find some common ground or be in a position to convince each other. You can't throw caution to the winds and allow every single idea the privilege of rational evaluation, though. There's still the problem of cognitive expense. Nobody has enough time or brain power to think through everything; you might as well try to read every book in the Library of Congress. Maybe the best plan is just to be as open-minded as you can. Good ideas and true propositions that are outside of your Overton Window remain off the grid, and a radical proposal like a full-length movie animated with expensive hand-painted cels will be dismissed out of hand. There's really no way around it—we can't give honest consideration to every wacky idea that comes down the pike. We'll still think those ideas come from someone who stopped payment on his reality check.

The openness, closedness, or general location of the Overton Window in epistemic possibility space is largely a matter of circumstantial luck. For example, there is such a strong correlation between the religious, political, and broadly scientific beliefs of parents and those of their children that it is apostasy, not conformity, that needs explaining. If your parents are conservative, then you are very likely conservative, if they are liberal then you are very likely to be liberal. If you are born and raised in Saudi Arabia, it is not coincidence that you are a Muslim; it is not a viewpoint you came to by independent reason. Sunni vs. Shiite might be a debate worth having, but atheism is well outside the window. The sorts of ideas on all kinds of topics that you think are radical or even unthinkable are so heavily determined by circumstance that it is just good luck if what's actually true is within your Overton Window.

Another way to see this point is the physicist Max Planck's remark that "a new scientific truth does not triumph by convincing its opponents and making them see the light, but rather because its opponents die, and a new generation grows up that is familiar with it."[22] A more concise paraphrase is *science advances one funeral at a time*. The luminiferous aether is not totally defeated by relativity theory until its last supporter is buried. Even within what one might think is the purely rational community of scientists, the movement of the Overton Window is not a matter of evidence alone, but of sociological forces that shift what was once radical into what is now sensible.

The Overton Window illustrates the ubiquity of circumstantial epistemic luck. How troubled we should be by this sort of luck depends on whether you think that there's something meritorious about having knowledge, whether you know something only if it is a credit to you. You don't really deserve praise for having a true belief that is no more than the fortunate result of your socialization, any more than you would deserve praise for inherited wealth.[23]

# Serendipity

Epistemic privilege is in some ways like moral privilege. Moral privilege, recall, was the idea of possessing advantages because of an unjust systematic differential distribution of unearned or unmerited advantages or benefits. Just as there was nothing wrong with having moral privilege, there's nothing wrong with having epistemic privilege. There's nothing unseemly about fortuitously being in the right place at the right time, or living in an environment in which the truth is within your Overton Window. What's bad is lacking privilege, of being unfortunate enough that the truth is in that category of ideas you consider radical or unthinkable, and so you miss out on the opportunity of gaining it.

Universal access to education is supposed to help, to reduce the chance that someone won't have access to the truth because of bad circumstantial luck. Equality of education aims to help with reducing epistemic underprivilege just as equality of treatment under the law aims to reduce moral underprivilege. A common complaint about public schools in every country is that their quality is uneven, and so children lucky enough to attend the good schools will perpetually outshine (on average) the children who went to inferior schools. In the aggregate, their level of education has less to do with individual pluck and initiative and more with the roll of the dice. Everyone thinks the fix is to make all the schools good ones. Really the hope is to achieve the dream of Lake Wobegon: a place where everyone is above average. Math is going to stop us from making every school above average, but presumably we could find ways to reduce the width of the bell curve, and produce narrower standard deviations. Make it so the worst schools are not that much worse than the best ones. In large societies diverse in population density, wealth, native language, ethnic background, and religious and political attitudes, that's a lot easier said than done. Suppose we could pull it off.

Fortuna isn't thwarted that easily. No matter how much education one has, or how good it is, or how diligent one is as an inquirer, luck seems to find a way. If improved education eliminated bad circumstantial luck, then the best educated in a society ought to be free of it entirely. The scholars, the scientists, the epistemically privileged should be cured of the taint of luck. But they aren't.

The May 30, 1953 issue of *Nature* contained a paper by James Watson and Francis Crick in which they gave the first correct description of the double-helix structure of DNA, the large molecule that encodes the blueprint of life. They explained its structural stability, how it can mutate, and how the molecule can replicate itself. The Nobel Laureate Sir Peter Medawar has said that "it is simply not worth arguing with anyone so obtuse as not to realize that this complex of discoveries is the greatest achievement of science in the twentieth century." In 1951 Jim Watson left America for England to be a postdoctoral researcher at Cambridge. There was nothing particularly noteworthy about him that anyone would expect him to be world-famous by 1953. How did that happen?

Certainly, diligence and cleverness were essential ingredients to Watson's success, but so was the role played by circumstantial luck. For one, Watson was lucky to have pursued science at all. According to Medawar, "In England a schoolboy of Watson's precocity and style of genius would probably been steered towards literary studies." Moreover, Watson was lucky to have entered a privileged inner circle of scientists and made privy to cutting-edge research prior to its publication, well before he had done anything to deserve such access. Most importantly, Watson was lucky to have made friends, and pursued collaborative research, with the brilliant Francis Crick. Watson and Crick were like

Lennon and McCartney—their creative insight was a joint product that neither would have achieved on his own.[24]

Watson may have been lucky, but his good fortune was a background condition for his success. The *discoveries* of Watson and Crick weren't due to luck. Indeed, the two were feverishly trying to unlock the secrets of DNA and were relieved when a competitor's idea fell through and failed to scoop them. On a traditional picture, human knowledge advances like the building of a cathedral, with scores of scientific laborers cutting and laying blocks and a handful of masters designing naves or bell towers. The sanctuaries of biology, chemistry, physiology all arise by different designs, but are still unified in their engineering and purpose. The history of science is merely the archaeology of finding a Romanesque chapel buried under the gothic edifice above. No one builds cathedrals by luck, and it is Athena, not Fortuna, who is the patron of the mighty temple of knowledge. Watson and Crick were personally fortunate to contribute to the building, but their scientific contribution itself was not luck.

The citadel of knowledge is an ennobling picture that, no matter how well it holds up at the large scale,[25] belies the unexpected and coincidental discoveries that cement the whole.

In 1302, the Persian poet Ab'ul Hasan Yamīn ud-Dīn Khusrau wrote *Hasht-Bihisht*, or "The Eight Paradises," a poem that involved seven princesses telling a different story each day of the week. One of the stories they told was about three princes of Serendip (the ancient Persian name for Sri Lanka) who were sent abroad by their father. The princes have a knack for keen observation. They notice that something chewed the grass on one side of the road, but left the greener, more attractive grass on the other side untouched. They spot lumps of masticated grass about the size of a camel's tooth and see the prints of three hooves, with a fourth being dragged. On the left side of the road ants feasted on butter and right side had honey covered in flies. They spot various other things of this sort as well.

The princes weren't especially looking for anything camel-related, but when they run into a merchant who was missing one, they say, "oh, you mean the lame, one-eyed camel who is missing a tooth, carrying honey on one side and butter on the other, and is being ridden by a pregnant woman? That camel? Haven't seen it." Naturally they are charged with theft. The three princes story was told and re-told by various people, including Horace Walpole and Voltaire, and it's not hard to see the princes' method of close observation and inference as a precursor to Poe's Auguste Dupin and Conan Doyle's Sherlock Holmes.

Serendipitous discoveries come about when someone is paying attention, or even looking for something, but nevertheless encounters the unanticipated. Columbus was looking for a new passage to the Indies, but found a new continent in its place. Mike Smith, a Welsh gardener, was trying to develop a novel entry for the Chelsea flower show and accidentally created the world's hottest chili pepper instead.[26] There are long lists of scientific discoveries that came about serendipitously.[27] Possibly the most famous is Sir Alexander Fleming's discovery of penicillin.

Fleming was a bacteriologist, working with Staphylococcus, a bacterium that can cause various ailments, including boils, sore throats, and food poisoning. Fleming was also a bit shambolic. In August, 1928, he went off on holiday while leaving various uncovered and unwashed petri dishes lying around his lab. When he returned September 3, he found that some of the dishes had gotten moldy. Closer inspection showed dots of Staphylococcus colonies, except where the mold spots were. Apparently, the mold was secreting something—mold juice, Fleming called it—that was killing off Staphylococcus. Fleming lucked out that some Penicillium notatum spores had floated in and settled in just the right environment in his slovenly lab.

Of course, Fleming had been looking for something like Penicillin for over a decade, and he had enough sense to understand what he was seeing in the petri dish. So maybe it wasn't all that lucky. Like looking for your lost keys all over the house, it is not luck when you find them in the couch cushions. You had been looking, after all. On the other hand, as Medawar observes, most antibiotics "are murderously toxic, because they arrest the growth of bacteria by interfering with metabolic processes of a kind that bacteria have in common with higher organisms. Penicillin is comparatively innocuous because it happens to interfere with a synthetic process peculiar to bacteria, namely the synthesis of a distinctive structural element of the bacterial cell wall."[28] Fleming was lucky that the right kind of mold juice grew in his dirty dishes.

Serendipitous discoveries are examples of society's most highly educated citizens devoting themselves to science and the advancement of knowledge, and still being subject to circumstantial luck when they finally get hold of the truth. When even the achievements of the cognitive elite are so infected with luck, it is hard to imagine what antibiotic will cure the contagion. It may be that how these stories are told determines how we view them. Is someone like Fleming a heroic scientist struggling against the formless chaos of ignorance, or is he a lucky slob who serendipitously stumbled onto a great discovery? The next chapter will investigate the question of narrative framing much more closely.

# Out of Control

All right, epistemic luck, in its various forms, looks like a real and present danger to knowledge. The *epistemic* part of that we've been trying to explore so far this chapter. Let's turn to the *luck* part. What's the notion of luck at work here? So far in this book we've examined the probability, modal, and control theories of luck. We saw in Chapter 3 that those theories have deep intrinsic problems. Let's set those aside and focus on what could possibly capture the idea of epistemic luck. Chapter 4 demonstrated that the modal and probability theories aren't any good for moral luck. Unless we adopt the control theory, moral luck turns out to not be a real thing at all. Actually, even if we accept the control theory we run that risk, since it might well collapse into one of the other ideas about luck. Nonetheless, let's assume for the sake of argument that the control theory of luck is autonomous and can stand on its own.

Remember, the control idea is that something is lucky for you only if its occurrence is outside of your control. Is the control theory the thing to use to explain *epistemic* luck? No, and for a surprising reason: it makes everything about knowledge a matter of luck. Almost nothing about knowledge is within your control. Take belief for example. You look outside the window and as a result believe that it is a warm sunny day. Did you voluntarily decide to form that belief? Could you decide to believe instead that it is dark and snowing? It's extraordinarily unlikely that the answer to either question is yes. Mostly our beliefs are just caused in us by what we encounter. A direct perception of a warm sunny day produces that belief without any voluntary choosing. It's hard, if not impossible, to overrule that testimony.

You might deliberate over what action to take, but it is far more difficult to deliberate over what to believe, and then have the results of that deliberation actually cause your belief. Pascal's famous Wager is in part about this very issue. In his *Pensées*, Pascal argues that it is rational to believe that God exists. His argument goes like this. There are only two possibilities: God exists or he does not. If there is no God but you mistakenly believe in him, Pascal reasons, you lose nothing by your error. If you correctly deny his existence, you gain nothing by being right. On the other hand, suppose there is a God. In that case, if you (accurately) believe in him then you win big, and if you erroneously deny his existence then you lose big. Given this set up, Pascal concludes that you have excellent decision-theoretic reasons—it is in your best interest as you yourself conceive of it—to believe that God exists.

At the end of his discussion, Pascal considers someone who reads his wager and responds along the lines of "you know, Blaise, that's a terrific argument. You've completely convinced me that I should believe in God. I have nothing to lose and everything to gain. The problem is that I just can't get myself to do it. It's like trying to believe that you are the Incredible Hulk just because you promise me a suitcase full of cash. It's definitely in my best interest to believe that you are the Incredible Hulk, but I just can't pull it off. I mean, I could lie and tell you that I think you are the Hulk, but I still wouldn't really believe it. Money aside, it's just too incredible to believe that you are Incredible."

Pascal thinks that's a serious problem. We *don't* have voluntary control over our beliefs. Pascal offers a solution that, after all his subtle reasoning, is surprising. Go hang around with the Christians, he writes, go to mass, have some holy water. That's what everyone else did to first start believing. You'll come around. Pascal thinks that at best we have a kind of indirect control over our beliefs.

Even Pascal's proposed indirect control must be uncommon. When Bill Wilson founded Alcoholics Anonymous in 1935, it was because he wanted to overcome his own drinking problem but found that he couldn't do it alone. Even though Bill W. called alcoholism "a death sentence," willpower wasn't enough to get him to stop drinking. It was only by working together with other alcoholics who also wanted to quit that they could find a system of mutual support that enabled them to get sober. It's extraordinarily hard to overcome addiction, long-standing habits, and powerful first-order desires, and the failure rate is high. As with desires, it can take a lot to change beliefs, and you may not be able to do it at all. Willpower alone—merely deciding to believe something—is not very likely to work. In *Through the Looking Glass*, the Red Queen declared, to Alice's amazement, that she could believe in half a dozen impossible things before breakfast. While it is ridiculous to believe impossible things, it is just as ludicrous to believe that the Red Queen had as much command over her beliefs as over her subjects. That's what gives the scene its absurdist humor.

We're assuming that something is lucky when its occurrence is outside of your control. It follows that to whatever degree you don't have control of what you believe, it's lucky when things pan out and your beliefs turn out to be true (and unlucky if they are false). To the extent that you don't have control over your beliefs, they are infected with luck. Since belief is an essential ingredient of knowledge, it too is largely a matter of luck.

Belief is part of knowledge, but so is truth. You may have little control over your beliefs, you have none at all over what is true. Objective facts that you believe like *it is a warm sunny day, Canada is north of Mexico,* and *the universe is more than a month old* all hold no matter what you do. Act however you like, those things are still going to be true; you have no control over them at all. You don't even have much, if any, control over subjective facts. It may be true that you like Islay scotches more than Speyside, or think Star Trek is better than Star Wars, but you certainly have no direct command over whether those are true facts about you. As we saw earlier, the best you can hope for is indirect and limited control, if that. Neither your beliefs nor what's true are within your control. All that remains to knowledge is whatever the proper connection is between your beliefs and the truth. Do we have any control over that connection?

Everyone has her own secret sauce for what elevates the rustic dish of true belief to the banquet of knowledge. Some epistemic chefs think the key ingredient is adding the requirement that whatever means you used to acquire your belief, it was a reliable method. Beliefs are justified by reliable methods. A true belief that was reliably formed is knowledge. Of course, you might have no clue at all about how reliable your methods are, whether you're using the scientific method, the method of least squares, or the eeny-meeny-miny-moe method. A second idea is this: if you couldn't have easily gone wrong, then you have knowledge. In other words, your true belief is modally safe. For example, when you look out of the window and see it is a warm sunny day, it would have been pretty hard to get it wrong and come away complaining about the vile winter weather. Here too, you might have no sense at all about whether your beliefs are modally safe ones or not.

Those are two ideas about what we've been loosely calling "justification." Here's a third. It could be that what converts true belief into knowledge is when your own virtuous character as a believer connects you with the truth. Knowledge is a kind of achievement from ability, the cognitive analogue of hitting a baseball or roller skating without falling down. Kant thought you couldn't accidentally do the right thing, since it had to spring from your good intent. Maybe you can't accidentally gain knowledge either, if it has to be the result of your mad knowledge-acquiring skills. Once again, you probably have no idea about whether you are some kind of saintly cognizer with only the purest of epistemic characters.

All of these ideas about the secret sauce have one thing in common: they set up a connection between your belief and the truth that you might not even know is there. Here's the kicker. You don't have any meaningful control over whether some connection holds when you're not even aware of it. The upshot is that you don't have any more control over whether your beliefs are justified than you do over whether they are true, or if you even have those beliefs. Just as we would say of someone who cannot control any of her limbs that she can't control her body, likewise we can't control any of the parts of knowledge, so we have no control over knowledge itself.

Luck poses all sorts of problems for knowledge. There's the difficulty of showing why knowledge is better than a lucky guess, the outcome luck threats of the Gettier problem and global skepticism, and the circumstantial luck of the Overton Window and scientific serendipity. Those are bad enough, but at least there is still some hope of salvation. Tossing the control theory of luck into this stew is like tossing in a grenade—now knowledge is *inherently* lucky; it is so riddled with the shrapnel of luck that it is beyond saving at all. To sum up so far: moral luck feels like it is a real thing. But if we adopt the probability or modal theories of luck then it doesn't exist. So we have to accept the control theory to preserve moral luck.[29] However, if we use the control theory of luck in epistemology, it turns out that everything about knowledge is pure luck, and knowledge doesn't exist. Damned if we do, damned if we don't.

# Divide and Conquer

The obvious move here is to declare that there are two kinds of luck: one kind has to do with a lack of control, and the other kind has to do with modal fragility or improbability.[30] Language is a slippery, tricky thing, though. It's tough to tell when the same word really means different things, or even when words are synonymous. "I'm sorry" and "I apologize" mean the same thing—except at a funeral. Other words are like the Roman god Janus, with two faces pointing in opposite directions.

"To trim" can mean "to remove things from," as in "I trimmed the grass." It can also mean "to add things to," as in "Let's trim the Christmas tree." Usain Bolt is fast, unless you hold him fast. The stone house will weather the storm, although the stone will eventually weather away. It's easy to be mad about (angry with/in love with) contronyms, the ideal form of ambiguous words.

We shouldn't rush to insist on ambiguity, though. Often that's just a cop-out, a lawyerly ploy to get around something as plain as day.[31] President Bill Clinton was impeached for, more or less, trying that very thing. He was charged by Congress for lying under oath about having an affair with Monica Lewinsky. Clinton's lawyer had said in a deposition that "there is absolutely no sex of any kind in any manner, shape or form, [between Lewinsky and] President Clinton." Clinton was directly asked under oath if that statement was true. His infamous reply was, "It depends on what the meaning of the word 'is' is."

Clinton was instantly and robustly mocked, although he did have a point. There's a difference between "there is [at this moment or very recently] no sex between Lewinsky and Clinton," and "there is [at any point in history] no sex between them." It's the same difference between "the sky is cloudy" and "the hypotenuse of a right triangle is the square root of the sum of the squares of the two remaining sides." The Pythagorean Theorem is true at every moment in time and but "the sky is cloudy" is not, even if it is true right now. Nonetheless, Clinton's attempt to draw attention to the difference between the tensed and tenseless senses of "is" was seen as a cheap dodge. One only imagines him trying that same argument with Hillary when he came home with lipstick on his collar.

"Bill, are you having an affair with another woman?"

Bill examined his trousers, and saw that he was wearing them. "Nope," he replied.

On the other hand, sometimes an appeal to ambiguity is exactly the right way to go. In 1907, the Harvard philosopher and psychologist William James opened his lecture *What Pragmatism Means* with a wonderfully homey example of settling a dispute through disambiguation.

> Some years ago, being with a camping party in the mountains, I returned from a solitary ramble to find everyone engaged in a ferocious metaphysical dispute. The corpus of the dispute was a squirrel—a live squirrel supposed to be clinging to one side of a tree-trunk; while over against the tree's opposite side a human being

was imagined to stand. This human witness tries to get sight of the squirrel by moving rapidly round the tree, but no matter how fast he goes, the squirrel moves as fast in the opposite direction, and always keeps the tree between himself and the man, so that never a glimpse of him is caught. The resultant metaphysical problem now is this: Does the man go round the squirrel or not? He goes round the tree, sure enough, and the squirrel is on the tree; but does he go round the squirrel? …

"Which party is right," I said, "depends on what you practically mean by 'going round' the squirrel. If you mean passing from the north of him to the east, then to the south, then to the west, and then to the north of him again, obviously the man does go round him, for he occupies these successive positions. But if on the contrary you mean being first in front of him, then on the right of him, then behind him, then on his left, and finally in front again, it is quite as obvious that the man fails to go round him, for by the compensating movements the squirrel makes, he keeps his belly turned towards the man all the time, and his back turned away. Make the distinction, and there is no occasion for any farther dispute. You are both right and both wrong according as you conceive the verb 'to go round' in one practical fashion or the other.[32]

Once James was able to make clear two different senses of "to go round," there was no longer any dispute to be had. James offered the squirrel story as an example of his pragmatic approach to "settling metaphysical disputes that otherwise might be interminable." That didn't work out to be quite the panacea that James had hoped for. Even in the squirrel case, James's solution did not make everyone a happy camper: "one or two of the hotter disputants called my speech a shuffling evasion, saying they wanted no quibbling or scholastic hair-splitting, but … just plain honest English."

It would be nice if we could simply run to the dictionary to settle debates about plain honest English. Unfortunately, dictionaries only report what lexicographers discover about how people use words, and the way words are used won't help much in discovering what the world is really like. If that were a good approach, then Newton or Einstein could have just looked up "gravity" and saved themselves a lot of effort. Or take a look at dictionary.com's definition of "murder": the unlawful premeditated killing of one human being by another. The Holocaust involved a lot of premeditated killing, but it was not unlawful under the Third Reich. Given the dictionary definition, it follows that the Nazis did not murder the Jews. When we wind up with a result that badly wrong, we have a good reason to think that the dictionary isn't going to tell us very much about what's going on in reality. It's not going to give us the true nature of gravity, murder, or luck.

We'll need a more systematic approach. Are there good theoretical reasons to think that "luck" is ambiguous? One thing we can try is to apply semantic tests for ambiguity and see whether "luck" passes them. There is no one universally accepted test, although one of the most popular is the contradiction test.[33] This is the idea. Some sentences that apparently contradict themselves really don't. There's just a superficial contradiction that dissolves when we realize that the sentence uses a word twice but with two different meanings. Here're a few examples.

1 This ball is not a ball.

2 Fido is a dog but not a dog.

3 Amber rented an apartment but did not rent an apartment.

4 Bruce Lee hit the man with a stick, but did not hit the man with a stick.

5 The barber shaves 20 times a day and yet always has a beard.

6 The man saw his wife drunk, but not drunk.

They are all superficially, syntactically contradictory. As soon as we realize that some of the words used have more than one distinct meaning, then the sentences can turn out to be true. It can be the case that the formal dance is not a sporting object. Fido is a domesticated carnivorous mammal with a long snout, an acute sense of smell, non-retractile claws, and a barking, howling, or whining voice, and is kept as a pet or for hunting, herding livestock, guarding, or other utilitarian purposes (Oxford English Dictionary), but Fido is not a male of the species. Amber is a landlord, not a tenant. Bruce Lee used his fists to hit a man who was wielding a stick. The barber is not miraculously hirsute—he merely shaves other men than himself. The sober man saw his drunken wife. All those sentences pass the contradiction test, which means that all have ambiguous parts.

Language is full of other kinds of weirdness. Take vagueness for example. A vague term is one that doesn't have sharp boundaries, like "aunt." That's vague as to whether she is your mother's or your father's sister, or possibly even sister-in-law. Or "purple." There's no precise point at which purple shades off into being purplish red or purplish blue. Or "middle-aged." There's no particular moment at which one ceases to be young and begins to be middle-aged, or stops being middle-aged and starts being old. Bob Hope quipped that middle age is when you still believe you'll feel better in the morning, but you're old when you stop buying green bananas. That may be accurate, but it is not exact.

Vague terms fail the contradiction test, as they should.

7   Your aunt is not your aunt.

8   That purple shirt is not purple.

9   A middle-aged man is not yet middle-aged.

Those sentences aren't just superficially contradictory—they are deeply and completely contradictory. There's no disambiguation that will save them. So what about "luck"? How does it fare on the contradiction test? Not well. It looks more like *aunt*, *purple*, and *middle-aged*.

10   Megan is lucky.

11   Megan is lucky but not lucky.

"Luck" is vague. Whether Megan is lucky or not could be at some imprecise border and open to interpretation. Suppose she accidentally left her wallet on a café table and walked to her car in the parking lot, only to realize she forgot her wallet. She's back at the café in five minutes and safely retrieves her wallet. Was she lucky to get it back? Maybe it's not completely clear.[34] None of that matters for the contradiction test, though. Make "lucky" as precise as you like. It still makes no sense to say that "Megan is lucky and unlucky."

There's more than one way to be lucky. Could that mean "luck" is ambiguous? In *The Three Musketeers*, d'Artagnan tells Porthos that he can't have all the privileges. "You know the saying: lucky in love, unlucky at cards. You're too lucky in love for the cards not to revenge themselves." Megan could be like Porthos: lucky in love but not in cards, and in that sense she is both lucky and unlucky. The apparent contradiction is just superficial after all, and maybe "luck" really is ambiguous.

Not so fast. What that example actually shows is the need for context. "Lucky in love, unlucky at cards" doesn't show an ambiguity in luck any more than "Luke won" is ambiguous. It could be true that Luke won (at tennis) but false that Luke won (at poker). Neither "won" nor "is lucky" are ambiguous in these cases. They are just unspecific, and that's yet again a different curious thing about language. For example, a description of a missed connection may be unspecific, such as "you were a tall rugby player on the District Line tube and we exchanged a look," but it is not ambiguous. It describes one unique person. Similarly, plenty of straightforward sentences can be pragmatically equivocal when there are unstated presuppositions. "The cops are coming" isn't ambiguous, but it can be an assertion, a warning, or an expression of relief, all depending on the situation.

All in all, luck is not ambiguous. If there is anything to luck, it is something univocal. There's not one kind of luck for moral luck and a different sort of luck for epistemic luck. There's, at most, just one kind. Unfortunately, that conclusion kicks us right back to our earlier antinomy. The worm in the apple is that there just isn't one notion of luck that helps us explain the seeming reality of moral luck while at the same time allowing the possibility of knowledge. By now it is starting to look as if luck is like medieval alchemy. We went as far as we could go with that way of understanding the world and perhaps the Renaissance will come if we turn our backs on the old ways. The psychology of luck will help us see why we were ever attracted to luck in the first place.

# 6 THE IRRATIONAL BIASES OF LUCK

*"Of course I don't believe in it, but I understand it brings you luck, whether you believe in it or not."*

**—PHYSICIST NEILS BOHR, AFTER BEING ASKED WHY HE HAD A HORSESHOE HANGING OVER HIS DOOR**[1]

Are you to blame for how your life turned out, or was it just a matter of bad luck? To what extent do you deserve praise for your successes instead of attributing them to the mere blessings of fortune? Every aspect of life seems riddled with good and bad luck, but all attempts so far to pin down just what luck might be have either failed outright or led to even more puzzles. Surely there is *some* sensible, intuitive notion of luck to be had. Maybe working out the psychology of when we think an event is a lucky one and when we do not is a new tool to use on luck. It could be that there is a cognitive cluster of coherent concepts that social science can unpack. Of course, it would be even more bothersome if it turns out that the way we decide this event is lucky or that one is unlucky is inconsistent, biased, or somehow irrational. That would be one final blow to the viability of luck.

## The Frame Shop

In the 1940s, the idea that the universe might have a beginning was generally regarded as radical, if not heretical. General relativity, along with an observably expanding universe, implied such a beginning, but it still seemed like speculative theorizing. Among those who took the idea seriously were the American physicists George Gamow, Ralph Alpher, and Robert Herman. In papers published in 1948, they argued that the Big Bang would have left a residual heat uniformly everywhere in the universe, and calculated the temperature to be 5 degrees Kelvin.[2] This afterglow—called the Cosmic Microwave Background—was a purely theoretical prediction, and the technology did not exist to detect it. Since this was also a period when few people accepted the Big Bang model, nobody else believed in these conjectures about the CMB radiation and Gamow, Alpher, and Herman went ignored.

Fast forward to the 1960s, when Arno Penzias and Robert Wilson were working at AT&T's Bell Labs, a private research division like today's X (formerly Google X) devoted to oddball basic science that might one day pay off. Penzias and Wilson thought they would spend some time using the underutilized radiotelescope at Crawford Hill, New Jersey, to study celestial radio sources. Before they could get properly started, they needed to work closely with the telescope, figure out its quirks, and in particular scrutinize it for noise. Signals from distant sources like quasars, far-off galaxies, and the like are so faint that they could easily be drowned out by a telescope that hums like a refrigerator or crackles like a drive-thru speaker. The Crawford Hill telescope was a state-of-the-art 6-meter radio horn antenna, so Penzias and Wilson expected the level of noise to be negligible.

They were wrong. They kept getting a low background noise. The problem was not so severe that it would affect their measurements, and most radio astronomers would have disregarded it and gone on with their work. Penzias and Wilson, however, were determined to figure out the strange faint signal. They pointed the telescope to the emptiest patch of space they could find. Still had the problem. They pointed it at New York City. Still had the problem. Morning, noon, night, summer, fall, winter, spring, none of that mattered. They tore into the telescope itself, looking for faulty wiring, bad electronics, poor contacts, anything. They came up with nothing. They went on for a year, discussing the problem with colleagues, chasing down every possibility, until at last they managed to piece it all together. The noise was everywhere, and it was the signal of the birth of the universe. Other researchers who had noisy signals during their radio astronomy surveys shrugged it off as a minor defect in their instruments they were prepared to tolerate. They lacked the sheer determination and doggedness to solve the mystery that allowed Penzias and Wilson to discover the CMB radiation.[3] Big Bang skeptics were at last convinced: the CMB was predicted by theory and confirmed by observation. Our universe began with a bang. For this tremendous discovery, Penzias and Wilson were awarded the Nobel Prize in Physics in 1978.

Told as above, Penzias and Wilson were determined scientists who, when confronted with an anomaly, stop at nothing to get to the bottom of it. It was their dogged tenacity, attention to minute detail, and relentless experimentalism that led to their great discovery and fame. Or was it? Here's another take on their tale, as presented by a humor writer for *Cracked* magazine.

Meet Arno Penzias and Robert Woodrow Wilson, two scientists who basically tripped into fame and glory.

Before the 1960s, scientists had no idea how the universe was created. Some were arguing for the Big Bang Theory. Others took up the much less scientific position of "It just fucking happened." However, a few of the Big Bang guys realized that they could find proof: If the universe really was born in a huge Michael Bay explosion, there would still be traces of post-explosion energy left over in space. Three cosmologists predicted that said traces of the Big Bang would be in the form of microwave radiation, and would be distributed pretty evenly across the universe at a temperature of 5-Kelvin. Unfortunately nobody could find it.

That is until 1964, when Wilson and Penzias were working on a new antenna at the Bell AT&T Telephone Labs in New Jersey. When they pointed their super-sensitive antenna out to the sky, they picked up a faint, strange radio signal coming from all around them. The brilliant physicists' first guess? That it was interference from pigeon shit.

After cleaning out the pigeon crap that had built up inside the antenna and shooting every pigeon in sight, the two found that the noise was still there. They ruled out radio interference from New York City, the military and, presumably, aliens. Then they finally heard about the theoretical microwave radiation that better physicists than them had predicted. One scientist, Robert Dicke, was about to design an experiment to find it. Upon getting the call from Penzias, he turned to his colleagues and said, "Well boys, we've been scooped." Which is scientist for "FUUUCK!"

For their extraordinary work in being really lucky, Penzias and Wilson won the Nobel Prize in Physics in 1978.[4]

The facts in both accounts are accurate. In the second version, though, Penzias and Wilson are humorously presented as a pair of scientific bumblers who make a great discovery by accident. They weren't looking for the CMB and didn't know what it was when they found it. So which is it? Are Penzias and Wilson heroic experimentalists or a pair of lucky chumps? It isn't the facts that determine the answer. Rather, it is the way the facts are arranged and the manner in which they are structured that lead to one interpretation over the other. Within a decade of the discovery of the CMB, psychologists were sorting out just how altering the presentation of the same information can drive people to opposite conclusions.

Classical economics assumes that actors are rational, selfish, and consistent.[5] It's easy to reflect on the carnival of human foibles and laugh at those foolish economists who think that our interactions are all logically coherent. However, these classical assumptions aren't as arbitrary as they seem. For one thing, if people aren't generally rational, then they can be turned into money pumps. For example, suppose that Robin has the following preferences.

**A** Robin prefers pie to cake. In fact, she would trade her piece of cake, plus a dollar, to get a slice of pie.

**B** Robin prefers an ice cream cone to pie. She would trade a slice of pie, plus a dollar, to get an ice cream cone.

**C** Robin prefers cake to an ice cream cone. She would trade an ice cream cone, plus a dollar, to get a piece of cake.

A dessert shop could cheerfully take all of Robin's money while giving her exactly what she wants. If most people were like Robin, then some smart and greedy economists could just suck up all the money as they constantly satisfy all the preferences of their targets. Because by-and-large we *can't* turn people into money pumps, it stands to reason that economic actors must be largely rational, and that there have to be some behavioral axioms (like having transitive preferences) that we all subconsciously follow. At least, that's the argument. Unfortunately, the beautiful economic hypothesis of rationality has been slayed by the ugly facts of human nature. Even the best of us are a lot more irrational than might be guessed.

The psychologists Daniel Kahneman and Amos Tversky were the frontrunners on showing the predictably irrational decision-making of our subconscious minds. In a series of papers starting in the 1970s they launched a flotilla of research into our hardwired heuristics and biases, and laid the foundations for behavioral economics. Cancer claimed Tversky at a young age, but Kahneman went on to win the Nobel Prize in Economics (2002) for their joint discoveries.

One of the biases they uncovered was framing.

The framing bias is revealed when people have opposite reactions to logically equivalent situations that are merely presented in different ways. Here are some classic examples.[6]

- Would you accept a gamble that offers a 10 percent chance to win $95 and a 90 percent chance to lose $5?

- Would you pay $5 to participate in a lottery that offers a 10 percent chance to win $100 and a 90 percent chance to win nothing?

Far more people are ready to say yes to the second question than to the first one, despite the fact that the two cases are identical—you have to decide whether to accept an uncertain prospect that will leave you richer by $95 or poorer by $5. Furthermore, the odds are the same both times. Why? Well, the second version only talks about winning, never about losing anything. Pay $5 to have a 10 percent chance at winning $100? Sure, that sounds good. But accepting a gamble with a 90 percent of losing $5? No way.

In another experiment, physicians were given statistics about two outcomes of two treatments for lung cancer: surgery and radiation. In the short term surgery is riskier than radiation, although the five-year survival rates are better with surgery. Half the participants were told about survival rates and the other half got the same information in terms of mortality rates. Here's how the short-term outcomes of surgery were described:

- The one-month survival rate is 90 percent.

- There is 10 percent mortality in the first month.

Surgery was much more popular when the outcomes were presented in terms of survival (84 percent of physicians preferred it) than when framed latterly as mortality rates (in which case 50 percent favored radiation). Here is the exact same scenario, evaluated by medical professionals, and yet they give very different recommendations based solely on the wording.

Here's one more of Kahneman and Tversky's cases.

Imagine that the United States is preparing for the outbreak of an unusual Asian disease, which is expected to kill 600 people. Two alternative programs to combat the disease have been proposed. The estimates of the consequences of the programs are as follows:

[Frame 1]

- If program A is adopted, 200 people will be saved.

- If program B is adopted, there is a one-third probability that 600 people will be saved and two-thirds probability that no people will be saved.

[Frame 2]

- If program A* is adopted, 400 people will die.
- If program B* is adopted, there is a one-third probability that nobody will die and a two-thirds probability that 600 people will die.

Programs A and A* have identical outcomes, as do B and B*. When given the first framing, a large majority picked program A, preferring the sure thing of saving 200 people over the gamble (even though the expected utility of B was the same as A). With good outcomes (saving 200 people!) risk aversion takes over and decision makers go with the sure bet. In the second frame, though, a substantial majority chose B*. When the outcomes are bad ones (400 people dying) they become risk positive and are prepared to throw the dice. Again, the manipulation was purely a matter of language—the true variables of chance, risk, and results stayed the same.

Brains really dislike bad news. Anything presented negatively in terms of mortality, loss, or death is automatically seen as a risk that must be avoided. Conversely, good news is always welcomed. Our subconscious intuitions are happy to sign on for actions when they are sold as winning, survival, and success; it doesn't matter if the positive and negative versions are extensionally equivalent or not. Unfortunately, human beings are unbelievably lousy at statistics and probability. Even mathletes well-versed in Bayes Theorem get tricky problems like the Pancake Puzzle (discussed in Chapter 3) wrong. The subconscious mind is completely hopeless at statistics and doesn't even try—it just looks to how a situation is framed and decides accordingly. It takes concerted conscious effort and reasoning to overcome the powerful voting bloc in the mind's dark web.

Why does framing matter? One reason is that, like the physicians studied in the cancer treatment case, we will have personally inconsistent beliefs and practical judgments. We will not be basing our actions or attitudes on a dispassionate evaluation of the evidence—we'll keep buying the sizzle instead of scrutinizing the steak. More troubling is that unless we are aware that our decisions could merely be the result of how the data are presented to us, we are liable to be manipulated and controlled by clever salesmen in the marketplace of ideas. For example, in the 1970s, when credit cards became commonplace, some retailers wanted to add a surcharge for the using a card instead of cash. Credit card companies generally charge around 1 percent of each sale, and merchants didn't want to eat that cost. The card companies naturally were opposed to the surcharge idea, knowing many customers would refuse to use the cards as a result. The issue wound up in Congress, who passed a law that retailers couldn't add a fee for using a credit card. However, they *could* offer a discount to a customer spending cash. Even though surcharges and discounts are really the same thing, just framed differently, everyone walked away happy.[7]

Look how easily researchers could generate framing effects with thin and barely altered descriptions of the same information. When we are that prone to a cognitive bias, imagine how much more we are affected when that information is embedded in a detailed and persuasive narrative. Penzias and Wilson are intellectual heroes or lucky dopes depending solely on a few paragraphs selling different interpretations. Same facts, different framing. If Penzias and Wilson are seen as lucky because of narrative framing, perhaps other attributions of luck are as well. Maybe "luck" is just a way of telling a story.

# Dueling Vignettes

Tara Cooper hit five out of six numbers in the Megabuck$ lottery. Pretty lucky to get that close to riches, right? Suppose instead she missed hitting the Megabuck$ jackpot by one number. Now that's some terrible luck, barely missing out on the prize. Obviously, it is the same event. Equally obviously, Cooper couldn't be both lucky and unlucky in the same way for the same thing. So which is right? Is there a right answer? There may be nothing to see here but the framing.

Here is a slate of luck stories, with only slight variations on the telling (Table 6.1).

**TABLE 6.1** Luck stories.

| | Positive framing | Negative framing |
|---|---|---|
| Tara Cooper lottery | "I hit five out of six! I've never come anywhere close to hitting the big jackpot before! It was just unbelievable," Cooper exclaimed, still stunned. Berwick bakery worker Tara Cooper stopped off at her usual place for a breakfast coffee and bagel, Brewed Awakening, and decided to pick up a lottery ticket before heading to first shift. "I don't usually play Megabuck$, and don't know why I did today." After work, she checked her numbers online. "I was like, oh my God!" | "I missed the jackpot by one lousy number! Story of my life. It was just unbelievable," Cooper exclaimed, still stunned. Berwick bakery worker Tara Cooper stopped off at her usual place for a breakfast coffee and bagel, Brewed Awakening, and decided to pick up a lottery ticket before heading to first shift. "I don't usually play Megabuck$, and don't know why I did today." After work, she checked her numbers online. "I was like, oh my God." |
| Mark Zabadi basketball | "I hit half my shots from the free throw line! Not bad for a beginner, huh?" Mark exclaimed with a grin. Even though he was one of the tallest kids in his class, Mark Zabadi had never picked up a basketball before. "I dunno," he said, "Guess I'm more of a gamer—not much of a team sports guy." But when some of his friends found themselves short a player for a pickup game, they convinced Mark to play. | "Yeah, I missed half my shots from the free throw line. Not great, huh?" Mark said with a frown. Even though he was one of the tallest kids in his class, Mark Zabadi had never picked up a basketball before. But when some of his friends found themselves short a player for a pickup game, they convinced Mark to play. "I dunno," he said, "Guess I'm more of a gamer—not much of a team sports guy." |
| Winter storm | "Half of the residents never lost their power," reported the mayor. "It could have been a lot worse. We dodged a bullet." Roads were slick for morning commuters, and icy trees knocked out electrical lines after a major winter storm blanketed the area in snow and ice this past weekend. Forecasters had predicted that the town would take the brunt of the worst storm of the season. | "Half of the residents lost their power," reported the mayor. "It can't get much worse. We weren't able to dodge this bullet." Roads were slick for morning commuters, and icy trees knocked out electrical lines after a major winter storm blanketed the area in snow and ice this past weekend. Forecasters had predicted that the town would take the brunt of the worst storm of the season. |

| | | |
|---|---|---|
| Vicki Mangano bowling | Last night Vicki Mangano bowled a 298 by hitting eleven strikes in a row, by far her best game ever. Her teammates, The Rolling Rocks, were taking her out for pizza and beer afterward to celebrate. "I just couldn't miss! I was totally in the zone." One of Vicki's teammates joked, "I just wish some of that lightning would strike me too." | Last night, Vicki Mangano just missed out on bowling a perfect game after missing two pins in the last frame. Her teammates, The Rolling Rocks, were taking her out for pizza and beer afterward to try to cheer her up. "I just couldn't miss!" she exclaimed. "I was totally in the zone." Said one of Vicki's teammates, "I just hope some of that lightning doesn't strike me too." |
| Derek Washington truck tire accident | "I walked away without a scratch! I must have a guardian angel. All my friends told me I should buy a lottery ticket tonight," said accident survivor Derek Washington. Washington was driving down the interstate when a loose tractor-trailer tire barreled into oncoming traffic. The massive 150-pound tire peeled back the roof of his Camry like a tin can and shattered his windshield. | "I was nearly killed! I'm driving to work, minding my own business, and my car is totally destroyed in some freak accident," said victim Derek Washington. Washington was driving down the interstate when a loose tractor-trailer tire barreled into oncoming traffic. The massive 150-pound tire peeled back the roof of his Camry like a tin can and shattered his windshield. |
| Michelle Simmons Tornado | "Half of my buildings look like nothing happened at all. They survived without losing a shingle," said Michelle Simmons. "There's no rhyme or reason to it. It's weird how the tornado just seemed to dance around." Simmons is a fifth-generation Oklahoma resident who owns several commercial rental properties right in the bull's-eye of the tornado's 220-mph winds. The governor of Oklahoma declared a state of emergency for the central part of the state after yesterday's F4 twister. | "Half of my buildings have been completely flattened. There's nothing but some shattered framing and pipes left," said Michelle Simmons. "There's no rhyme or reason to it. It's weird how the tornado just seemed to dance around." Simmons is a fifth-generation Oklahoma resident who owns several commercial rental properties right in the bull's-eye of the tornado's 220-mph winds. The governor of Oklahoma declared a state of emergency for the central part of the state after yesterday's F4 twister. |

(Continued)

**TABLE 6.1** Luck stories.

| | Positive framing | Negative framing |
|---|---|---|
| James Goldberg black ice accident | "I fishtailed and just missed hitting this guy walking to the pizza place. He moved out of the way just in time," said local driver James Goldberg. Drivers are well advised to look out for black ice, especially on the minor roads. The light drizzle on top of below-freezing ground temperatures has made the roads as slick as Teflon. The weather is expected to improve tomorrow. | "I hit a patch of black ice and practically killed this guy who was walking to the pizza place. One minute the road is fine and the next I almost run over a guy," said local driver James Goldberg. Drivers are well advised to look out for black ice, especially on the minor roads. The light drizzle on top of below-freezing ground temperatures has made the roads as slick as Teflon. The weather is expected to improve tomorrow. |
| José Ramirez baseball | "I'm feeling good about this season," said center fielder José Ramirez, who got on base twice in four at-bats yesterday in the season opener against Cleveland. "First game of the year. I trained so hard in the off-season. For whatever reason the pitches all looked slow to me today. It was like playing t-ball again. I can't believe it!" | "I should have done better," said center fielder José Ramirez, who got out twice in four at-bats yesterday in the season opener against Cleveland. "First game of the year. I trained so hard in the off-season. For whatever reason the pitches all looked slow to me today. It was like playing t-ball again. I can't believe it." |

The scenarios on the left and right are exactly the same; they are merely delivered in psychologically different packaging. Even though that packaging varies only slightly, when these vignettes were given to a group of test subjects, they reacted very differently to the two variants as a result. Study participants read each vignette and then decided how lucky the subject of the story was. For example, in the first one, participants were provided with the prompt "Tara Cooper was: *unlucky, somewhat unlucky, somewhat lucky, lucky.* Circle one." There were similar instructions for the Mark Zabadi, winter storm, and the other examples. The positive and negative frames were scrambled so everyone got some of each, but no one participant read both a positive and a negative version of the same case.

The results were striking. When Tara Cooper *hit five* out of six numbers in the lottery, practically everyone thought she was lucky to do so. But when she *missed one* out of six numbers in the lottery, that was universally judged to be bad luck, even though, of course, it was the identical event. The same pattern held for the other seven vignettes above. Two ways of describing equivalent things produced extremely different opinions about luck.[8] Overall, when events were presented positively (the left-hand column above in Table 6.1), participants considered the event "lucky" 83 percent of the time. The very same events when cast negatively (the right-hand column above) were considered "lucky" only 29 percent of the time. The statistical p-value was $< .001$. Social scientists think that if there is only a 1/20 probability that the results of a study were due to random chance ($p = .05$) then it is a statistically significant result. The luck framing effect was dramatic—there is less than a 1/1000 chance that it was a random result.

There were other interesting things buried in the data too. The Mark Zabadi basketball, Vicki Mangano bowling, and José Ramirez baseball examples were all cases of skilled action. Mangano's near-perfect bowling game involved a great deal of skill, whereas, say, Derek Washington's near-death in a bizarre truck tire accident was pure chance. As we saw in Chapter 2, most writers on luck are keen to contrast skill and luck. Either skillful results can't be lucky (or unlucky) because they just aren't a matter of luck at all,[9] or there is a continuum between pure luck and pure skill and we need to find the right spot on the scale for any particular event.[10] If any of that is right, then there ought to be some kind of noticeable difference between how people react to the mostly skill cases (Zabadi, Mangano, Ramirez) and how they respond to the pure chance cases (Cooper, winter storm, Washington, Simmons, Goldberg). Are the skill examples seen as involving less luck than the all-chance scenarios? It turns out no, not at all. In fact, the test subjects saw the skill cases as containing a tiny bit more luck than the pure chance ones. Statistically, skill vs. chance really didn't matter when it came to luck—the framing effect swamped any perceptions of difference between them.

The Tara Cooper lottery case is a near-miss scenario, where she almost, but not quite, won the lottery. The Derek Washington and James Goldberg cases are also examples of near-misses, where Washington was almost killed in a freak accident with a runaway tractor-trailer tire and Goldberg came close to hitting a pedestrian on an icy road. All of the other vignettes above are ones with half positive and half negative results. Half the town lost power and half didn't, half of the free throws went in and half didn't, and so on. The Norwegian psychologist Karl Teigen interviewed eighty-five Norwegian tourists several months after they narrowly escaped the 2004 tsunami in Southeast Asia. Every single one thought that they had been lucky, and nobody said they had been unfortunate or unlucky. Teigen concluded that luck implies closeness to disaster, and that people judge themselves luckier in cases of a near miss, where they just skirted a terrible outcome, than in cases where they were comfortably separated from trouble.[11] In other words, it is near-miss scenarios that trigger attributions of luck. If Teigen is right that luck is a matter of a near-miss, then we should expect that study participants would consider near-miss cases to be more an issue of luck than cases where the outcome was 50–50. But they didn't. Once again, it was framing, more than anything else, which determined the attribution of good luck or bad. Subjects perceived the presence of luck in the 50–50 cases just as much as they did in the near-miss ones.

Manipulating the words describing an event predictably manipulates how people react to those events and whether they see them as lucky or unlucky. Sometimes things are ambiguously lucky—without changing the description at all the very same occurrence can be seen as amazingly good luck or spectacularly bad luck. Recent studies have found that there is a neat psychological explanation for not only why that is, but how you personally will interpret ambiguous events. Here are a few to consider.

# The (Un)Luckiest Man in the World

Tsutomu Yamaguchi was a technical draughtsman for oil tankers when his employer Mitsubishi Heavy Industries sent him to Hiroshima, Japan, in the summer of 1945 for a lengthy business trip. His visit abruptly ended when the bomber Enola Gay dropped the Little Boy atomic bomb on August 6, and the equivalent of 15 kilotons of TNT exploded less than two miles away. Even though Yamaguchi was inside the "instant death zone," he managed to escape with only burns, temporary blindness, and ruptured eardrums. He headed back home to Nagasaki and, despite his injuries, was able to report to work on August 9. Yamaguchi's supervisor couldn't believe a wild story about a single bomb that instantly destroyed a city, and just as he told Yamaguchi that his tale was crazy talk, the room filled with an unearthly, solar-white light as Fat Man detonated over Nagasaki.[12] Yamaguchi somehow survived that blast too, and lived until 2010, when he died at the ripe old age of ninety-three.

Was Yamaguchi lucky or unlucky? On the one hand, he was a simple businessman who was nuclear-bombed twice, which sounds about as unlucky as someone could possibly be. On the other hand, he was a survivor of the two deadliest bombs ever used in war, and still lived to old age, facts which make him seem wondrously lucky. Individuals like Yamaguchi show up on internet lists of the World's Unluckiest People and also the World's Luckiest People; whether they are lucky is ambiguous. Pick up any newspaper and you'll find similar stories—survivors of terrible plane or auto crashes or patients with dread diseases who live past their predicted expiration date. Invariably they are described as hugely lucky. That's puzzling on the face of it; you'd think that somebody really lucky wouldn't have gotten cancer or been in a terrible wreck to start with. Here are a few other real-life tales of ambiguous luck to toss into the mental hopper.

A rocket-propelled grenade (RPG) is a small rocket with a charge of explosives. Designed as a tank-killer, it can punch a two-inch hole through a foot of armor, and has become a handy and commonplace battlefield weapon. In 2006, Private Channing Moss got to know one in a personal way. Moss was on patrol with an Alpha Company platoon in eastern Afghanistan when their convoy started taking fire. One enemy RPG exploded a soft-skin pickup truck, another shredded the protective armor of a Humvee, and a third hit Moss, lodging in his abdomen. Although Moss was still alive, the unexploded grenade inside his body could blow at any time. In the view of one commentator, "Moss was either the luckiest or unluckiest soldier in the entire U.S. Army, and no one knew for sure." The platoon commander called for emergency medical pickup and a very nervous Blackhawk helicopter flight crew ferried Moss to the nearest medical outpost. The doctors and an explosive ordnance disposal tech managed to remove the RPG, patch Moss up and defuse the weapon. Several surgeries later, he went back home to his family.[13]

In 1999, Australian Bill Morgan was crushed in a traffic accident. If that wasn't bad enough, the medication he was given afterwards caused an extreme allergic reaction to the point that his heart stopped. For fourteen minutes. Followed by a coma. His doctors expected severe brain damage, and advised his family to remove life support, predicting that in the best possible case, Morgan would be in a persistent vegetative state. Needless to say, everyone was astonished when, after nearly two weeks in the coma, Morgan woke up feeling completely fine, with no apparent brain damage or long-term problems.[14]

Construction worker Eduardo Leite was on the job in Brazil when a six-foot long piece of iron rebar toppled off the building he was working on and shot down five stories directly at his head. The bar went right through Leite's hard hat, entered the back of his skull, and exited between his eyes. He rode to the hospital with the bar still impaled through his brain, but conscious and cogent. In a five-hour surgery, the neurosurgeons wound up pulling the bar right back out the entry hole. They later marveled that it had been just a few centimeters from taking out Leite's right eye and paralyzing him on one side. Leite has since made a full recovery.[15]

Roy Sullivan is in the *Guinness Book of World Records*, but is unlikely to have many people chasing after his record. According to *Guinness*, no one has ever been struck by lightning more times. Sullivan had a forty-year career as a park ranger in The Shenandoah National Park, and was struck by lightning *seven* times. The odds of this happening are $4.15 \times 10^{32}$; no wonder he was nicknamed "the Spark Ranger." The various bolts blew his big toe off, singed his eyebrows, knocked him unconscious, set his hair on fire, and blasted his shoes off. After a while, no one wanted to go walking in the woods with him. Sullivan later died of unrelated causes.[16]

Luck judgments are a matter of perspective. What's going on in these cases isn't framing. It's not that if the story of Leite or Morgan were presented in one way that they look lucky and if presented in another way that they look unlucky. Rather, there is a clear sense in which something happened to them that had both a definitely unlucky component and a definitely lucky one. Overall, though, what should we think? At the end of the day, was Moss the luckiest or the unluckiest soldier in the US Army? Was Yamaguchi the luckiest or unluckiest person in the world? Sullivan could be seen as lucky for surviving seven lightning strikes or unlucky for suffering them at all. It turns out that there is a simple variance in personality that determines one's perspective on luck.

Take the following quiz.

1  In uncertain times, I usually expect the best.

   **a.** I agree a lot

   **b.** I agree a little

   **c.** I neither agree nor disagree

   **d.** I disagree a little

   **e.** I disagree a lot

2  It's easy for me to relax.

   **a.** I agree a lot

   **b.** I agree a little

   **c.** I neither agree nor disagree

   **d.** I disagree a little

   **e.** I disagree a lot

3  If something can go wrong for me, it will.

   **a.** I agree a lot

   **b.** I agree a little

   **c.** I neither agree nor disagree

   **d.** I disagree a little

   **e.** I disagree a lot

4  I'm always optimistic about my future.

   **a.** I agree a lot

   **b.** I agree a little

   **c.** I neither agree nor disagree

   **d.** I disagree a little

   **e.** I disagree a lot

5  I enjoy my friends a lot.

   a.  I agree a lot

   b.  I agree a little

   c.  I neither agree nor disagree

   d.  I disagree a little

   e.  I disagree a lot

6  It's important for me to keep busy.

   a.  I agree a lot

   b.  I agree a little

   c.  I neither agree nor disagree

   d.  I disagree a little

   e.  I disagree a lot

7  I hardly ever expect things to go my way.

   a.  I agree a lot

   b.  I agree a little

   c.  I neither agree nor disagree

   d.  I disagree a little

   e.  I disagree a lot

8  I don't get upset too easily.

   a.  I agree a lot

   b.  I agree a little

   c.  I neither agree nor disagree

   d.  I disagree a little

   e.  I disagree a lot

9  I rarely count on good things happening to me.

   a.  I agree a lot

   b.  I agree a little

   c.  I neither agree nor disagree

   d.  I disagree a little

   e.  I disagree a lot

**10** Overall, I expect more good things to happen to me than bad.

   **a.** I agree a lot

   **b.** I agree a little

   **c.** I neither agree nor disagree

   **d.** I disagree a little

   **e.** I disagree a lot

This is the Life Orientation Test (Revised) developed by psychologists to measure generalized optimism vs. pessimism.[17] Questions 2, 5, 6, and 8 are "fillers"—just random noise to keep readers from guessing what the test is really all about and then skewing their natural responses. It is not hard to see which answers to the remaining six questions would indicate an optimistic or a pessimistic outlook. That outlook isn't some transitory emotion, either; it's stable over time and at least partly heritable.[18]

A study was done to see what optimists thought about the cases of Yamaguchi, Moss, Morgan, Leite, and Sullivan, and what the pessimists thought about the same cases.[19] Study participants were first given the Life Orientation Test (Revised) above to determine where they fell on the pessimism–optimism continuum. Then they were asked whether Yamaguchi and the others were unlucky, somewhat unlucky, somewhat lucky, or lucky. It turned out there was a significant positive correlation between their level of optimism and their luckiness ratings of those scenarios. That is, the more optimistic someone was, the more likely they were to judge people in the vignettes as lucky. Likewise, the more pessimistic someone was, the more likely they were to judge the people in the vignettes as unlucky. One of the things this means is that the more optimistic *you* are, the more you think *others* are lucky. If you are more of a pessimist, you're likelier to see others as suffering bad luck.

One worry about that study is the possibility that the subjects were effectively ignoring half of the information they received. Perhaps the optimists were just setting aside the negative component of the case and focusing solely on the good aspect, and the pessimists were doing the same by focusing on the bad portion and ignoring the positive features of the vignette. If that was going on, then the optimists and pessimists were essentially talking past each other; they were not really assessing the *total* situation for luck. To obviate this concern, a follow-up study was done. This time the good and bad parts were separated, and study participants were forced to consider each one. For example:

- Australian Bill Morgan was crushed in a car versus truck accident. He was clinically dead for more than fourteen minutes followed by a twelve-day coma during which his family removed life support. Bill Morgan was (circle one): *unlucky, somewhat unlucky, somewhat lucky lucky.*

- Now Bill Morgan is fine. Bill Morgan was (circle one): *unlucky, somewhat unlucky, somewhat lucky, lucky.*

Pretty much everyone recognized the good part—survival—as being lucky and the bad part—the accident—as being unlucky. Optimists and pessimists can clearly agree upon what constitutes good versus bad luck. However, optimists and pessimists varied in their judgments of the severity of the bad luck components. The more pessimistic the person, the *more* unlucky she considered the bad luck component. The more optimistic the person, the *less* unlucky she considered the bad luck component. In other words, if you're an optimist, you just don't see the cruel or miserable parts of life as being all that terrible. These results supported and even explained those in the first study. When Channing Moss had an RPG embedded in his abdomen, that was unlucky. When he survived the whole ordeal, that was lucky. However, for optimists, getting impaled with an RPG was not all *that* bad so it made the getting-impaled-and-surviving event a luckier one than the pessimists believed. For pessimists, his getting skewered with an RPG was so unlucky that it diminished the good fortune of his survival.

Tsutomu Yamaguchi's own take on his life confirms the optimism/pessimism study results. A reporter for *The Times of London* recounts:

I asked Mr. Yamaguchi if he felt optimistic about the future. He hesitated, then said: "I have hope for the future."

Where did that hope come from? "I believe in love, in human beings," he said, and he was weeping again. "The reason that I hate the atomic bomb is because of what it does to the dignity of human beings. Look at the photographs of the aftermath of the atomic bombing, those dead bodies in the photographs. When you forget the dignity of individual human beings, that it is when you are heading towards the destruction of the earth."

What did it mean, I asked, to have lived through two atomic bombs? "I think that it is a miracle," he said.[20]

Yamaguchi could have easily been a pessimist and viewed his story as a tragedy, as spectacular misfortune. Instead, after a long life he remained optimistic about the future, and saw his life as a miracle, as luck. It is hard to read this interview and not think of Friedrich Nietzsche, who was impoverished, unappreciated, suffered chronic migraines, insomnia, and digestive problems, and died after years of insanity. Nonetheless the epigraph to his autobiography was the joyous affirmation, "how could I fail to be grateful to my whole life?"[21] Seen though the powerful lens of positive optimism, the world is filled with good luck.

# Sailing Stones and Flying Witches

If luck is real, a genuine property of persons or events, then there must be an objective fact as to whether Yamaguchi, Moss, Morgan, Leite, and Sullivan were truly lucky. Sure, the optimists say that, taken all in, they were lucky whereas the pessimists insist that they were unlucky. But which is it? Who is right? This is the point where a theory of luck should ride to the rescue. When we have perplexing experiences or inconsistent perceptions, that's exactly when we want a theoretical explanation to sort everything out and set the world aright. A kayak paddle half in the water looks bent, and out of the water it does not. Parallel train tracks disappearing into the distance appear to converge. A decent theory should (1) tell us that in fact the paddle is not really bent and the tracks do not truly converge and (2) explain away the competing perceptions. A theory of optics that couldn't do those things would be rejected as inadequate for that very reason.

Or take the mystery of the racing stones. In California's Death Valley National Park, there is a dry lake bed known as Racetrack Playa. It is extraordinarily flat and level; the northern end is only 1.5 inches higher than the southern end nearly three miles away. Nothing grows in the desert of Racetrack Playa and, since it only rains three to four inches per year, nearly all of the time it is bone-dry cracked mud. Scattered across its surface are hundreds of rocks, some of them several hundred pounds. Racetrack Playa is perfectly flat, totally dry, remote, and uninhabited. But these boulders move, leaving trails hundreds of meters long. There are no footprints or tire tracks which would indicate a prank. On top of that, their movements are unpredictable; one can sit still for a decade and then decide to head out across the valley floor. Not exactly an easy phenomenon to study.

A few researchers proposed that it was occasional hurricane-force winds that moved the rocks. Others suggested slick algal films, dust devils, or thick sheets of ice. In 2011 some scientists showed up with a dozen rocks loaded with motion-activated GPS transmitters and a high-resolution weather station. They expected to wait a long time for any results but, after only two years, they discovered that the rocks move when a rare combination of events takes place. First, there must be some winter rains, enough to shallowly cover the playa with water. Second, there must be an overnight freeze that causes thin sheets of windowpane-like ice to form. This must be followed by enough sun to melt the ice and break it up into large floating panels. Finally, there must be sufficient wind to drive these very thin ice floes into the rocks, causing them to slide across the soft mud.[22] Some rocks were observed to slide for sixteen minutes, but very slowly—only a few inches per second. The rocks seldom move because the confluence of necessary conditions is rare. Is the mystery then solved? Perhaps, although as one of the investigators involved comments, "So we have seen that even in Death Valley, famous for its heat, floating ice is a powerful force driving rock motion. But we have not seen the really big boys move out there ... does that work the same way?"[23]

With the sailing stones of Racetrack Playa, there is a real phenomenon that can be plainly observed, and the puzzle is to explain how it could happen at all. Observation alone couldn't solve the puzzle, though; we needed a theory that could unite the ideas of thin, half-melted ice, wind, and slippery mud. There are other cases where it is much less clear that there is a genuine phenomenon to explain. Sometimes a thing long accepted turns out to be completely incompatible with everything else we know about the world, and permanently resists a theoretical accounting. There're many examples from the history of science, like the luminiferous ether, spontaneous generation, and the miasma hypothesis of contagion. In those cases, the challenge is to illuminate why we ever thought there was something there to start with. When that happens, we have an *error theory*: a theory that explains original phenomena and is able to tell us why we misunderstood it all along.

One example is witches. Beliefs in magic, sorcery, and witchcraft date back to ancient times, but the Western idea of a witch was made canonical in the Middle Ages. According to the *Malleus Maleficarum*, the famous medieval inquisitors' manual, witches were mostly women, and the bewitched mostly men.[24] Witches were unattractive social outcasts who flew about on broomsticks, such a popular notion that in Normandy they were called *scobaces*, or "women with brooms."[25] Flying was only possible once, according to Inquisitor Pierre le Broussard, "they spread an ointment, which the Devil has given them, on a wooden stick … then they put the stick between their legs and fly off over towns, woods, and stretches of water" to engage in sodomy, orgies, bestiality, and basically whatever sacrilegious carnal acts the fourteenth-century mind could imagine.[26] One confessed witch told the Inquisition that "she found a huge he-goat and after greeting him she submitted to his pleasure. The he-goat in turn taught her all kinds of secret spells; he explained poisonous plants to her and she learned from him words for incantations and how to cast spells."[27] The *Malleus Maleficarum* confirmed that once a witch has smeared a broomstick with the devil's unguent, they were "immediately carried up into the air."[28]

Witches were also famed as master herbalists, with knowledge of nightshade plants like henbane, belladonna, and mandragora. The power of herbs was so associated with witchcraft that would-be exorcists worried that they were stepping into the dark side if they used herbs in their ceremonies.[29] With the development of modern science in the Renaissance, skepticism about witches gradually began to appear. Some physicians began to suspect that all the incredible things witches were supposed to have done could be mere visions brought on by their ointments and potions. A Spanish doctor experimented with a balm found in the home of two accused sorcerers, and caused a deep stupor and fantastic dreams in a test subject.[30] The philosopher Nicolas Malebranche suggested that too much wine and the power of suggestion could lead to vividly imagining the Witches' Sabbath.[31] Such doubts were not well received in their time, although in the end the scientific view of the world eclipsed the world of magic.

Many contemporary scholars have unified these ideas: lonely women, estranged from society, rub psychoactive substances that are easily absorbed through mucous membranes onto broomsticks which they place between their legs. They then promptly fly off to a realm of sexual abandon.[32] Lacking any other interpretive tools, these women understand their own experiences through the filter of the church and see them as unholy rituals supervised by demons. Add to that a pinch of misogyny, a dash of prudery, and a measure of superstition and you have a recipe for the *auto-da-fé*. These perfectly empirical, naturalist explanations obviate the need for a supernatural one.

In the case of witches, we have an error theory. They turned out to not be authentic things after all, just a pre-Enlightenment shibboleth properly erased from The Big Book of Reality. The point of the error theory is to help us understand why anyone ever thought they were genuine to start with. Once we're able recognize that things in fact went wrong, it's much more satisfying to figure out why. Like any theory, the error theory recounted above could be wrong in whole or in part—the point is to illustrate what one is and why we would want it, and how it's enlisted for a different kind of project than theories of what is real. Racetrack Playa's sailing stones are real, and we needed a theory to tell us how they worked. Medieval-style witches aren't real, and we needed an error theory to tell us why we ever thought otherwise.

So which is for luck? Our assignments of luck are affected by both framing effects and one's own personal tendency toward optimism or pessimism. If luck is a fully paid-up member of reality then some positive theory of luck should be able to make sense of those results and tell us, for example, whether Tara Cooper is truly lucky or truly unlucky, and whether Channing Moss's luck was good or bad overall. If no theory can do that and there're no prospects of a new-and-improved one in sight, then maybe it is time to turn to an error theory.

Sadly, the hope of a bailout by theory is in vain. The available theories of luck are incapable of solving the problems raised in the psychological studies. To settle the framing cases here is what we want: a defensible account of luck to tell us whether Tara Cooper really is lucky or whether she really is unlucky. Then we could dismiss one frame as misleading and accept that the other frame is better at leading us to the truth. So, for example, if she really is lucky, then we can say, well, our inclinations to see good luck in "she hit five out of six numbers in the Megabuck$ lottery" track the truth more accurately than our predilections to see bad luck in "she missed one out of six numbers in the Megabuck$ lottery."

Consider first the probability theory of luck. According to it, something's luckiness is a function of its importance and probability of occurrence. Under the probability theory, Cooper is lucky to hit five out of six numbers in the Megabuck$ lottery if and only if (1) hitting five numbers mattered to her in a positive way and (2) it was improbable that she would hit five of six numbers. Obviously, it mattered to her that she got as many numbers right as she did, and equally obviously it was very, very unlikely that she does so. It follows that Cooper was lucky to hit five numbers in the lottery. The problem is that the same reasoning works for the other frame just as well. Also according to the probability theory, she was unlucky to miss one of six numbers in the Megabuck$ lottery if and only if (1) missing one of the numbers mattered to her in a negative way, and (2) it was improbable that she would hit all six numbers. Surely missing one of the numbers mattered to her in a negative way (no jackpot!), and we all know it's mighty improbable to get all the numbers right in a lottery. So she was unlucky to miss one of the six numbers.

We get the same result under the modal theory. According to the modal theory, a very small change in the world, such as one ball in the Megabuck$ lottery hopper rotating an extra 20 degrees, would have meant that Cooper did not hit five of six numbers in the lottery, and so her hitting those numbers was modally fragile. Thus her success in getting five out of six was lucky. It is also the case that a very small change in the world would have meant that she got all six numbers right in the lottery, and she was unlucky not to find herself in this very close possible world instead. Again, Tara Cooper is both lucky and unlucky for the same thing.

The control theory of luck lines up with the others. The fact that Cooper got five of six lottery numbers correct was wholly outside her control. Coupled with the fact that getting those numbers mattered to her, under the control theory she was lucky to get five of six numbers in the lottery. However, it was also not within her control to hit all six numbers, although she would have surely loved to. Thus the fact that she missed one number was a case of bad luck. While Tara Cooper was lucky to have hit five out of six numbers in the lottery, she was unlucky to have missed one number.

Tara Cooper was not simultaneously lucky and unlucky for the exact same event. In the snowstorm example, the town's residents were not both lucky and unlucky; those are contrary properties in the same way that *being red all over* and *being blue all over* are contraries, or *skydiving* and *swimming* are contraries. No one can skydive and swim simultaneously, and no one can be both lucky and unlucky for the same thing in the same way. An adequate theory of luck should tell us, in any given case, whether the subject of luck is objectively lucky or objectively unlucky, just as probability theory tells a gambler whether he is objectively likely to be dealt good cards after a run of bad ones, or not. If probability theory could not do that, we'd still be stuck with the Gambler's Fallacy. To pick another example, suppose we look to a moral theory to solve some ethical dilemma and the result is "yep, you both should and should not steal bread to feed your hungry family." That *leaves* us with a puzzle—it's not a solution to one. And it's a reason to reject that particular moral theory. Likewise, if a theory of luck cannot render a consistent, univocal, and objective decision about a putative case of luck, then we have no solution.

Maybe the probability, modal, or control elements of a theory of luck aren't suitable to parse good luck from bad. Instead, it's the idea of an event's being significant that does that work. It is not enough to know that an event is chancy, or that a chancy event affects someone; we need to know whether it affects them in a good or bad way. The way that we do that is to consider for whom the event is significant, and the manner in which it matters to them. For example, the central set-piece of the 2006 film *Casino Royale* features James Bond playing Texas Hold 'Em poker in a high stakes tournament. One of the other players is the terrorist mastermind LeChiffre. In the final hand of the tournament there are four players remaining. When the first two cards are dealt, Bond is holding a lowly 7♠5♠. He has only a 12.3 percent chance of winning the hand; he's the least likely person at the table to win. There are three rounds of community cards, with Bond's chance of victory gradually increasing until he is holding the unbeatable straight flush 8♠7♠6♠5♠4♠. With over 100 million dollars in the pot, Bond's victory was great good luck—beating the odds for a substantial purse and triumph over the bad guy. Of course, it was equally lucky for LeChiffre, just bad luck. We can identify them both as lucky (and not merely subject to the chanciness of the cards) because of the significance of the poker tournament to them both. Furthermore, we recognize Bond's luck as good and LeChiffre's as bad because Bond's win was positively important for him and negatively important for LeChiffre.

Unfortunately, a significance constraint is no help sorting out whose attributions of luck are the right ones in the psychological studies. Consider the optimism/pessimism results. Optimists think that Tsutomu Yamaguchi is, overall, lucky, and pessimists don't. They agree that he was lucky to survive two atomic blasts, and agree that he was unlucky to have been subject to them in the first place. There's no dispute about the facts, no quarrel about whether luck had a big impact on his life, no debate that it was a negative thing to get bombed and a positive thing to survive, and no disagreement about how significant those things were for Yamaguchi. As far as significance is concerned, there's no disparity whatsoever between the opinions of the pessimists and those of the optimists. Still the optimists think Yamaguchi was lucky and the pessimists think he was unlucky. The significance condition can't sort out who is correct.

# Machine Gambling

Many ideas once held dear—like the reliability of eyewitness testimony, or that belief in obvious facts wouldn't be undone by peer pressure, or that ordinary citizens wouldn't commit atrocities at the slightest encouragement—have been tossed to the curb by experimental psychology. Luck is destined to the same fate. Luck is less like the sailing stones and more like witches: there's no successful positive theory of luck or even a path to find one. The concept of luck is long past its expiration date, and looks ready to be consigned to the trash heap of history. Nonetheless, it's hard to concede that luck skepticism is right. Belief in luck and references to luck are so deeply ingrained that giving up luck is a seismic shift in how we think about the world. One of the natural responses to luck skepticism is to insist that clearly *a gambling win* is lucky, especially when it is a game of pure chance. Recall Cicero's mention of winning at "morra, dice, or knuckle-bones" as the quintessential example of luck. We can argue about the skill involved in blackjack or horse racing, but roulette, slots, video poker, keno—denying the existence of luck when one wins at a slot machine is like denying that the sky is blue. Samuel Johnson once commented about free will, "all theory is against it, but all experience is for it." All theory may be against luck, but all experience is surely for it. One imagines Dr. Johnson hitting a jackpot on Invaders From Planet Moolah and declaring "I refute luck skepticism thus."

There is little doubt that for a casual, occasional gambler such an experience does feel powerfully lucky, in the same way that a near-miss experience at video poker or slots feels unlucky. Part of the appeal of gambling for the sporadic card player or infrequent casino patron is the adrenaline high, or the shot of dopamine, that comes with a big score. So one might naively imagine that gambling addicts want that but more of it, that they are adrenaline junkies, chasing the green dragon, jonesing for another rush. Or perhaps it is the very random, chance element of machine gaming that holds the appeal—an aleatory process that injects excitement into the predictable, humdrum everyday world. Luck spices a bland existence.

However, harrowing and eye-opening scholarship shows that none of those things is the experience of gambling addicts. Theirs is an eschatological inversion: the total reversal of final expectations no less complete than Jesus's declarations in *Luke* chapter 6 that it will be woe unto the rich, well-fed, and popular, but it is the poor, hungry, and reviled who are blessed and will inherit the kingdom of God. Sociologist Natasha Dow Schüll writes, "As machine gamblers tell it, neither control, nor chance, nor the tension between the two drives their play; their aim is not to *win* but to *continue*."[33] One gambler explains:

> Most people define gambling as pure chance, where you don't know the outcome. But at the machines I do know: either I'm going to *win*, or I'm going to *lose*. I don't care if it *takes* coins, or *pays* coins: the contract is that when I put a new coin in, get five new cards, and press those buttons, I am allowed to *continue*.
>
> So it isn't really a gamble at all—in fact, it's one of the few places I'm certain about anything. If I had ever believed that it was about chance, about variables that could make anything go in any given way at any time, then I would've been scared to death to gamble. *If you can't rely on the machine, then you might as well be in the human world where you have no predictability either.*[34]

The house always has its edge, which veteran gamblers know from ingrained experience; in the long run the gambler not only can't win, but isn't even playing to win.[35] Both the casino and manufacturers of gambling machines, as well as the gamblers themselves, have the same goal: to maximize time-on-device. The former employs a deep knowledge of human psychology to keep gamblers seated at their machines. Casinos have found that circuitous paths through a maze of shops, restaurants, restrooms, and gambling options that lead to semi-private grottos of machines are far more appealing than open hangars with endless rows of one-armed bandits. Gambling machines themselves are ergonomically designed for comfort, with ease of access to controls, self-leveling seats, plenty of legroom, and closeness to the screen for total absorption. The machines are smooth, rounded, with arm support, and requiring minimal motion to insert more money or hit the Play buttons. Their sounds and lights are designed to be neither too harsh nor excessively frenetic; they are immersively choreographed to game outcomes.

Moreover, the programming of the machines incorporates numerous features to keep the human rats pressing the levers for occasional pellets (a metaphor used by machine addicts to describe themselves).[36] Reinforcement (i.e., payout) schedules are carefully calibrated to different types of gamblers, from those who require infrequent large payouts to those who need small, regular wins. Slot machines constantly run random number generators, whether being played or not. The instant a player hits the SPIN button, the outcome of the game is fully determined by the random number generator. While in old-school slot machines the mechanical action of the reels fixes the result, in digital devices the spinning reels are completely irrelevant and unconnected to game outcome. Yet machines often have a STOP button, so that the player can manually terminate the spinning of one or all of the reels before they stop on their own, creating the illusion of control.[37]

Machine gamblers crave "the zone"—a trancelike state in which there is nothing but the machine, nothing but tunnel vision to the screen while the rest of the world melts away. All of the engineering, programming, and design described above aim at pulling players into this zone as swiftly and completely as possible. They are designer drugs. "You go into the screen, it just pulls you in, like a magnet. You're there in the machine, like you're walking around in it, going around in the cards," says one gambler.[38] "I resent someone breaking my trance … the machine is like a really fast-working tranquilizer," says another.[39] These players do not want excitement, or the gratification of agency, but uninterrupted flow, assimilation, and self-erasure.

New technology allows real-time changes in game parameters in accordance with player desires, giving them mastery over the variables of the game, such as the payout rates, game speed, and complexity. That feeling of control obviates luck; machine gambling addicts don't want luck, chance or randomness. They want the opposite of thrill-seeking. They want the oblivion of the zone. In an ironic confluence of interests, the casino aims for the very same goal, which is to reduce the gambler's personal agency to zero and make them merely a means of entering money into a machine until all available funds are exhausted, a state that they call *player extinction*.[40] The cosmology of the machine is certain— just as the inevitable fate of the universe is entropic heat death, so too the gambler knows that her destiny is dissipation and annihilation.

For such gamblers, winning a jackpot is not lucky at all. "When I hit a jackpot nowadays," says one gambler, "I don't even blink, I don't miss a beat … one time I won a jackpot and I wasn't even sure what the cards were."[41] Another confirms, "I don't even experience the joy of [a] win—in fact I cut it off to get back into the game."[42] One gambler states, "Winning can disappoint me, especially if I win right away." Another explains: "if it's a moderate day—win, lose, win, lose—you keep the same pace. But if you win big, it can prevent you from staying in the zone."[43] "Every now and then," observes one gambler, "I was so exhausted that I actually wanted to lose, so that I could go home. If I'd get close to losing and win again, I'd think *Oh great, now I've got to sit here until its gone.*"[44] For infrequent gamblers, hitting a bonanza is experienced as a lucky event. But for the addicts of machine gambling, wins are neither lucky nor unlucky. Jackpots mean nothing; they are a matter of non-luck—merely another station of the cross, a waypoint on the path to extinction. Even in the case of gambling, the original motivation to develop probability to master chance, the domain where luck should reside in its purest form, luck arises from the idiosyncrasies and perspectives of the gamblers themselves.

# Against Luck

The full argument against luck has many moving parts and has required this whole book to spell out in sufficient detail. The present effort is not the first to declare the death of luck, although hopefully it has provided much more ammunition to achieve that end. Mathematicians from the Renaissance to the present day have thought that probability theory eradicated luck. By understanding that chance is not divine caprice but governed by mathematical laws, they thought to show that luck too is predictable and law-like. As we saw early on, though, the reach of probability to anticipate the future is limited not only by the true randomness found at the atomic scale, but by the fact that chaos theory makes exact predictions of the future impossible in principle. All the probability theory and computational power in the world is not going to tell us how our lives will turn out. The entire universe cannot even solve by brute force the simple game of Go. In that sense then, the best grasp of probability will be incapable of eliminating the role of luck in our lives.

If probability has a role to play, it is as a *theory* of luck. To be acceptable, it will have to do the work we'd like to see for an adequate understanding of luck, such as parsing skill from luck. Unfortunately, the probability theory of luck fails at this task. For one thing, mere success above chance performance (or failure below chance) might not show anything about skill. Tossing coins gives streaks of heads and runs of tails. That is, true randomness isn't smooth but clumpy, and we have to find a way to distinguish that sort of clumpiness from that of skillful performance. A basketball player on a hot streak might be playing with uncommon skill, or just luckily fluctuating above his normal performance; a statistical model struggles to decide. Uncommon skill might just *be* temporarily deviating above the mean.

There is also the reference class problem. The probability of an event is dependent on what background conditions are assumed to do the calculation. Are you lucky if your plane lands safely? A probability theory of luck will require that we figure out how probable it is that the plane safely lands before we can answer the question. Suppose your plane is landing in a Boston blizzard. What's the chance that a commercial airliner lands safely? What's the chance that a plane lands in Boston safely? What's the chance that a plane in a blizzard lands safely? What's the chance that AA #3356 with Capt. Smith lands safely? There are different answers to each of those questions—there's no natural or unique answer to the probability question. For luck that means inconsistent results about whether an event is a lucky one or not. It may be very lucky that the marginal pilot Capt. Smith safely landed in a blizzard, but not at all lucky that a commercial airliner landed safely. Even when those are the same flight.

The probability theory of luck also stumbles on the problem of noisy signals. Even cautious statistical analyses aren't able to say much—if anything—about one-off lives in a world of nonlinear processes. So much of our lives are singular occurrences where the choices we make lead to unpredictable results. You move to a new town for college and meet your spouse or move to a different town and meet a different spouse. You pick one job over another and thereby have a different set of relationships and connections. You keep in touch with some friends and not others, you invest in Betamax instead of VHS or Apple instead of Enron. Like a caffeinated squirrel, we leap from branch to branch through a vast decision tree. Probability theory does best over easily quantified data sets with fixed rules of action, and isn't able to say much about whether it was good luck when we find a nut, or bad luck when don't.

Additionally, there is a normative component to how we usually think about luck; no one deserves praise for a lucky success in the same way that they do for skillful achievement. An acceptable theory of luck must be able to tell us how much credit someone deserves for their success or failure and to what extent that outcome was the result of luck. Once again, probability fails to meet the job requirements. If Roger Federer's first serve percentage is 62 percent, does that mean each first serve he hits in is 62 percent skill and 38 percent luck or does it mean it is 100 percent skill up to the point that he is hitting exactly 62 percent of his first serves in? As we saw in Chapter 2, both alternatives are problematic. Chance, odds, statistics—they are purely technical tools and tell us nothing about merit, desert, and praise (or blame) worthiness. We care about luck not only for gamblers wishing to predict their future play, but because of the human element of understanding the credit we deserve for how our own lives have turned out. On that topic, mathematics is silent.

The idea that luck is somehow chancy survives the downfall of the probability approach. Under the modal theory of luck, luck is modal fragility; luck means that things could have easily been different. One small change in the world and Sabotai's Mongol warriors overrun Europe, so it was good luck that the death of the Khan forced Sabotai to return to China. Another small change and your ticket wins the lottery, so it was bad luck that you lost, despite the immense probability that you do so. These are alternative realities, other possible ways the world might have gone. It is events that are modally robust, ones that would occur even given substantial changes in the world, that aren't lucky. The modal theory of luck depends upon an intrinsic metric of close and distant worlds to make sense of fragility and robustness. As we saw with the example of the Transworld 2000, the dichotomy of "close" and "distant" possibilities is a questionable one. But without it we can't systematically distinguish between lucky and non-lucky events after all.

A further problem for the modal theory was that it seems perfectly reasonable to think that even necessarily true facts might be lucky. We're lucky to live in a universe that has physical constants within just the right parameters to permit life. Such a fact is supposed to be as robust a thing as we could want—the most basic nature of the universe would have to change for it to be different—which means that the modal theory forbids it from being a matter of luck at all. A modal conception of luck can't allow lucky necessities.

The control theory of luck looks to escape some of these difficulties by proposing that lucky events are those that are out of your control, instead of focusing on their improbability or fragility. The "lack of control" idea comes with its own set of challenges, though. Our intuitive sense of control gives some wonky results. Was Ty Cobb in control of his baseball hits? If he was, then it's hard to understand why he missed most of the time. If he was not, then every hit in baseball is just a matter of luck.

Neither alternative is very appealing. Was underdog Lukas Rosol lucky to beat champion Rafael Nadal at Wimbledon? He was lucky to be playing at the very top of his game, but that is when his control over his play is the *greatest*, not when it is the weakest. Rosol didn't lack control; he had the most control, and still he seems lucky.

More generally, we are lousy intuitive judges of when we have or lack control over an event. Those subject to the rubber-hand illusion believe they have control over a rubber hand when of course they lack it, and sincere séance-goers believe they lack control over a moving table when they actually have it. As soon as we try to avoid reliance on these intuitive judgments by working out a more precise understanding of what it is to be in control, we get an even worse problem. If being in control over some result means that you can usually bring that result about, then you're in control just in case there is a high probability of success. If being in control over some result means that it would have been difficult for you to fail to bring it about if you tried, then you're in control just in case success is modally robust. The control theory of luck turns out to not be a new and interesting theory in its own right; instead it collapses to either the probability or modal theories.[45] There might not be three distinct ideas about what luck is—rather, there are just two. Two that already faced serious problems.

All three theories stumble over the problem of synchronic and diachronic luck. The very same event looks lucky when seen from the perspective of its location in a series of events, but not lucky at all when considered in isolation. When the third slot machine reel comes up lemon, it's very lucky, given its location in a series of other lemons. It feels much luckier than the preceding two lemons, even though three lemons are needed for the jackpot. On its own a single lemon is neither lucky nor unlucky; it means nothing. The theories of luck on offer can't tell us which perspective is the right one: the synchronic point of view where we only consider events on their own, sequestered from others and assess them for luck, or the diachronic standpoint where an event's temporal location and relationships to other events must also be gauged. Already luck begins to look like a matter of perspective.

One of the reasons we wanted a theory of luck in the first place was to help us understand certain philosophical issues. We saw in Chapters 4 and 5 that there are many puzzles in ethics and epistemology that get explained in terms of outcome and constitutive luck. How much are we to be praised or blamed for the outcomes of our actions when luck interferes with those outcomes? Our life's trajectory, the range of possible decisions we could make, and ideas of moral privilege are all built on the foundation of good and bad luck. Similarly, figuring out the value and nature of knowledge, or even the possibility of knowledge in light of skeptical threats is set against the background risk of getting the truth by luck alone. These luck-based approaches get off the ground only if there is a coherent theory of luck behind them. However, only the probability or modal theories have any possible traction with epistemic luck, and only the control theory has any chance at all in the case of moral luck (assuming the control theory isn't really one of the other two in disguise). There is no unified theory of luck to which we can appeal for both moral and epistemic luck. Even more, we saw that there were good reasons to deny that "luck" is ambiguous. Luck does not and cannot do the work for which it is tasked. It remains to future research to decide whether the puzzles of moral and epistemic luck are in fact nonissues after all, or whether there are conceptual tools not based on luck that properly sort them out.

Finally, this chapter has shown that luck attributions are determined by framing effects and predicted by personal optimism and pessimism. That's not a showstopper as long as we have a viable theory of luck to fall back on, one that can tell us whether Tara Cooper really is lucky or not, or the degree to which Tsutomu Yamaguchi is lucky. But we don't have such a theory. Even the luck in gambling jackpots turns out to be a matter of perspective. All theories of luck on offer are profoundly, irredeemably flawed: they fail on their own terms, can't handle a whole panoply of counterexamples, aren't able to distinguish skill from luck, aren't serviceable for moral and epistemic luck, and founder in the face of psychological biases.

Concepts aren't arbitrary. We develop them to help us make sense of the world, and when they turn out to be no longer useful to us, or somehow incoherent, we toss them aside. That was the fate of the Olympian gods and medieval witches—once common notions found to be explanatorily worthless in a post-Enlightenment world and now relegated to metaphor or fantasy. Likewise, "luck" has proven to be a crudely thrown-together junk drawer of vaguely connected ideas, none of which lives up to its billing alone or in tandem. It is time to find a new approach, new tools to untangle the thorny issues that talking about luck failed to solve.

At least an error theory of luck is close at hand. It is easy to confuse luck and fortune, but they are not synonymous. Someone on a long-planned vacation to Hawaii may be fortunate to be enjoying the beach in such a lovely place, but it isn't luck; she paid for the plane ticket herself. It's unfortunate to lose one's job as a pilot, but if the reason was that he kept showing up for work drunk, he can't complain that it was bad luck. The rejection of luck is not the rejection of good and ill fortune, although those ideas are probably more suitable for casual and informal reflections than high-pressure theoretical use. No one denies that we often feel that things are going well for us or badly, or that some events affect us positively or negatively. Those feelings, however, are inconsistent and manipulable, the result of framing effects and idiosyncratic personality traits. Similarly, it is tempting to conflate luck and chance, especially because chance seems tractable by mathematics, and many of our thoughts about luck are connected to the unknown or unexpected. To deny that luck is merely ignorance of statistics is not the same as rejecting the theory of probability. Fortune and chance may be real, but luck is not. Luck is a cognitive illusion.

# Go Luck Yourself

Nietzsche once commented that his own brilliant and vituperative criticisms of popular morality had no more effect than an anarchist shooting stray arrows at the prince. The only result is the prince sits more firmly on his throne.[46] It's hard not to suspect that despite the many quivers of arrows shot at luck throughout this book that belief in luck will persist nonetheless. Once you see that luck is a cognitive illusion, that doesn't make the feeling of it disappear. Look at the two table tops in Roger Shepard's marvelous drawing "Turning the Tables" (Figure 6.1).[47]

What's the length-width ratio of the table top on the left? What about the one on the right? Whatever they are, they certainly can't be the same ratio; the left-side table top looks decidedly longer and skinnier. Now take a ruler and measure them. As you might have guessed—rightly suspecting a trick—they are exactly the same. But even knowing that, they still do not *look* the same. Our perceptions of difference are spontaneous and involuntary, and even when we know better, it is a losing struggle to shake the feeling that the table tops must be different. Likewise, feeling of luck's presence in the world remains even after acknowledging that it is illusory. Even people who probably should have known better fall prey

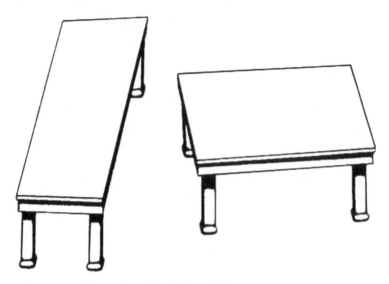

**FIGURE 6.1** Turning the tables. Wikimedia Commons.

to luck's seduction. For example, Daniel Kahneman is a firm believer in luck, writing in his magnum opus, "a recurrent theme of this book is that luck plays a large role in every story of success; it is almost always easy to identify a small change in the story that would have turned a remarkable achievement into a mediocre outcome."[48] It is deeply ironic that the discoverer of so many cognitive biases fails to see that luck too dissolves in the acid of his own making.

In the end, nothing precludes us from using the word "luck." We cross our fingers for good luck, or wish each other luck, or modestly attribute our success to luck. Most of this is a sort of ceremonial speech, not to be taken literally, or done with a wink to the superstition it represents. To take seriously the demise of luck is to recognize all uses of luck as the lingering traces of old and failed paradigms, no different from calling an unemotional man phlegmatic (harkening back to Galen's theory of bodily humors), or noting that the sun sets in the west (a result of Ptolemy's astronomy). We should not take these things seriously, as components of the true story of the world, even if they are a kind of harmless legacy code that lives on in our cultural milieu.

In Plato's Myth of Er, Lachesis insisted that the blame for an unlucky life rested on the person who chose that life. Even though the gods arranged the lottery of birth and might capriciously meddle in our lives, still they were faultless. Unexpectedly, Lachesis was right. It is, in a sense, all on us. Whether we perceive winning at video poker as lucky or not an issue of luck at all, whether we consider nearly winning the lottery a lucky event or an unlucky one, whether we optimistically think that dire events in our lives fail to undermine the good ones or pessimistically view them as fatally corrupting the good—these judgments are a matter of the perspectives we take. Luck is not an objective quality of the world, and upon dissection proves to be only a point of view, a subjective assessment that we bring to bear on our circumstances. There is no more to being lucky or unlucky than seeing yourself as so. Our fortunes may be tenuously connected to our deeds and ambitions, but our luck is constructed by us alone. None of this is to suggest that changing one's point of view is an easy task, or that a pessimist can become an optimist by mere force of will. But still—you do make your own luck.

# NOTES

## Chapter 1

1   (Annas 1981) pp. 349, 353.

2   (Pindar 2007).

3   (Polybius 1889) §402.

4   Cited in (Eidinow 2011) p. 49.

5   (Plutarch 1962) §320.

6   (Ferguson 1970) p. 87.

7   (Putzi 2009) p. 151.

8   (Lawrence 1898).

9   (Putzi 2009) p. 194.

10  (Petronius 1960) ch. 60.

11  "Let us study such a collection, worn in the form of little silver pendants: the four-leaf clover, a pig, a mushroom, a horseshoe, a ladder, and chimney-sweep. The four-leaved clover has taken the place of the three-leaved one which is really suited to be a symbol. The pig is an ancient fertility symbol. The mushroom is an obvious penis-symbol: there are mushrooms which owe their systematic name (*Phallus impudicus*) to their unmistakable resemblance to the male organ. The horseshoe copies the outline of the female genital orifice, which the chimney-sweep, who carries the ladder, appears in this company on account of his activities, with which sexual intercourse is vulgarly compared." (Freud 1917) p. 64.

12  (Rowling 2005).

13  (Hesiod 2006) §822.

14  (Redford 2001), "Horoscopes"; (Kadish 2013).

15  (Baroja 2001) p. 132.

16  (Putzi 2009) p. 199.

17  (Ogden 2002) p. 225.

18  (Cohen 1960) p. 127.

**19** (Frazer 1890) chs. 57 and 58.

**20** (Seddon 2005).

**21** (Nussbaum 1994).

**22** (Aurelius 2002), IV.

**23** (Seneca 1917), IX.

**24** (Nussbaum 1994) ch. 10.

**25** (Camus 1955).

**26** (Sextus Empiricus 1998) §309–310.

**27** Cf. (Kneale and Kneale 1962) pp. 118–22.

**28** (Boethius 2008).

**29** (Calvin 1559) p. 173.

**30** (Calvin 1559) p. 180.

**31** (Edwards 1754).

**32** (Edwards 1741) pp. 11–12.

**33** (Edwards 1858) p. 292.

**34** (Mazur 2010) pp. 5–6.

**35** (Decker et al. 1996).

**36** (Casanova 1957) ch. 20.

**37** (Aquinas 1963) Cf. (Bennett 1998) ch. 3.

**38** (Cicero 1923) book 2, §41.

**39** Cited in (David 1962) p. 14.

**40** (Mlodinow 2008) ch. 3.

**41** (Galilei 1962) p. 192.

**42** (David 1962) ch. 7, (Mlodinow 2008) ch. 4.

**43** (Hacking 1975) p. 61.

**44** (David 1962) p. 144.

**45** (de Moivre 1718) p. iv.

# Chapter 2

**1** (Boscovich 1966) §540.

**2** Compare Ralph Waldo Emerson writing 100 years later, "Shallow men believe in luck, believe in circumstances: it was somebody's name, or he happened to be there at the time, or it was so then, and another day it would have been otherwise. Strong men believe in cause and effect. The man was born to do it, and his father was born to be the father of him and for this deed, and, by looking narrowly, you shall see there was no luck in the matter, but it was all a problem in arithmetic, or an experiment in chemistry" (Emerson 1904b) p. 220.

3   (Gleick 1987) p. 43.

4   (Laplace 1902) p. 4. Compare Boscovich's very similar, if less elegant, remarks at (Boscovich 1966) §385. There is a nice discussion contrasting Boscovich and Laplace on this matter in (Kožnjak 2015).

5   (Tromp and Farnebäck 2016).

6   (Dewdney 1989).

7   (Lloyd 2002).

8   (Lloyd 2002).

9   See for example (Smith 2016), (Mazur 2010) p. xvii and (Rosenthal 2006) ch. 16.

10  (Ballantyne 2012) and (Whittington 2016) offer excellent discussions of a significance condition for luck.

11  (Rescher 1995) p. 32.

12  (Rescher 1995) p. 211.

13  Some writers have attempted to distinguish skill from luck while providing no theory of luck whatsoever, ostensibly assuming that the nature of luck is somehow obvious. Examples include (Heesen 2017) and (Christensen et al. 2016). At the very least the present book should dispel the assumption of obviousness.

14  (Gladwell 2008) pp. 54–5. Cf. (Mlodinow 2008) pp. 208–9 and (Frank 2016) ch. 2.

15  (Hanauer 2014).

16  (Gladwell 2008) p. 55.

17  Nicely refuting E. B. White's remark that "luck is not something you can talk to economists about, because it does not fit into the hard-earned grooves of social thought" (White 1944) p. 342.

18  (Frank 2016) pp. 3–4.

19  (Emerson 1904a) p. 100.

20  (Drucker 2006) p. 151.

21  http://en.espn.co.uk/facupstories/sport/player/1139.html. Accessed 24 March, 2020.

22  (Bleck 2014).

23  (Weber 1946) p. 271. Cf. (Frank 2016) p. 93: "Overlooking luck's role makes those who've succeeded at the highest levels feel much more entitled to keep the lion's share of the income they've earned."

24  (James Jr. 2008).

25  (Freedberg 2009).

26  Personal communication.

27  "Luck [is] the result of insufficient information—an inability to pinpoint cause and effect" (Mauboussin 2012) p. 190.

28  These examples are all discussed in depth in (Kucharski 2016).

29  Ernest Sosa also endorses something like this. See (Sosa 2017) p. 77 and p. 122.

30  It is used by, for example (Mauboussin 2012), (Levitt and Miles 2011), and (Croson et al. 2008).

31  (Mauboussin 2012) p. 77.

32  Compare Cicero, *De Natura Deorum* (5.12), "sensations are *probable*, that is, though not amounting to a full perception they are yet possessed of a certain distinctness and clearness, and so can serve to direct the conduct of the wise man."

33  http://www.golfdigest.com/story/want-to-know-your-odds-for-a-hole-in-one-well-here-they-are. Accessed 24 March, 2020.

34  (Taleb 2007).

35  These ideas are from (McKinnon 2014), and she is subject to the *reductio ad absurdum* argument that follows.

36  Non-probability accounts of skill have a better chance of success. See (Stanley and Williamson 2017) and (Pavese 2016). Of course, assuming the central thesis of this book is correct, no account of skill that hopes to contrast it with luck can be right.

37  (White 1944) p. 342.

# Chapter 3

1  (Leibniz 1768).

2  The idea of an infinity of possible worlds branching from our own is nicely imagined in (Crouch 2016).

3  Presumably, this means there's a reason why the Principle of Sufficient Reason is true too, but that's another story.

4  (Leibniz 1710) part 1, §8.

5  Quoted in (Kendrick 1955) pp. 137–8.

6  According to the twentieth-century social critic Theodor Adorno, "the earthquake of Lisbon sufficed to cure Voltaire of the theodicy of Leibniz" (Adorno 1973) p. 361. (Voltaire 1759).

7  (Holland 1999).

8  This scenario has been played out a few times, incidentally. Cf. *The Amazing Spider-Man* 14, 120, 328; *The Amazing Spider-Man king size special* 3; *Peter Parker* 14; *The Incredible Hulk* 349; *Marvel Team-Up* 27, 53, 54; *Web of Spider-Man* 7, 69; *Marvel Treasury Edition* 25, 28. The Hulk has the edge. (Hat tip to Rob Ledford's encyclopedic knowledge of all things comic.)

9  A good recent summary of Pritchard's view is (Pritchard 2014b). He does idiosyncratically, and without much explanation, reject the significance condition; but that is not germane to the present discussion.

10  (Dawkins 1998) p. 1.

11  See Derek Parfit's essay "Why Is Reality as It Is?" in (Hales 1999), Robert Nozick's longer discussion of why there is something rather than nothing in (Nozick 1981), and Jim Holt's book (Holt 2012).

12  Cited in (Holton 1978) p. xii.

13  Proof that the correct answer is 2/3: Your pancake could only be golden/golden or golden/black. Of the three golden sides you could be seeing, two of them have golden on the other side. Another way of putting it is that before you get any pancake, the chances that you'll select one with matching sides are two out of three. So then if you get a pancake and see a black side, the chances that the other side is also black is two of three. If you get a pancake and see a golden side, the chance that the other side matches is also two of three.

14  (Smith 2012) chapter 7.

15  (Smith 2012) p. 71.

16  See (Coffman 2009), (Mele 2006) p. 7, (Greco 2010) p. 130, and (Levy 2011) p. 36 for some examples. More are discussed in the chapter on moral luck.

17  (Hofstadter 1985) p. 353.

18  An expression first coined by the American colonial statesman Thomas Paine (Paine 1792).

19  (Lamont 2013) p. 64.

20  Faraday described his experiments in "On Table-Turning" and "Experimental Investigation of Table-Moving", both reprinted in (Faraday 1859) pp. 382–91.

21  (Carpenter 1852). An excellent recent discussion is (Hyman 1999).

22  (Botvinick and Cohen 1998).

23  (Ramachandran and Blakeslee 1998) pp. 59–62.

24  (Ramachandran et al. 2011).

25  (Ramachandran et al. 2011) p. 370.

26  The neurologist Oliver Sacks describes a "man who fell out of bed" because his proprioceptive map no longer acknowledged his leg as being his own, and a "disembodied lady" who lost all sense of proprioception, both due to neurological deficits (Sacks 1985).

27  (Shepherd 2014) defends this point.

28  http://espn.go.com/tennis/wimbledon12/story/_/id/8106990/wimbledon-2012-rafael-nadal-upset-second-round-lukas-rosol. Accessed 24 March, 2020.

29  The philosopher Ernest Sosa also rejects this high standard in (Sosa 2011) p. 53.

30  (Johnson 1795) p. 219.

31  Compare (Gould 1991) p. 467.

32  (Whittingham 1989) p. 315.

33  (Arbesman and Strogatz 2008).

34  (Arbesman and Strogatz 2008) p. 11.

35  (Whittingham 1989) p. 315.

36  http://www.basketball-reference.com/players/w/willimi02.html, http://www.nba.com/history/records/regular_freethrows.html. Accessed 24 March, 2020.

37  An example attributed to J. B. S. Haldane by Richard Dawkins (Dawkins 2009) p. 147.

# Chapter 4

1  *As You Like It*, Act 1, Scene 2.

2  (Martin and Cushman 2016) p. 190.

3  (Plus Media Solutions 2013), http://blogs.seattletimes.com/today/2014/01/teen-sentenced-to-probation-in-oregon-leaf-pile-hit-and-run/, http://www.oregonlive.com/forest-grove/index.ssf/2017/09/decision_overturning_convictio.html, Accessed 24 March, 2020.

**4** (Nietzsche 1888), "What the Germans Lack" §7.

**5** (Kant 1784) chapter 1.

**6** Cf. *Hamlet*, Act 3, Scene 1: "The dread of something after death, the undiscovered country from whose bourn no traveler returns, puzzles the will and makes us rather bear those ills we have than fly to others that we know not of."

**7** Cf. (Nelkin 2013).

**8** (Sacks 2010) chapter 4. One of Sacks's best-known case studies was of a music professor who was so severely prosopagnosic that he couldn't distinguish between his wife and a hat, as related in the titular essay in (Sacks 1985).

**9** See, for example, chapter 22 in (Garrison 1999).

**10** (Nagel 1976) p. 137.

**11** (Garrison 1999) pp. 159–60.

**12** Note Harrison Ford's astonished reaction to a David Blaine trick performed in Ford's own kitchen: "get the fuck out of my house." https://youtu.be/rB0wzy-xbwM. Accessed 24 March, 2020.

**13** (Benzoni 1857) p. 17. Compare (Kant 1790), book II, "Analytic of the Sublime," §43, fn 1: "In my part of the country, if you set a common man a problem like that of Columbus and his egg, he says, 'There is no art in that, it is only science': i.e., you can do it if you know how; and he says just the same of all the would-be arts of jugglers. To that of the tight-rope dancer, on the other hand, he has not the least compunction in giving the name of art."

**14** (Roese and Vohs 2012).

**15** (Whitehead and Popenoe 2001).

**16** Merely 71 percent of Americans know that the earth revolves around the sun instead of the other way around. Europeans are apparently even less informed—only 66 percent know this fact. See National Science Foundation, *Science and Engineering Indicators 2006*, Appendix Tables 7–10 (http://www.nsf.gov/statistics/seind06/append/c7/at07-10.pdf).

**17** (Munroe 2014) has an amusing chapter explaining exactly why.

**18** As does Robert Frank in chapter 2 of (Frank 2016).

**19** (Adams and Alinder 1985) p. 382.

**20** Cf. (Driver 2013).

**21** (Nietzsche 1887) essay II, §6.

**22** (Milgram 1974), (Zimbardo 2008).

23 This is the position argued for in (Martin and Cushman 2016).

24 The best account of the twins is (Segal 2005), chapter 3. The historical details in the present discussion derive from that.

25 (Pocock 1975) p. 167.

26 (Reich 1989).

27 (Trump and Zanker 2007) p. 105.

28 https://en.wikipedia.org/wiki/Richard_Arvine_Overton.

29 (Eknoyan 2006).

30 (Kyle 2012) p. 108.

31 The luck egalitarian/insurance argument is developed in (Dworkin 2000), chapter 9.

32 (Hurley 2005).

33 (Bailey 1998) p. 111 and (Monahan 2014) p. 73.

34 (Gordon 2004). Also see (Monahan 2014).

35 (Card 1996) is devoted to just these sorts of cases.

36 Spoiler alert: it doesn't.

# Chapter 5

1 (Dollar 1986).

2 See (Zagzebski 2003).

3 Official name of the statue: Phra Phuttha Maha Suwana Patimakon. It is now in the temple of Wat Traimit, Bangkok, Thailand.

4 For more discussion of relativism, see (Hales 2006) and (Hales 2011).

5 (Dreyfus 1997) pp. 292–3. For more discussion of the mirage example, see (Krasser 1995) pp. 251–2.

6 (Boh 1993) p. 114.

7 (Russell 1948) p. 170.

8 Adding to his citation count: (Gettier 1963).

9 Gettier's own examples are tedious. The one that follows, from Keith Lehrer, is structurally identical to one of Gettier's cases.

10 (Zagzebski 1994), cf. (Pritchard 2014a).

11 (Unger 1968).

**12** (Pritchard 2014a) p. 154; of course there's disagreement. (Turri et al. 2015) write that "like any human achievement, knowledge is usually due to a mix of ability and luck." p. 386. (Hetherington 2014) thinks that knowledge and luck are fully compatible. But these are minority views.

**13** (Plato 1961) p. 853.

**14** Historical information from (King 2012) and (Maysh 2016).

**15** (Descartes 1641), meditation 1.

**16** The best discussion of the problem of the criterion is in (Chisholm 1982).

**17** Epistemologists typically use the expression "environmental epistemic luck" instead of "circumstantial epistemic luck" as I do here. That's unfortunate, because it keeps them from recognizing the parallels with circumstantial moral luck.

**18** http://www.slate.com/articles/news_and_politics/dispatches/2009/07/donkey_business.html.

**19** Obviously, the zebra example is structurally identical to what philosophers call a "barn case," which refers to a widely discussed hypothetical example of Carl Ginet's. It is much nicer to use real-life examples, though.

**20** The Overton Window could no doubt be represented with a Gaussian distribution, with unacceptable views a certain number of standard deviations from the mean. Social scientists could figure out how to map Overton's intuitive distinctions onto an empirically generated curve.

**21** https://www.washingtonpost.com/news/worldviews/wp/2016/06/13/here-are-the-10-countries-where-homosexuality-may-be-punished-by-death-2/?. Accessed 24 March, 2020.

**22** (Planck 1949) pp. 33–4.

**23** There is a hot debate in epistemology between those who think that virtue epistemology is adequate to solve the Gettier problem, barn cases, and related issues (e.g., Sosa and Greco), and those who think that it needs to be supplemented with an anti-luck condition (e.g., Pritchard). Regardless of whether virtue epistemology is on the right track, including an anti-luck condition is pointless. Since luck is nonexistent, adding such a clause amounts to adding a zero.

**24** (Medawar 1968).

**25** A good point for the expected reference to (Kuhn 1970).

**26** http://www.telegraph.co.uk/news/2017/05/17/welsh-grown-hottest-ever-chilli-line-chelsea-flower-show-prize/. Accessed 24 March, 2020.

**27** For examples, see (Roberts 1989), (Meyers 2007), and (Donald 2017).

**28** (Medawar 1968).

29 The control theory is the default position in discussions of moral luck already. (Hartman 2017) chapter 2 calls it the Standard View.

30 (Levy 2011) does this.

31 Compare Saul Kripke on this point. "It is very much the lazy man's approach in philosophy to posit ambiguities when in trouble. If we face a putative counterexample to our favorite philosophical thesis, it is always open to us to protest that some key term is being used in a special sense, different from its use in the thesis. We may be right, but the ease of the move should counsel a policy of caution: Do not posit an ambiguity unless you are really forced to, unless there are really compelling theoretical or intuitive grounds to suppose that an ambiguity really is present." (Kripke 1977) p. 268.

32 (James 1907) pp. 43–5.

33 Originating in (Quine 1960), qualifiedly endorsed by (Sennet 2011), (Dunbar 2001) and (Gillon 1990).

34 Example from (Pritchard 2005) p. 143.

# Chapter 6

1 https://quoteinvestigator.com/2013/10/09/horseshoe-luck/, Accessed 24 March, 2020.

2 (Alpher and Herman 1948) (Gamow 1948). The modern calculation of the CMB is about 2.73K. For a more detailed but accessible account of the CMB, see (Evans 2015).

3 (Singh 2010) pp. 70–1.

4 (Espino 2010).

5 See (Kahneman 2011) p. 269.

6 Examples from (Kahneman 2011), ch. 34.

7 Cf. (Thaler and Sunstein 2008) p. 36, (Kahneman 2011) p. 364.

8 The original presentation of these studies was in (Hales and Johnson 2014).

9 (Pritchard and Smith 2004) p. 24, "An outcome that is brought about via an agent's skill is not, we argue, properly understood as a 'lucky' outcome." Compare (Littlejohn 2014).

10 (Mauboussin 2012) p. 24, for example.

11 (Teigen 2005; Teigen and Jensen 2011).

12  https://youtu.be/9_VsNZl6LGU.

13  (Farwell 2015).

14  http://www.todayifoundout.com/index.php/2013/10/man-died-came-back-life-won-lotto-twice-second-time-re-enacting-first-media/.

15  http://nationalpost.com/news/brazilian-construction-worker-survives-after-surgery-for-iron-bar-that-pierced-his-skull.

16  (Conradt 2015).

17  (Scheier et al. 1994).

18  (Carver et al. 2010; Carver and Scheier 2014).

19  (Hales and Johnson 2018).

20  (Parry 2009).

21  (Nietzsche 1908).

22  (Norris et al. 2014).

23  https://www.nps.gov/deva/planyourvisit/the-racetrack.htm.

24  (Kramer and Sprenger 1971), Part II, Question II, Chapter II.

25  (Baroja 2001) p. 90.

26  (Baroja 2001) pp. 90–1.

27  (Baroja 2001) p. 85.

28  (Kramer and Sprenger 1971), Part II, Question I, Chapter III.

29  (Kramer and Sprenger 1971), Part II, Question II, Chapter V.

30  (Baroja 2001) pp. 107–8.

31  Book II, Part III, Chapter IV.

32  (Escohotado 1999) ch. 6, (Rudgley 1993) ch. 6, (Schultes and Hofmann 1979) pp. 89–90, (Baroja 2001) pp. 254–6.

33  (Schüll 2012) p. 12.

34  (Schüll 2012) p. 12.

35  (Schüll 2012) p. 75.

36  (Schüll 2012) pp. 102–5.

37  On this point, see (Langer 1982).

38  (Schüll 2012) p. 174.

39  (Schüll 2012) p. 193, p. 248.

40  (Schüll 2012) cf. p. 233.

41 (Schüll 2012) p. 130, p. 177.

42 (Schüll 2012) p. 177.

43 (Schüll 2012) p. 198.

44 (Schüll 2012) p. 225.

45 This idea is developed in technical detail in (Hales 2019).

46 (Nietzsche 1888) "Maxims and Arrows" §36.

47 (Shepard 1990) p. 48.

48 (Kahneman 2011) p. 9.

# BIBLIOGRAPHY OF WORKS CITED

Adams, Ansel, and Mary Street Alinder. 1985. *Ansel Adams: An Autobiography*. Boston, MA: Little, Brown and Company.

Adorno, Theodor. 1973. *Negative Dialectics*. New York: Seabury Press.

Alpher, Ralph, and Robert Herman. 1948. "On the Relative Abundance of the Elements." *Physical Review* 74: 1737–42.

Annas, Julia. 1981. *An Introduction to Plato's Republic*. Oxford: Oxford University Press.

Aquinas, Thomas. 1963. *Liber De Sortibus (on Lots)*. Dover, MA: Dominican House of Philosophy.

Arbesman, Samuel, and Steven H. Strogatz. 2008. "A Monte Carlo Approach to Joe Dimaggio and Streaks in Baseball." *arXiv*:0807.5082v2 [physics.pop-ph] 1–14.

Aurelius, Marcus. 2002. *Meditations*. New York: Modern Library.

Bailey, Alison. 1998. "Privilege: Expanding on Marilyn Frye's 'Oppression.'" *Journal of Social Philosophy* 29 (3): 104–19.

Ballantyne, Nathan. 2012. "Luck and Interests." *Synthese* 185 (3): 319–34.

Baroja, Julio Caro. 2001. *The World of the Witches*. London: The Phoenix Press.

Bennett, Deborah J. 1998. *Randomness*. Cambridge, MA: Harvard University Press.

Benzoni, Girolamo. 1857. *History of the New World*. London: Hakluyt Society.

Bleck, Tammy. 2014. "Does Luck Have Anything to Do with Success?" *Huff/Post* 50, March: 30.

Boethius, Anicius Manlius Severinus. 2008. *The Consolation of Philosophy*. Cambridge, MA: Harvard University Press.

Boh, Ivan. 1993. *Epistemic Logic in the Later Middle Ages*. London: Routledge.

Boscovich, Roger. 1966. *A Theory of Natural Philosophy*. Cambridge, MA: MIT Press.

Botvinick, Matthew, and Jonathan Cohen. 1998. "Rubber Hands 'Feel' Touch That Eyes See." *Nature* 391 (6669): 756.

Calvin, John. 1559. *The Institutes of the Christian Religion*. Edinburgh: The Calvin Translation Society.

Camus, Albert. 1955. *The Myth of Sisyphus and Other Essays*. New York: Vintage Books.

Card, Claudia. 1996. *The Unnatural Lottery: Character and Moral Luck*. Philadelphia, PA: Temple University Press.

Carpenter, William Benjamin. 1852. "On the Influence of Suggestion in Modifying and Directing Muscular Movement, Independently of Volition." *Royal Institution of Great Britain* 10: 147–53.

Carver, Charles S., and Michael F. Scheier. 2014. "Dispositional Optimism." *Trends in Cognitive Science* 18 (6): 293–9.

Carver, Charles S., Michael F. Scheier, and Suzanne C. Segerstrom. 2010. "Optimism." *Clinical Psychology Review* 30: 879–89.

Casanova, Giacomo. 1957. *The Memoirs of Jacques Casanova.* New York: Modern Library.

Chisholm, Roderick M. 1982. *The Foundations of Knowing.* Minneapolis: University of Minnesota Press.

Christensen, Clayton M., Taddy Hall, Karen Dillon, and David S. Duncan. 2016. *Competing against Luck: The Story of Innovation and Customer Choice.* New York: HarperCollins.

Cicero, Marcus Tullius. 1923. *On Divination.* Cambridge, MA: Harvard University Press.

Coffman, E. J. 2009. "Does Luck Exclude Control?" *Australasian Journal of Philosophy* 87 (3): 499–504.

Cohen, John. 1960. *Chance, Skill, and Luck: The Psychology of Guessing and Gambling.* Baltimore, MD: Penguin Books.

Conradt, Stacy. 2015. "Meet the Man Struck by Lightning 7 Times." *Mental Floss,* August 6.

Croson, Rachel, Peter Fishman, and Devin G. Pope. 2008. "Poker Superstars: Skill or Luck? Similarities between Golf—Thought to Be a Game of Skill—and Poker." *Chance* 21 (4): 25–8.

Crouch, Blake. 2016. *Dark Matter.* New York: Crown.

David, F. N. 1962. *Games, Gods, and Gambling.* New York: Hafner Publishing.

Dawkins, Richard. 1998. *Unweaving the Rainbow.* New York: Houghton Mifflin.

Dawkins, Richard. 2009. *The Greatest Show on Earth: The Evidence for Evolution.* New York: The Free Press.

de Moivre, Abraham. 1718. *The Doctrine of Chances, or, a Method of Calculating the Probability of Events in Play.* London: W. Pearson for the author.

Decker, Ronald, Thierry Depaulis, and Michael A. E. Dummett. 1996. *A Wicked Pack of Cards: The Origins of the Occult Tarot.* New York: St. Martin's Press.

Descartes, Rene. 1641. *Meditations on First Philosophy.* Indianapolis, IN: Hackett Publishing.

Dewdney, A. K. 1989. "A Tinkertoy Computer That Plays Tic-Tac-Toe." *Scientific American,* October 1: 119–23.

Dollar, John. 1986. "Prisoner of Consciousness." Film.

Donald, Graeme. 2017. *The Accidental Scientist: The Role of Chance and Luck in Scientific Discovery.* London: Michael O'Mara Books Limited.

Dreyfus, Georges B. J. 1997. *Recognizing Reality: Dharmakārti's Philosophy and Its Tibetan Interpretations.* Albany: State University of New York Press.

Driver, Julia. 2013. "Luck and Fortune in Moral Evaluation." In *Contrastivism in Philosophy,* edited by Martin Blaauw, 154–73. London: Routledge.

Drucker, Peter F. 2006. *Managing for Results.* New York: HarperBusiness.

Dunbar, George. 2001. "Towards a Cognitive Analysis of Polysemy, Ambiguity, and Vagueness." *Cognitive Linguistics* 12 (1): 1–14.

Dworkin, Ronald. 2000. *Sovereign Virtue*. Cambridge, MA: Harvard University Press.

Edwards, Jonathan. 1741. *Sinners in the Hands of an Angry God*. Boston, MA: S. Kneeland and T. Green.

Edwards, Jonathan. 1754. A *Careful and Strict Enquiry into the Modern Prevailing Notions of That Freedom of Will, Which Is Supposed to Be Essential to Moral Agency, Virtue and Vice, Reward and Punishment, Praise and Blame*. Boston, MA: S. Kneeland.

Edwards, Jonathan. 1858. "The End of the Wicked Contemplated by the Righteous." In *The Works of President Edwards*, Vol. 4, 287–99. New York: Leavitt and Allen.

Eidinow, Esther. 2011. *Luck, Fate and Fortune: Antiquity and Its Legacy*. Oxford: Oxford University Press.

Eknoyan, Garabed. 2006. "A History of Obesity, or How What Was Good Became Ugly and Then Bad." *Advances in Chronic Kidney Disease* 13 (4): 421–7.

Emerson, Ralph Waldo. 1904a. *The Conduct of Life: Wealth*. New York: Houghton Mifflin.

Emerson, Ralph Waldo. 1904b. *The Conduct of Life: Worship*. New York: Houghton Mifflin.

Escohotado, Antonio. 1999. *A Brief History of Drugs: From the Stone Age to the Stoned Age*. Rochester, VT: Park Street Press.

Espino, Fernando. 2010. "The Six Most Baffling Nobel Prizes Ever Awarded." *Cracked*, https://www.cracked.com/article_18382_the-6-most-baffling-nobel-prizes-ever-awarded.html. Accessed 6 April, 2020.

Evans, Rhodri. 2015. *The Cosmic Microwave Background: How It Changed Our Understanding of the Universe*. New York: Springer.

Faraday, Michael. 1859. *Experimental Researches in Chemistry and Physics*. London: Richard Taylor and William Francis.

Farwell, Matt. 2015. "A True Story about RPGs and the Reality of the Battlefield." *Vanity Fair: Hive*, https://www.vanityfair.com/news/2015/02/rpgs-lies-battlefield-afghanistan, Accessed 7 April, 2020. February 24.

Ferguson, John. 1970. *The Religions of the Roman Empire*. Ithaca, NY: Cornell University Press.

Frank, Robert H. 2016. *Success and Luck: Good Fortune and the Myth of Meritocracy*. Princeton, NJ: Princeton University Press.

Frazer, James George. 1890. *The Golden Bough: A Study of Magic and Religion*. London: Macmillan.

Freedberg, J. 2009. "Appeal from the Order Entered January 14, 2009 in the Court of Common Pleas of Columbia/Montour County Criminal Division At No(s): Cp-19 Cr-0000733-2008 and Cp-19-cr-0000746-2008." Pennsylvania Superior Court 47 167 and 168 MDA 2009 1–16.

Freud, Sigmund. 1917. *Introductory Lectures on Psychoanalysis*. New York: Penguin.

Galilei, Galileo. 1962. "Sopra Le Scoperte Dei Dadi (on a Discovery Concerning Dice)." In *Games, Gods, and Gambling*, edited by F. N. David, 192–5. New York: Hafner Publishing.

Gamow, George. 1948. "The Evolution of the Universe." *Science* 162: 680–2.

Garrison, Webb. 1999. *Friendly Fire in the Civil War*. Nashville, TN: Routledge Hill Press.

Gettier, Edmund. 1963. "Is Justified True Belief Knowledge?" *Analysis* 23: 121–3.

Gillon, Brendan S. 1990. "Ambiguity, Generality, and Indeterminacy: Tests and Definitions." *Synthese* 85 (3): 391–416.

Gladwell, Malcolm. 2008. *Outliers*. New York: Pantheon.

Gleick, James. 1987. *Chaos: Making a New Science*. New York: Viking Penguin.

Gordon, Lewis R. 2004. "Critical Reflections on Three Popular Tropes in the Study of Whiteness." In *What White Looks Like: African-American Philosophers on the Whiteness Question*, edited by George Yancy, 173–93. New York: Routledge.

Gould, Stephen J. 1991. *Bully for Brontosaurus*. New York: W. W. Norton.

Greco, John. 2010. *Achieving Knowledge: A Virtue-Theoretic Account of Epistemic Normativity*. Cambridge: Cambridge University Press.

Hacking, Ian. 1975. *The Emergence of Probability*. Cambridge: Cambridge University Press.

Hales, Steven D. 1999. *Metaphysics: Contemporary Readings*. Belmont, CA: Wadsworth.

Hales, Steven D. 2006. *Relativism and the Foundations of Philosophy*. Cambridge, MA: MIT Press (A Bradford Book).

Hales, Steven D., ed. 2011. *A Companion to Relativism*. Malden, MA: Wiley-Blackwell.

Hales, Steven D. 2019. "Moral Luck and Control," *Midwest Studies in Philosophy* 43: 42–58.

Hales, Steven D., and Jennifer Adrienne Johnson. 2014. "Luck Attributions and Cognitive Bias." *Metaphilosophy* 45 (4–5): 509–28.

Hales, Steven D., and Jennifer Adrienne Johnson. 2018. "Dispositional Optimism and Luck Attributions: Implications for Philosophical Theories of Luck," *Philosophical Psychology* 31 (7): 1027–45.

Hanauer, Nick. 2014. "The Pitchforks Are Coming. For Us Plutocrats." *Politico* July/August.

Hartman, Robert J. 2017. *In Defense of Moral Luck*. New York: Routledge.

Heesen, Remco. 2017. "Academic Superstars: Competent or Lucky?" *Synthese* 194 (11): 4499–518.

Hesiod. 2006. *Works and Days*. Cambridge, MA: Harvard University Press.

Hetherington, Stephen. 2014. "Knowledge Can Be Lucky." In *Contemporary Debates in Epistemology*, edited by Mattias Steup, John Turri, and Ernest Sosa, 164–76. Somerset, MA: Wiley-Blackwell.

Hofstadter, Douglas R. 1985. *Metamagical Themas: Questing for the Essence of Mind and Pattern*. New York: Basic Books.

Holland, Cecelia. 1999. "The Death That Saved Europe." In *What If?: The World's Foremost Military Historians Imagine What Might Have Been*, edited by Robert Cowley, 93–106. New York: G. P. Putnam's Sons.

Holt, Jim. 2012. *Why Does the World Exist? An Existential Detective Story.* New York: W. W. Norton.

Holton, Gerald. 1978. *The Scientific Imagination: Case Studies.* Cambridge: Cambridge University Press.

Hurley, Susan. 2005. *Justice, Luck, and Knowledge.* Cambridge, MA: Harvard University Press.

Hyman, Ray. 1999. "The Mischief-Making of Ideomotor Action." *The Scientific Review of Alternative Medicine* 3 (2): 34–43.

James, William. 1907. *Pragmatism, a New Name for Some Old Ways of Thinking.* New York: Longman, Green, and Co.

James Jr., Thomas A. 2008. "Commonwealth of Pennsylvania V. Diane A. Dent and Walter Watkins." In the Court of Common Pleas for the 26th Judicial District, Columbia County Branch, Pennsylvania Criminal Division cases 733 and 746 of 2008 1–15.

Johnson, Samuel. 1795. *Lives of the English Poets and a Criticism of Their Works.* London: R. Dodsley.

Kadish, Gerald E. 2013. "Calendar of Lucky and Unlucky Days." In *The Encyclopedia of Ancient History*, edited by Roger S. Bagnall, Kai Brodersen, Craige B. Champion, Andrew Erskine, and Sabine R. Huebner, 1265–6. Oxford: Wiley-Blackwell.

Kahneman, Daniel. 2011. *Thinking Fast and Slow.* New York: Ferrar, Straus, and Giroux.

Kant, Immanuel. 1784. *Groundwork for the Metaphysic of Morals.* London: Routledge.

Kant, Immanuel. 1790. *Critique of Judgment.* Oxford: Oxford University Press.

Kendrick, Thomas Downing. 1955. *The Lisbon Earthquake.* Philadelphia, PA: J. B. Lippincott Company.

King, Gilbert. 2012. "The Smoothest Con Man That Ever Lived." *Smithsonian*, August 22.

Kneale, William, and Martha Kneale. 1962. *The Development of Logic.* Oxford: Oxford University Press.

Kožnjak, Boris. 2015. "Who Let the Demon Out? Laplace and Boscovich on Determinism." *Studies in History and Philosophy of Science* 51: 42–52.

Kramer, Heinrich, and James Sprenger. 1971. *Malleus Maleficarum.* New York: Dover Occult.

Krasser, Helmut. 1995. "Dharmottara's Theory of Knowledge in His *Laghuprāmāṇyaparīkṣā.*" *Journal of Indian Philosophy* 23: 247–71.

Kripke, Saul. 1977. "Speaker's Reference and Semantic Reference." *Midwest Studies in Philosophy* 2 (1): 255–76.

Kucharski, Adam. 2016. *The Perfect Bet: How Math and Science Are Taking the Luck Out of Gambling.* New York: Basic Books.

Kuhn, Thomas S. 1970. *The Structure of Scientific Revolutions.* Chicago, IL: University of Chicago Press.

Kyle, Chris. 2012. *American Sniper.* New York: HarperCollins.

Lamont, Peter. 2013. *Extraordinary Beliefs: A Historical Approach to a Psychological Problem.* Cambridge: Cambridge University Press.

Langer, Ellen J. 1982. "The Illusion of Control." In *Judgment under Uncertainty: Heuristics and Biases*, edited by Daniel Kahneman, Paul Slovic, and Amos Tversky, 231–8. Cambridge: Cambridge University Press.

Laplace, Pierre Simon. 1902. *A Philosophical Essay on Probabilities*. New York: John Wiley and Sons.

Lawrence, Robert Means. 1898. *The Magic of the Horseshoe*. Boston, MA, and New York: Houghton, Mifflin, and Co.

Leibniz, Gottfried Wilhelm. 1710. *Theodicy*. London: Routledge and Kegan Paul.

Leibniz, Gottfried Wilhelm. 1768. *Opera Omnia, Nunc Primum Collecta, in Classes Distributa, Praefationibus & Indicibus Exornata*, Studio Ludovici Dutens. Génève: Frères de Tournes.

Levitt, Steven D., and Thomas J. Miles. 2012. "The Role of Skill versus Luck in Poker: Evidence from the World Series of Poker." *Journal of Sports Economics* 15 (1): 31–44.

Levy, Neil. 2011. *Hard Luck: How Luck Undermines Free Will and Moral Responsibility*. Oxford: Oxford University Press.

Littlejohn, Clayton. 2014. "Fake Barns and False Dilemmas." *Episteme* 11 (4): 369–89.

Lloyd, Seth. 2002. "Computational Capacity of the Universe." *Physical Review Letters* 88 (23): 237901.

Martin, Justin W., and Fiery Cushman. 2016. "The Adaptive Logic of Moral Luck." In *A Companion to Experimental Philosophy*, edited by Justin Sytsma, and Wesley Buckwalter, 190–202. Oxford: Wiley-Blackwell.

Mauboussin, Michael J. 2012. *The Success Equation: Untangling Skill and Luck in Business, Sports, and Investing*. Boston, MA: Harvard Business School Press.

Maysh, Jeff. 2016. *Handsome Devil*. NP: Amazon Digital Services, LLC.

Mazur, Joseph. 2010. *What's Luck Got to Do with It?: The History, Mathematics, and Psychology of the Gambler's Illusion*. Princeton, NJ: Princeton University Press.

McKinnon, Rachel. 2014. "You Make Your Own Luck." *Metaphilosophy* 45 (4–5): 558–77.

Medawar, Peter B. 1968. "Lucky Jim." *The New York Review of Books*, March 28.

Mele, Alfred R. 2006. *Free Will and Luck*. Oxford: Oxford University Press.

Meyers, Morton A. 2007. *Happy Accidents: Serendipity in Modern Medical Breakthroughs*. New York: Arcade Publishing.

Milgram, Stanley. 1974. *Obedience to Authority: An Experimental View*. New York: Harper and Row.

Mlodinow, Leonard. 2008. *The Drunkard's Walk: How Randomness Rules Our Lives*. New York: Pantheon Books.

Monahan, Michael J. 2014. "The Concept of Privilege: A Critical Appraisal." *South African Journal of Philosophy* 33 (1): 73–83.

Munroe, Randall. 2014. *What If?: Serious Scientific Answers to Absurd Hypothetical Questions*. New York: Houghton Mifflin.

Nagel, Thomas. 1976. "Moral Luck." *Proceedings of the Aristotelian Society* 50: 137–51.

Nelkin, Dana K. 2013. "Moral Luck," *The Stanford Encyclopedia of Philosophy* (Summer 2019 Edition), Edward N. Zalta (ed.). https://plato.stanford.edu/archives/sum2019/entries/moral-luck/.

Nietzsche, Friedrich. 1887. *On the Genealogy of Morals.* New York: Vintage Books.

Nietzsche, Friedrich. 1888. *Twilight of the Idols.* London: Penguin Classics.

Nietzsche, Friedrich. 1908. *Ecce Homo.* Leipzig: Insel-Verlag.

Norris, Richard D., James M. Norris, Ralph D. Lorenz, and Brian Jackson. 2014. "Sliding Rocks on Racetrack Playa, Death Valley National Park: First Observation of Rocks in Motion." *PLOS One* 9 (8): e105948.

Nozick, Robert. 1981. *Philosophical Explanations.* Cambridge, MA: Harvard University Press.

Nussbaum, Martha. 1994. *The Therapy of Desire: Theory and Practice in Hellenistic Ethics.* Princeton, NJ: Princeton University Press.

Ogden, Daniel. 2002. *Magic, Witchcraft, and Ghosts in the Greek and Roman Worlds: A Sourcebook.* Oxford: Oxford University Press.

Paine, Thomas. 1792. *The Rights of Man*, Part 2. London: J. S. Jordan.

Parry, Richard Lloyd. 2009. "The Luckiest or Unluckiest Man in the World? Tsutomu Yamaguchi, Double A-Bomb Victim." *The Times of London*, March 25.

Pavese, Carlotta. 2016. "Skill in Epistemology 1: Skill and Knowledge." *Philosophy Compass* 11: 642–9.

Petronius. 1960. *Satyricon.* New York: New American Library.

Pindar. 2007. *The Complete Odes.* Oxford: Oxford University Press.

Planck, Max. 1949. *Scientific Autobiography and Other Papers.* New York: Philosophical Library.

Plato. 1961. "Theaetetus." In *Plato: The Collected Dialogues*, edited by Edith Hamilton, and Huntington Cairns, 845–919. Princeton, NJ: Princeton University Press.

Plus Media Solutions. 2013. 2 Arraigned in Deaths of Young Sisters. *Newswire.*

Plutarch. 1962. *Moralia.* Cambridge, MA: Harvard University Press.

Pocock, J. G. A. 1975. *The Machiavellian Moment: Florentine Political Thought and the Atlantic Republican Tradition.* Princeton, NJ: Princeton University Press.

Polybius. 1889. *The Histories of Polybius.* London: Macmillan.

Pritchard, Duncan. 2005. *Epistemic Luck.* Oxford: Oxford University Press.

Pritchard, Duncan. 2014a. "Knowledge Cannot Be Lucky." In *Contemporary Debates in Epistemology*, edited by Mattias Steup, John Turri, and Ernest Sosa, 152–64. Somerset, MA: Wiley-Blackwell.

Pritchard, Duncan. 2014b. "The Modal Account of Luck." *Metaphilosophy* 45 (4–5): 594–619.

Pritchard, Duncan, and Matthew Smith. 2004. "The Psychology and Philosophy of Luck." *New Ideas in Psychology* 22: 1–28.

Putzi, Sibylla, ed. 2009. *A to Z World Superstitions and Folklore: 175 Countries: Spirit Worship, Curses, Mystical Characters, Folk Tales, Burial and the Dead,*

*Animals, Food, Marriage, Good Luck, Bad Luck, Totems and Amulets and Ancestor Spirits*. Petaluma: World Trade Press.

Quine, W. V. 1960. *Word and Object*. Cambridge, MA: MIT Press.

Ramachandran, V. S., and Sandra Blakeslee. 1998. *Phantoms in the Brain: Probing the Mysteries of the Human Mind*. New York: William Morrow and Company.

Ramachandran, V. S., Beatrix Krause, and Laura C. Case. 2011. "The Phantom Head." *Perception* 40: 367–70.

Redford, Donald B. 2001. *The Oxford Encyclopedia of Ancient Egypt*. Oxford: Oxford University Press.

Reich, Steve. 1989. *Different Trains*. New York: Elektra Nonesuch. Recording. 79176-2.

Rescher, Nicholas. 1995. *Luck: The Brilliant Randomness of Everyday Life*. New York: Farrar, Straus, Giroux.

Roberts, Royston M. 1989. *Serendipity: Accidental Discoveries in Science*. New York: John Wiley and Sons.

Roese, Neal J., and Kathleen D. Vohs. 2012. "Hindsight Bias." *Perspectives on Psychological Science* 7 (5): 411–26.

Rosenthal, Jeffrey S. 2006. *Struck by Lightning: The Curious World of Probabilities*. Washington, DC: Joseph Henry Press.

Rowling, J. K. 2005. *Harry Potter and the Half-Blood Prince*. London: Bloomsbury.

Rudgley, Richard. 1993. *Essential Substances: A Cultural History of Intoxicants in Society*. New York: Kodansha International.

Russell, Bertrand. 1948. *Human Knowledge: Its Scope and Limits*. London: Allen & Unwin.

Sacks, Oliver. 1985. *The Man Who Mistook His Wife for a Hat*. New York: Summit Books.

Sacks, Oliver. 2010. *The Mind's Eye*. New York: Alfred A. Knopf.

Scheier, Michael F., Charles S. Carver, and M. W. Bridges. 1994. "Distinguishing Optimism from Neuroticism (and Trait Anxiety, Self-Mastery, and Self-Esteem): A Re-Evaluation of the Life Orientation Test." *Journal of Personality and Social Psychology* 67: 1063–78.

Schultes, Richard Evans, and Albert Hofmann. 1979. *Plants of the Gods: Origins of Hallucinogenic Use*. New York: McGraw-Hill Book Company.

Schüll, Natasha Dow. 2012. *Addiction by Design: Machine Gambling in Las Vegas*. Princeton, NJ: Princeton University Press.

Seddon, Keith. 2005. *Epictetus' Handbook and the Tablet of Cebes*. New York: Routledge.

Segal, Nancy L. 2005. *Indivisible by Two: Lives of Extraordinary Twins*. Cambridge, MA: Harvard University Press.

Seneca, Lucius Annaeus. 1917. *Moral Epistles*. Cambridge, MA: Harvard University Press.

Sennet, Adam. 2011. "Ambiguity," *The Stanford Encyclopedia of Philosophy* (Spring 2016 Edition), Edward N. Zalta (ed.). https://plato.stanford.edu/archives/spr2016/entries/ambiguity/.

Sextus Empiricus. 1998. *Against the Grammarians*. Oxford: Oxford University Press.

Shepard, Roger. 1990. *Mind Sights*. New York: W. H. Freeman and Company.

Shepherd, Joshua. 2014. "The Contours of Control." *Philosophical Studies* 170 (3): 395–411.

Singh, Simon. 2010. "Cosmological Serendipity." In *Serendipity*, edited by Mark de Rond, and Iain Morley, 65–72. Cambridge: Cambridge University Press.

Smith, ed. 2012. *Luck: What It Means and Why It Matters*. London: Bloomsbury.

Smith, Gary. 2016. *What the Luck?* New York: The Overlook Press.

Sosa, Ernest. 2011. *Knowing Full Well*. Princeton, NJ: Princeton University Press.

Sosa, Ernest. 2017. *Epistemology*. Princeton, NJ: Princeton University Press.

Stanley, Jason, and Timothy Williamson. 2017. "Skill." *Noûs* 51 (4): 713–26.

Taleb, Nassim Nicholas. 2007. *The Black Swan: The Impact of the Highly Improbable*. New York: Random House.

Teigen, Karl Halvor. 2005. "When a Small Difference Makes a Large Difference: Counterfactual Thinking and Luck." In *The Psychology of Counterfactual Thinking*, edited by David R. Mandel, Denis J. Hilton, and Patrizia Catellani, 129–46. London: Routledge.

Teigen, Karl Halvor, and Tine K. Jensen. 2011. "Unlucky Victims or Lucky Survivors? Spontaneous Counterfactual Thinking by Families Exposed to the Tsunami Disaster." *European Psychologist* 16: 48–57.

Thaler, Richard H., and Cass R. Sunstein. 2008. *Nudge: Improving Decisions about Health, Wealth, and Happiness*. New Haven, CT: Yale University Press.

Tromp, John, and Gunnar Farnebäck. 2016. "Combinatorics of Go." https://tromp.github.io/go/gostate.pdf.

Trump, Donald J. 2016. *Great Again: How to Fix Our Crippled America*. New York: Threshold.

Trump, Donald J., and Bill Zanker. 2007. *Think Big and Kick Ass in Business and Life*. New York: HarperCollins.

Turri, John, Wesley Buckwalter, and Peter Blouw. 2015. "Knowledge and Luck." *Psychonomic Bulletin & Review* 22: 378–90.

Unger, Peter. 1968. "An Analysis of Factual Knowledge." *The Journal of Philosophy* 65 (6): 157–70.

Voltaire. 1759. *Candide: Or, All for the Best*. London: J. Nourse at the Lamb Opposite Katherine Street in the Strand.

Weber, Max. 1946. "The Social Psychology of the World Religions." In *From Max Weber: Essays in Sociology*, edited by H. H. Gerth, and C. Wright Mills, 267–301. Oxford: Oxford University Press.

White, E. B. 1944. *One Man's Meat*. New York: Harper & Brothers Publishers.

Whitehead, Barbara Dafoe, and David Popenoe. 2001. "Who Wants to Marry a Soul Mate?" In *The State of Our Unions*, New Brunswick, NJ: National Marriage Project.

Whittingham, Richard, ed. 1989. *The Dimaggio Albums: Selections from Public and Private Collections Celebrating the Baseball Career of Joe Dimaggio*. New York: G. P. Putnam's Sons.

Whittington, Lee John. 2016. "Luck, Knowledge, and Value." *Synthese* 193 (6): 1615–33.

Zagzebski, Linda. 1994. "The Inescapability of Gettier Problems." *Philosophical Quarterly* 44 (174): 65–73.

Zagzebski, Linda. 2003. "The Search for the Source of the Epistemic Good." *Metaphilosophy* 34 (1–2): 12–28.

Zimbardo, Philip. 2008. *The Lucifer Effect*. New York: Random House.

# INDEX